ECOLOGY, IDEOLOGY AND POWER

ECOLOGY, IDEOLOGY AND POWER

DONALD GIBSON

Ecology, Ideology and Power

160 pages. List Price: $14.95
ISBN 1-61577-530-7, EAN 978-1-61577-530-9

Facsimile of the Original 2002 Edition
released by Nova Science Publishers
under the title *Environmentalism: Ideology and Power*

Library of Congress Subject Headings
1. Environmentalism
2. Malthusianism
3. Aristocracy; Oligarchy
LC: GE195, G43 2002. Dewey: 363.7

BISAC Subject Area Codes
NAT011000   Nature / Environmental Conservation & Protection
POL042020   Political Science / Political Ideologies / Conservatism & Liberalism
BUS068000   Business & Economics / Development / Economic Development
SOC046000   Social Science / Abortion & Birth Control
SOC033000   Social Science / Philanthropy & Charity
(N.B. The BISG have yet to allocate a code to any such topic as the class system, social élites, or oligarchy as a form of government.)

This book warns against the effort to sell a reactionary economic, political and social agenda dressed up as concern for and protection of the environment. The author is in no way opposed to any genuine ecological concerns, but his work demonstrates that what we call "environmentalism" is primarily an expression of the world view of segments of the world's upper class. When they talk to us about pollution, resource scarcity, and overpopulation, they are actually talking about their own fears and hatreds of the common people, and their ambitions for themselves. Whatever label we affix to today's environmentalism, it is certain that it carries over into the 21st century the same kinds of reactionary, aristocratic and elitist tendencies evident two centuries ago in England and Germany. Such tendencies also emerged in a significant way in the late 1800's in the United States, involving Malthusianism, social Darwinism and the eugenics movement.

CONTENTS

Chapter One

AN INTRODUCTION, HUMAN NATURE AND ENVIRONMENTALISM

About 2500 years ago Aeschylus celebrated the dawning of human creativity in the person, or god-person, of Prometheus. Aeschylus thereby defined humanity in terms of the ability to reason and understand the world, create knowledge and technology, and transform and improve the world.

Aeschylus speaks to us across time, place, and culture about our nature and the nature of human existence. That he could do this is itself evidence against relativism, nihilism and post-modernism. The idea of Prometheus is also evidence that there is a human nature and there are trans-historical truths. Prometheanism is human nature. Prometheanism has also been viewed by powerful groups as something that must be constrained or destroyed.

Aeschylus is able to speak to us with clarity and in a familiar voice even though he lived in Greece twenty-five hundred years ago because there are constants in human nature and the human circumstance. Briefly, the story is as follows.[1] In primitive times the world was ruled by gods, the most powerful of which was Cronos. Humans were "kept in a state of wretchedness and total subservience" by the gods. There was also a race of stupid giants, or Titans, who were "sons of Earth begotten by gods." One of these Titans, Prometheus, possessed capabilities for rational thought and moral judgment, and a love of freedom and justice.

Zeus, a son of Cronos, enlisted Prometheus in a successful effort to overthrow Cronos. Prometheus then learned that Zeus hated humanity and planned to destroy them. Prometheus believed humans were capable of infinite development and he acted to save them. Prometheus is seized and on the orders of Zeus is taken to a mountain top where he is to be tortured so that he will "accept the sovereignty of Zeus" and "cease acting as champion of the human race."[2]

---

[1] Vellacott, 1961, pp. 7-9.
[2] Aeschylus, 1961, p. 20.

On the mountain Prometheus engages in an exchange with the Chorus of the Daughters of Oceanus in which he explains why Zeus is punishing him. Prometheus relates that he gave fire to humans and also did the following for humanity.[3]

> What I did
> For mortals in their misery, hear now. At first
> Mindless, I gave them mind and reason. -What I say
> Is not in censure of mankind, but showing you
> How all my gifts to them were guided by goodwill.-
> In those days they had eyes, but sight was meaningless;
> Heard sounds, but could not listen; all their length of life
> They passed like shapes in dreams, confused and purposeless.
> Of brick-built, sun-warmed houses, or of carpentry,
> They had no notion; lived in holes, like swarms of ants,
> Or deep in sunless caverns; knew no certain way
> To mark off winter, or flowery spring, or fruitful summer;
> Their every act was without knowledge, till I came.
> I taught them to determine when stars rise or set -
> A difficult art. Number, the primary science, I
> Invented for them, and how to set down words in writing -
> The all-remembering skill, mother of many arts.
> I was the first to harness beasts under a yoke
> With trace or saddle as man's slaves, to take man's place
> Under the heaviest burdens; put the horse to the chariot,
> Made him obey the rein, and be an ornament
> To wealth and greatness. No one before me discovered
> The sailor's wagon - flax winged craft that roam the seas.
> Such tools and skills I found for men: myself, poor wretch,
> Lack even one trick to free me from this agony.
> ....
> Now hear the rest of what I have to tell, what crafts,
> What methods I devised - and you will wonder more.
> First in importance: if a man fell ill, he had
> No remedy, solid or liquid medicine,
> Or ointment, but for lack of drugs they pined away;
> Until I showed them how to mix healing herbs
> And so protect themselves against all maladies.
> ....
> Next the treasures of the earth,
> The bronze, iron, silver, gold hidden deep down - who else
> But I can claim to have found them first? No one, unless
> He talks like a fool. So, here's the whole truth in one word:

---

[3] Ibid., pp. 28, 33-34, 35.

All human skill and science was Prometheus' gift.

The human being is the only self-conscious thing that we know of in the universe. In spite of the vastness, perhaps the infinity, of the universe, we have yet to learn of one other kind of living thing that has a demonstrated ability to reflect on itself and wonder about the purpose of it all. The human species is still the only thing in the universe that we know of that has the capacity for self-development. We are, likewise, as far as we know, the only living thing capable of the conscious transformation of our life environment. What Aeschylus portrays for us is the central importance of the creative potential of mankind. It is the ability to understand and create that Prometheus gives to humanity, Prometheus himself perhaps being a symbol of the power of reason. What raises humanity out of their misery is the development of the capacity to comprehend the universe and act on it. The realization of that potential yields science, engineering and medicine. A case can be made that the human capabilities which are mobilized to achieve progress are what define us as human.

HUMAN NATURE

Only humans are capable of intentionally generating knowledge about the world for the purpose of creating moral and material progress. This potential is part of our nature; it is what makes us unique. We are the only known species capable of creating, seeking and assimilating knowledge which transcends immediate experience. The 'knowledge' acquired by all other life forms is a product of the interplay of physical needs, instincts and sensory experience. By contrast, the object, scope and purpose of human knowledge, while including that related to need, instinct and senses, transcends the immediate. Not even the highest forms of animal life show any inclination, or capacity, to want to know about things which are beyond their immediate sensory experience. The scope of human knowledge as it is exhibited in astronomy, geology, physics and philosophy is qualitatively different from 'knowledge' sought by or possessed by any other species. The objects of human curiosity are unique inasmuch as humans seek to understand not only that which can be seen, felt or touched but also that which is impenetrable to our senses. The internal workings of the sun, earth, biological entities and atoms are all objects of human interest that provide obvious examples. Principles governing radiation or the movement of distant objects in space are of potential interest to us but not to the brightest dolphin.

Unique also to humans is the range of purposes that are the reasons for and goals of knowledge. Humans are alone in their capacity to seek knowledge that may be of service to those outside of immediate experience in space or time. No animal displays any concern for or interest in even the members of its own species unless direct contact exists. Only humans seek knowledge in the service of nation, humanity, other species or the future.

For humans only, the purpose of knowledge may be the knowledge itself. Acquiring knowledge can be a conscious activity rooted not in need or necessity, but in the desire to comprehend. This desire to comprehend or know, whatever its ultimate source, clearly separates humans from all other living things. As philosopher Bernard J. F. Lonergan observed,

> When an animal has nothing to do, it goes to sleep. When a man has nothing to do, he may ask questions. The first moment is an awakening to one's intelligence. It is release from the dominance of biological drive and from the routines of everyday life. It is the effective emergence of wonder, of the desire to understand.

This desire to know

> ... pulls man out of the solid routine of perception, conation, instinct and habit, doing and enjoying. It holds him with the fascination of problems. It engages him in the quest of solutions. It makes him aloof to what is not established. It compels assent to the unconditional. It is the cool shrewdness of common sense, the disinterestedness of science, the detachment of philosophy. It is the absorption of investigation, the joy of discovery, the assurance of judgment, the modesty of limited knowledge. It is the relentless serenity, the unhurried determination, the impeturbable drive of question following appositely on question in the genesis of truth.[4]

Where this desire to know is fully developed, either in the formal practice of science or in the general exercise of intelligence and reason, the object of the desire is everything that can be known.[5] In this respect, intelligence and reason differ from common sense which stops at the practical solution of problems rooted in particular times, places and situations.[6] In an interview Lonergan added that there must be feelings and emotions which support this desire to know.[7] Lonergan seems to have had something like love of humankind or love of justice in mind.

It is a distinctly human trait that the effort to solve a problem may have no direct connection to the negative impact or experiences related to that problem. Human problem solving, particularly that undertaken in a scientific mode, bears no resemblance to that engaged in by rats and pigeons. V. Gordon Childe observed that while animals are capable of solving immediate problems with direct solutions,

> What is distinctive of human reasoning is that it can go immensely farther from the actual present situation than any other animal's reasoning ever seems to get it. In this distinctive advance language has surely been a very great help.[8]

---

[4] Lonergan, 1970, pp. 348-349.
[5] Ibid., pp. 349, 352.
[6] Ibid., pp. 175, 179.
[7] Ibid., pp. 220-223.
[8] Childe, 1942, p. 19.

Elsewhere Childe noted that while the invention of writing allowed people to learn from past generations and from contemporaries living far off, upper classes for thousands of years had a monopoly on writing and they had no interest in applied science or the physical labor process.[9]

Our development as individuals and as a species occurs when we come to understand that the universe operates according to certain principles and that such principles cannot be changed or can be changed only when the system in question is understood on its own terms. Such understanding requires that humans treat the world and its components as separate objects.[10] This is part of the foundation for scientific knowledge and for general intelligence and it is necessary in order for humans to establish a capacity to alter natural or social systems. In relation to this, Carroll Quigley has observed that the Western outlook that has produced progress

> assumes, first, that there is a truth or goal for man's activity. Thus it rejects despair, solipsism, skepticism, pessimism, and chaos. It implies hope, order, and the existence of a meaningful objective external reality. And it provides the basis for science, religion, and social action as the West has known these.[11]

In general, then, humans are distinct because we are the only known species capable of a self conscious search for knowledge which transcends desire and instinct in its purposes, which transcends particular times, places and situations in its scope and which is based on a felt separation between known and knower. The creation, internalization and application of knowledge are activities. Passivity will not do, there must be a desire, intent or will which activates individuals. Whether that will is an instinct, a tendency or only a potential of human nature, it must be there to fuel the search for knowledge. Will springs from many sources. In its higher form, it involves love of truth, progress and life.

Will must also appear in order for knowledge to bear fruit. If knowledge is to have meaning and value beyond its role in satisfying the desire to know, it must have an impact on the world beyond the mind of the knower. Will translates what is known into the actions of individuals and the policies of groups, institutions and nations. Failure to act upon what is known, the truth, reduces and undermines the significance of the knowing itself and such failure constitutes a failure of will which may become habitual.[12] One form this takes is the rationalization that alters knowing to make it consistent with action or lack of action. Consistency between knowing and doing is necessary for rational consciousness to emerge and endure, but consistency achieved through sacrifice of the truth cannot be the basis for rational consciousness.[13]

Conscious and willful action produces a causal relationship between the actor and the world that is acted upon, as in the application of science and the use of technology. In this way humanity raises itself above nature and both individuals and collectivities act as

---

[9] Childe, 1951, pp. 140, 142.
[10] Lonergan, 1970, pp. 474, 543.
[11] Quigley, 1979, p. 339.
[12] Lonergan, 1970, p. 562.
[13] Ibid., pp. 599, 613, 621.

creators and modifiers of their environment. In the process humans separate themselves from all other life forms, which exist as merely part of nature, acting as neither knowers nor creators. The existence of such will, as opposed to instinct, allows humans to actively undertake courses of action which are self-motivated and self-generated, not merely responses to external forces. This potential for willful action means that humans, unlike the builders of anthills, may decide to affect changes for the better or worse, i.e., make moral choices.

Whereas animals act within the limits of sensory experience, instinct and the pressures of environment, humans can opt to behave in accordance with moral or ethical principles and, beyond this, to construct systems of morals that are binding, as in the case of law. Questions of right and wrong have been the subject of intense analysis throughout the history of human civilization. Humans display the full range of orientations toward morality from deep commitments through indifference to consciously anti-moral intent. The very existence of morality and moral systems, however, is a fact which demonstrates how very different humanity is from all else that lives in this world.

Not only do we take the issues of right and wrong and of responsibility to be topics for reflection, debate and study, but we have formulated systems of morals in the form of laws which regulate the behavior of people who never see, touch or hear one another, but who are nevertheless bound together under commonly observed views of right and wrong.

The capacity for moral choice places human beings in the position of being free, but also of being responsible. Moral freedom, as Lonergan points out,[14] is thoroughly intertwined with will and knowledge. Knowledge, will and morality are interrelated and interdependent. Taken together, they are the source of human progress and progress is the condition for the cultivation of each, particularly morality.

Knowledge is related to will in two general ways. First, knowledge shapes the decisions leading to action. Without adequate knowledge, the individual's actions, organizational decisions, or a nation's policies may be off target, leading to failure or unforeseen consequences. Secondly, knowledge, as opposed to impulse or emotion alone, provides a sustainable and rational basis for action, with a concomitant increase in the probability of effectiveness.[15]

The acquisition of knowledge is based on the desire to know. This will to know may be called alertness of mind, intellectual curiosity, the spirit of inquiry or active intelligence.[16] As already noted, it is fueled by feelings and emotions. Whatever it is called, it is the force within the individual that leads to learning and the creation of knowledge. This force may be cultivated, discouraged or distorted, but it probably cannot be eliminated entirely.

Morality provides the ability to discern the value and significance of knowledge and it shapes the purposes to which knowledge is put, as well as the purpose for which it is sought. In the absence of morality, will becomes merely the tool of emotions, desires or

---

[14] Ibid., p. 627.
[15] Ibid., p. 286.
[16] Ibid., pp. 9, 74, 283-285.

calculated interests of individuals or groups. In the absence of will, morality becomes ineffective. The failure to act, taking the form of passivity, fatalism, or withdrawal, produces an inconsistency which is removed by a revision of the moral sentiments.[17]

Sufficient knowledge, a developed morality and the will to act permit humanity to transform both the material world and its own social organization for the purposes of generating progress. Improvements in material existence are both a goal of progress and a condition for further progress. Nowhere is human nature more fully on display than when people act over time and in a planned way to increase knowledge and create new ways of doing things in order to produce a better world in the future. In the modern world science, technology and industry have been central ingredients in any such effort. What makes human beings different from other species, what constitutes our nature, is deeply connected to our potential for economic, social and cultural progress. The natural environment for humans is the city, not the forest. The natural tool is the laser, not the unsharpened stick.

While the actual possibilities for progress at any given moment are limited by the conditions inherited from previous generations, a choice of direction is constant. Each generation is in the position of affecting, within limits, its own life and the range of possibilities it bequeaths to the next generation. In this sense, each generation's actions are affected by the past, but so is every generation free to decide how it will affect the range of possibilities for the generation that follows.

Progress has never been universally desired. Progress has always had enemies. What Aeschylus conveyed to us through the story of Prometheus is that the creation and use of knowledge to make the world conform to an idea of justice is a direct challenge to those who wish to dominate and suppress the rest of humanity. What angered Zeus and the other gods is what angers the ideological environmentalist today. It is the disruptive and threatening potential of science and its applications, it is material progress.

ENVIRONMENTALISM

Environmentalism is not an attempt to solve specific problems. It is not primarily an effort to protect nature from unnecessary destruction. Environmentalism is a political doctrine. It is an expression of the worldview of certain groups. For two centuries those who have spoken against human progress in the name of protecting nature have played the role of Zeus, seeking to deny to humanity what humanity must by its own nature seek to do. The modern day gods are actually talking about their own fears, hatreds and ambitions when they talk to us about pollution, resource scarcity and overpopulation.

If protecting the environment were actually the reason for ecologism and environmentalism, then its proponents would act as if that were the goal. That is, a real concern for the environment would look one way, a political agenda dressed up as a concern for the environment would look another way. Let me suggest that a real concern for the environment, one not shaped by a fear of or hatred of human progress, would be

---

[17] Ibid., p. 599.

based on a determination to learn the truth. That means being open to all facts. It means a desire to know if environmental problems really exist. It would include a full and open discussion of the assumptions and implications of all ideas. It would be open to all facts and information. It would focus on specific problems, seeking solutions consistent with human well being. It would be dispassionate and objective. It would acknowledge and recognize the value of science and technology. It would proceed from an assumption that human life has value. It would also place a value on the development and wellbeing of people. Such a concern for the environment should be acceptable to all of us.

Environmentalism, on the other hand, would treat problems, real or alleged, as an opportunity to attack progress. As part of a broader political agenda, the truthfulness of the claims made is secondary to their propaganda value. The presentation of facts would be highly selective, sweeping generalizations would be used, along with inflammatory rhetoric. Human needs and desires would be portrayed as problems in themselves. Progress, science and technology would all in general be disparaged. This 'ism' would promote pessimism and anti-human elitism. Environmental problems, real or not, would be focused on to support the broader political agenda.

The present work is in no way opposed to a concern with the environment. It is against the effort to sell a reactionary economic, political and social agenda dressed up as concern for and protection of the environment. This book will demonstrate that what we call 'environmentalism' is an expression of the worldview of segments of the world's upper class. When they talk to us about pollution, resource scarcity, and overpopulation, they are actually talking about their own fears, hatreds, and ambitions.

Whatever label we affix to today's environmentalism, it is certain that it carries over into the twenty-first century the same kinds of reactionary, aristocratic and elitist tendencies evident two centuries ago in England and Germany. Such tendencies also emerged in a significant way in the late-1800s in the United States.

Commenting on the anti-progress tendencies in environmentalism, William Tucker observed in his book *Progress and Privilege* that

> What is important to recognize first, though, is that the impulse to slow growth, to suspect invention, and to place natural or agrarian values above material progress has been the consistent pattern of aristocratic politics wherever and whenever it has asserted itself. Like most social impulses, these values are always present in society. They are only briefly unrecognizable when they disguise themselves as something new. These aristocratic impulses have made important contributions to our political heritage, and we would probably do better to honor them for what they are. The only problem with the aristocratic viewpoint is that it has been consistently *undemocratic*. Far from being an issue of the underprivileged or the masses of people, it has usually been *people themselves* who have been its enemy.[18]

As we will see, it may be an understatement to simply say that people themselves are thought of as the enemy. To many environmentalists, people are nothing more than a cancer.

---

[18] Tucker, 1982, p. 42.

In a very general way, environmentalism and its predecessors express an upper class fear that the rise of other groups will diminish or threaten their power and status. Environmentalism is a political expression of upper class fears about progress. It is not a reasoned or objective or scientific concern about resources and pollution. Neo-colonialism and Social Darwinism are other expressions of that fear. When an upper class acts on these fears, they become a threat to progress.[19]

The current outburst of hostility toward human creativity and its fruits in science and technology, that is, against human nature, descends from German ecology of the early-1800s and, especially, the nineteenth century fears of English aristocrats.

---

[19] Lipset, 1968, pp. 132-133; Quigley, 1979, p. 139; Tucker, 1982, pp. 15-19.

Chapter Two

GERMAN ECOLOGISTS AND BRITISH ARISTOCRATS

Ecology emerged in Germany in close association with reactionary ideas. This connection has been analyzed by Peter Staudenmaier and the background and context have been described by George Mosse in his major work on the intellectual and cultural origins of the Nazi world view, *The Crisis of German Ideology: The Intellectual Origins of the Third Reich.*

In what is perhaps the first example of what we would call today environmentalist writing, Moritz Arndt, a fanatical German nationalist, connected ideas about nature and the need to protect German soil to racist nationalism. Arndt also expressed a theme in this 1815 essay, entitled "On the Care and Conservation of Forests," which is present in today's environmentalist arguments:

> When one sees nature in a necessary connectedness and interrelationship, then all things are equally important -shrub, worm, plant, human, stone, nothing first or last but all one single unity.[1]

The idea that nature is a web of interdependent relationships and that everything, even a stone, is as important as humans in this web is similar to contemporary biocentrism, perhaps less extreme than some of the current versions of this. In this concept, the value of a human life can be reduced to the value of a worm just as logically as can a worm's value be elevated to equality with humans.

In the mid-1800s Wilhelm Heinrich Riehl, one of Arndt's students, joined green ideas to racist nationalism and to rabid opposition to industrialism and urbanism. Riehl denounced urban, industrial society claiming that Germany's real roots were in the forests and the peasantry.[2] Riehl's romanticist, anti-modernist views were joined to anti-semitism and both became important ingredients in the Volkisch movements which appeared in the late-1800s. This tendency united ethnocentric populism with nature mysticism. The spokesmen for these groups claimed that alienation, rootlessness, and the destruction of

---

[1] Staudenmaier, 1995, p. 6.
[2] Dominick, 1992, pp. 22-23.

nature were consequences of the growing dominance of rational thought and urban civilization.[3]

According to Mosse,[4] disaffection with modernization and dislike of industrialism were part of German culture after the mid-1800s. The concept of 'Volk' was in part at least a response to this alleged feeling of alienation, offering to link the soul to nature or to the essence of nature. Although circulating in various parts of German society, particularly the educational system, it was not until after World War One, according to Mosse, that these views acquired active mass support.[5]

The green or ecological part of the Volkisch movement was carried forward in the late-1800s by Ernst Haeckel, a successor to Arndt and Riehl. Haeckel coined the term "ecology" in 1867 and in the process he brought together "aggressive nationalism, mystically charged racism, and environmentalist predilections."[6]

Like his predecessors, Haeckel joined right-wing social and political ideas to ecology. In this case it was his modification of the already reactionary ideas embodied in Social Darwinism. These he merged with the worshipping of nature.[7] Haeckel founded the German Monist League to promote his version of this Darwinist ecology, including his argument that the Nordic race is superior. During the period leading up to World War One, Haeckel increasingly promoted eugenics as a solution for what he viewed as the Jewish problem.[8] In Volkisch thought in general, Jews had come to represent the much-despised modernity. Although the hostility to Jews is absent, there has been a similar wave of anti-modernist thought in American intellectual circles since the early-1980s.

Near the end of his life Haeckel joined the Thule Society, an organization directly involved in the creation of the Nazi movement. That movement would reflect a conviction held by Haeckel that man's attempt to create a rational and just world is futile.[9]

Ecology came into 20th century German thought partly as an element of a youth movement which Staudenmaier describes as "a hodge-podge of countercultural elements, blending neo-Romanticism, Eastern philosophers, nature mysticism, hostility to reason, and a strong communal impulse."[10] They have been aptly labeled "right-wing hippies." Students of American cultural history will recognize similarities to the American counter-culture of the late-1960s and 1970s[11] and to so-called postmodernism after that.[12]

A passionate sensitivity to the natural world was part of this German youth movement. One of the exemplary writings of the period was the 1913 essay "Man and Earth" by Ludwig Klages. This essay, according to Staudenmaier, featured most of the themes of modern environmentalism. Klages' essay

---

[3] Staudenmaier, 1995, pp. 6-7.
[4] Mosse, 1964, pp. 2-4.
[5] Ibid., 1964, p. 5.
[6] Staudenmaier, 1995, p. 7.
[7] Bramwell, 1989, pp. 39-43.
[8] Staudenmaier, 1995, pp. 7-8.
[9] Ibid., 1995, pp. 8-9.
[10] Ibid., 1995, p. 10.
[11] Berger, Berger and Kellner, 1973, pp. 202-205.
[12] Devine, 1996.

decried the accelerating extinction of species, disturbance of global ecosystemic balance, deforestation, destruction of aboriginal peoples and of wild habitats, urban sprawl, and the increasing alienation of people from nature. In emphatic terms, it disparaged Christianity, capitalism, economic utilitarianism, hyperconsumption, and the ideology of 'progress.'[13]

Klages' essay was reprinted by ecologists to signify the birth of the Green movement in 1980.[14]

These kinds of themes were part of right-wing criticism of German culture in the 1920s. A part of this was the belief that German culture was undermined in the late-1800s by the spread of soulless materialism and by the nation's commitment to unfettered progress.[15] In this period the United States also came under attack in Germany as a symbol of runaway technology and that soulless materialism.[16]

The elevation of nature, the criticism of modern society, and the hostility toward Christianity were all part of the attraction for Nazis to Friedrich Nietzsche's ideas. This is exemplified in the following excerpt from an essay written in 1937 by Alfred Baeumler, one of the Third Reich's leading philosophers.

> Consciousness is only a tool, a detail in the totality of life. In opposition to the philosophy of the conscious, Nietzsche asserts the aristocracy of nature. But for thousands of years a life-weary morality has opposed the aristocracy of the strong and healthy. Like National Socialism, Nietzche sees in the state, in society, the 'great mandatory of life,' responsible for each life's failure to life itself. 'The species requires the extinction of the misfits, weaklings, and degenerates; but Christianity as a conserving force appeals especially to them.' Here we encounter the basic contradiction: whether one proceeds from a natural life context or from an equality of individual souls before God.
>
> Ultimately the ideal of democratic equality rests upon the latter assumption. The former contains the foundations of a new policy. It takes unexcelled boldness to base a state upon the race. A new order of things is the natural consequence. It is this order which Nietzsche undertook to establish in opposition to the existing one.[17]

The Nazi movement fed off of and absorbed basic Volkisch ideas. Among the core tendencies of the Volkisch movement were the elevation of the mystical and irrational over rationality and reason; pantheism; and the goal of living in accordance with nature, being in harmony with it rather than understanding and controlling it.[18] According to Mosse the Volkisch worldview was essentially "an ideology which stood opposed to the progress and modernization that transformed nineteenth-century Europe."[19]

---

[13] Staudenmaier, 1995, p. 11.
[14] Ibid., 1995, p. 12.
[15] Laqueur, 1974, p. 79.
[16] Ibid., 1974, p. 32.
[17] Mosse, 1966, p. 100.
[18] Ibid., 1964, pp. 8-10, 13, 15, 50, 115.
[19] Ibid., 1964, pp. 16-17.

The Volk was supposed to be the opposite of a "mechanical and materialistic civilization."[20] The primitive became associated with what is genuine and the countryside was linked to sincerity, integrity, and simplicity.[21] Rationalism, materialism, industrial progress, the city, and modernity in general were viewed as impediments to the achievement of union with nature and the cosmic life spirit.[22]

In its version of Volkisch views the Nazis made pragmatic compromises in certain areas. For example, not all science and mechanization could be opposed since some of it would be necessary to achieve the Reich's goals.[23] Nazism was nevertheless different from other forms of fascism in that it gave primacy to "Volk, nature and race."[24]

The Nazis absorbed much of ecological thought creating a "religion of nature" which combined "nature mysticism, pseudo-scientific ecology, irrationalist anti-humanism, and a mythology of racial salvation through a return to the land."[25] The idea that humans are a part of one organic whole was promoted in the 1930s by the director of the Reich Agency for Nature Protection and this idea was linked in Nazi ideology directly to both eugenics and nature protection. Neo-pagans in the Nazi movement, like Heinrich Himmler and Alfred Rosenberg, were preoccupied with finding man's lost connectedness to nature.[26]

Hitler and Himmler were strict vegetarians and nature mystics. Hitler considered himself to be very knowledgeable about renewable energy sources and future uses of water, wind and tides.[27] Himmler even preoccupied himself with issues of soil conservation in occupied Poland.[28]

After the Nazis took power in 1933 the leading 'greens' within the government were Walther Darre, Fritz Todt, Alwin Seifert and Reich Chancellor Rudolph Hesse, who fled to England during the War. Darre, Reich Peasant Leader and Minister of Agriculture from 1933 to 1942, justified taking land in the East on the basis of a need to reestablish harmony between Germany's people and the land.[29] With Hesse's backing a variety of environmental laws were enacted in 1933. This included legislation dealing with reforestation, protection of species, and prohibitions on industrial development. It is interesting to note that Hesse and an American we will focus on later, Henry Fairfield Osborn, both signed a manifesto supporting the German Nature Park Society.[30] This initial legislation was followed in 1935 by the Imperial Conservation Law, a law protecting flora, fauna, and wilderness. About this law Dominick remarks that:

> Not only did it protect plants, animals, special 'monuments of nature,' and official nature reserves, all of which had found some protection in various earlier laws, it also extended protection to the 'remaining portions of landscape in free Nature whose preservation on

[20] Ibid., 1964, p. 19.
[21] Ibid., 1964, pp. 19, 26.
[22] Ibid., 1964, pp. 22-23, 29, 56, 73, 154.
[23] Ibid., 1964, p. 97.
[24] Ibid., 1964, p. 315.
[25] Staudenmaier, 1995, p. 14.
[26] Ibid., p.15.
[27] Ibid., 1995, pp. 15-16.
[28] Ibid., 1995, p. 16.
[29] Ibid., pp. 17-19.
[30] Dominick, 1992, p. 55.

account of rarity, beauty, distinctiveness or on account of scientific, ethnic, forest or hunting significance lies in the general interest.[31]

Some leaders in the Nazi government, like Goebbels and Heydrich, were not supporters of green initiatives and the green effort lost its momentum as World War Two unfolded.[32]

Staudenmaier[33] concludes that the green wing of National Socialism was not a group of misled innocents but rather were "conscious promoters and executors of a vile program explicitly dedicated to inhuman racist violence, massive political repression and worldwide military domination." Ecological arguments were used to justify genocide, as in the claim that land taken in the east would be used with greater ecological sensitivity by Germans. Staudenmaier[34] also concludes that ecology becomes associated with conservative, reactionary and fascist politics when it involves the idea of a natural order or law to which humans must submit. As we will see, this last point needs further examination. Raymond Dominick,[35] although emphasizing the differences between German conservationists and Nazis, has acknowledged that the two shared racism, anti-modernism, anti-technology views, anti-materialism, and reactionary aesthetics. Some of this is part of the history of environmentalism in the United States and is still there today. Some of what Dominick thought separated Nazism and conservationism is irrelevant today. That is, he argued that German conservationists in the Nazi era never embraced militarism, the fuhrer principle, or extreme nationalism.[36] Even if this was true, and Staudenmaier's work and that of Mosse would dispute this in part at least, it would not mean that environmentalism is not a dangerous and anti-human ideology. If you take away those three elements, militarism, nationalism and the fuhrer principle, you would still have hostility toward reason, rationality, materialism, science, industrialism, and urbanism.[37] These ideas are themselves reactionary and aristocratic. The anti-modernism and nature mysticism which were part of German ecologism and part of the Nazi world view were elements of an aristocratic opposition to or disdain for progress that became an important part of English culture and politics.

ENGLAND AND THE ARISTOCRATIC OPPOSITION TO PROGRESS

An important element of contemporary environmentalism appeared early in modern English history and it gained wide acceptance in the upper levels of English society. These were concerns about population growth and its relationship to resources. Thomas Robert Malthus is usually credited with the first version of this that focused on land, food production, and population growth. Malthus was an Anglican clergyman and professor at

---

[31] Ibid., p. 108.
[32] Dominick, 1992, pp. 106-108; Staudenmaier, 1995.
[33] Staudenmaier, 1995, pp. 24-25.
[34] Ibid., pp. 25-26.
[35] Dominick, 1992, pp. 86-88.
[36] Ibid., p. 86.
[37] Ibid., pp. 87-88.

the East India Company's Haileyburg College, the training ground for the Indian Civil Service. Because Malthusian and neo-Malthusian ideas have played an important role in the development of today's environmentalism, we will examine Malthus' views and take a brief look at one example of a Malthusian governmental policy involving small pox.

Both versions of Malthus' *An Essay on the Principle of Population* (1798 and 1803) were ostensibly written to warn humankind about the dangers of unrestricted population growth. Assuming the necessity of food and unchanging "passion between the sexes," Malthus asserted in the 1798 version that there is a constant tendency for population growth, which progresses geometrically, to exceed the increase in agricultural production, which progresses arithmetically. This tendency means that there will be forces which act to suppress population growth with severe effects, including unemployment and poverty, on a large part of humanity. Malthus said he was making these points to refute those such as Condorcet who believed in virtually unlimited progress and in the "perfectibility of society." Against them, Malthus claimed "that the period when the number of men surpass their means of subsistence has long since arrived."[38]

In the second, much expanded version published in 1803, Malthus restated the arguments from the first essay, but gave more attention to the ways in which the two unequal forces of food and population increases are kept in balance. Since he believed that population growth always neutralizes improvements in food production, he focused on those forces that act to inhibit population growth. These he divided into two categories: preventive and positive checks. Preventive checks are those which reduce the numbers of people born. Primary is moral or self restraint, including non-marriage, late marriage and efforts to avoid reproducing. Also mentioned were forms of promiscuity and vice which do not increase reproduction. Positive checks are those which eliminate existing human beings. Malthus' list included war, severe labor, unwholesome occupations, extreme poverty, exposure, poor care of children, and what he called natural checks -- epidemics, plague and famine. All of the preventive and positive checks, said Malthus, are "resolvable into moral restraint, vice and misery."[39]

Although Malthus proclaimed an interest in mankind's happiness,[40] he did not hide his glee at the prospect of humans paying for their violations of the Malthusian law.

> Famine seems to the last, the most dreadful resource of nature. The power of population is so superior to the power in the earth to produce subsistence for man, that premature death must in some shape or other visit the human race. The vices of mankind are active and able ministers of depopulation; and often finish the dreadful work themselves. But should they fail in this war of extermination, sickly seasons, epidemics, pestilence, and plague, advance in terrific array, and sweep off their thousands and ten thousands. Should success be still incomplete, gigantic inevitable famine stalks in the rear, and with one mighty blow, levels the population with the food of the world.[41]

---

[38] Malthus, 1960, pp. 9-10, 14-15, 56-57.
[39] Ibid., pp. 151-165, 335-338, 356, 454, 470-476.
[40] Ibid., p. 151.

The enthusiasm for the extermination of excess people illustrates the vicious nature of this gentleman's views. So do his views on how to deal the poor. Malthus advocated openly and explicitly that government and society should adopt a policy of allowing the destitute to die. This is expressed in his attack on parish relief. For over two centuries this system had assigned responsibility to local officials and churches to give assistance to the poor in their area, or parish. Malthus argued that

> there is one right which man has generally been thought to possess, which I am confident he neither does nor can possess -- a right to subsistence when his labour will not fairly purchase it.[42]

Malthus recommended that public notice be given that anyone born after a certain date, sometime in the very near future, would not be eligible for any form of relief. Generations to come than will have "no claim of right on society for the smallest portion of food."[43]

Acknowledging that charity would become the only possible hope for survival, he went on to say that the uncertainty this would create for the poor would be desirable. The end of parish relief and the uncertainty of charity would force the poor to save more or risk having their families starve to death. This, he said, would discipline the poor to avoid having children they cannot care for. To further discourage childbearing Malthus recommended that policies should ensure a housing shortage.

Malthus' vicious attitudes toward the poor are derived from and justified by his arguments against the human capacity for progress. His pessimistic view of our ability to develop or expand resources leads him to warn that the only way to help the poor is through the redistribution of existing resources. Malthus:

> Poor-laws, indeed, will always tend to aggravate the evil by diminishing the general resources of the country; and in such a state of things can exist only for a very short time; but with or without them, no stretch of human ingenuity and exertion can rescue the people from the most extreme poverty and wretchedness.[44]

His assertion that the reduction of poverty is only possible through redistribution is repeated in various places as is the pessimistic conclusion that poverty and misery are inevitable.

This brings us to what seems to be the crux of Malthus' arguments and the reason for their creation. Ultimately, the reason that progress is not possible in Malthus' ideas and Malthus' motive for saying that progress is not possible appear to be one in the same. His condemnation of the attempts to negate the laws of nature as they relate to population growth and misery is actually a condemnation of all efforts to change what he sees as a

---

[41] Ibid., pp. 51-52.
[42] Ibid., p. 518.
[43] Ibid., pp. 530-531.
[44] Ibid., p. 537.

natural social order. Malthus' purpose was the defense of a quasi-feudal system of privilege and power that he considered natural.

This purpose becomes clear when one examines Malthus' constant tendency to intermix the natural with social and political reasons for the impossibility of progress. In both the natural and the socio-political arguments he portrays humans as a species which, like animals, exists within a fixed and unchanging environment. Such progress as had already taken place could not be refuted or denied by Malthus, so he simply ignored it or treated it as part of a futile endeavor by mankind to alter what is ultimately unchangeable.[45] Malthus argued that humans, like animals and plants, must live within the limits that nature provides. It is nature, not human creativity combined with nature, that sets the limits of food production. Substantial improvements for the poor are in Malthus' words "not in the nature of things."[46]

The limits to progress created by Malthus' natural world have their counterpart in the social, political and economic organization of society.

> In the actual circumstances of every country, the prolific power of nature seems to be always ready to exert nearly its full force; but within the limit of possibility, there is nothing perhaps more improbable, or more out of reach of any government to effect, than the direction of the industry of its subjects in such a manner as to produce the greatest quantity of human sustenance that the earth could bear. It evidently could not be done without the most complete violation of property, from which everything that is valuable to man has hitherto arisen.[47]

Here the system of property replaces the system of nature as the reason that limits exist and Malthus makes what might be called today a free enterprise of free market argument. It is apparent that Malthus was most concerned with the property owned by the upper layers of English society. For Malthus, the law of property, along with self-interest and legal marriage, is the basis "for all the noblest exertions of human genius, for everything that distinguishes the civilized from the savage state."[48] Following John Locke, Malthus saw property as the central value of society. What might be done can't be done because it would upset the property system that is the foundation of all that is good in the world.[49] It is obvious today that great economic progress can be made with moderate amounts of government interference with property and the market. It is also obvious that government passivity can be disastrous.

Having set forth the view that things cannot, or should not, be otherwise, Malthus relieved the rich of all responsibility for the conditions of the poor.

> That the principal and most permanent cause of poverty has little or no direct relation to the forms of government, or the unequal division of property; and that, as the rich do not

---

[45] Ibid., pp. 10, 79, 84-85, 100, 220-221, 337-338.
[46] Ibid., pp. 9-15, 100.
[47] Ibid., p. 370.
[48] Ibid., p. 593.
[49] Ibid., pp. 519, 593.

in reality possess the power of finding employment and maintenance for the poor, the poor cannot in the nature of things, possess the right to demand them...[50]

The social order is the unyielding system that presents the natural limit to progress. The relationship of population to nature is also an expression of Malthus' conception of the relationship of the poor, and perhaps all without property, to the property owner of eighteenth and nineteenth century England. Population growth puts pressure on available land; that land was owned by the English upper class.

Malthus was also an enthusiastic critic of two developments that were upsetting the world of the landowner - urbanization and industrialization. Malthus' hostility toward manufacturing is present in both versions of his book, although it is given greater emphasis in the first version. Even though Malthus does not deny that trade and manufacturing had been of benefit to the poor, he opposes the shift to manufacturing because it shifts resources, including labor, away from agriculture and because the urban-manufacturing environment is unhealthy and corrupt compared to that of the countryside.[51] Malthus claimed that employment in manufacturing was unreliable for the worker because such labor is less productive than agricultural labor. This was Malthus' version of the physiocrat's argument that agriculture was the source of all wealth.[52] These arguments are repeated in the second version of his book even though he frequently acknowledges general advantages in the combination of manufacturing and commerce with agriculture.[53] These inconsistencies, which he always resolved in general tone against manufacturing, were made more incoherent by his assertions that progress in creating wealth makes children more costly, his incredibly simplistic division of production into luxuries and food, and his argument that real wages of labor are always connected to the price of corn.[54] Malthus' view of cities was consistent with his ideas about manufacturing. He thought of them as unwholesome places of misery that were draining Europe of its vitality.[55]

Malthus had very elitist ideas about the majority of human beings. Only the upper class, in Malthus' view, possessed a spirit of independence and was capable of serious intellectual activity. He thought that most of humanity was by nature lazy and dull unless forced into activity by necessity and fear of pain.[56] While Malthus was pessimistic about human potential, he did hope that people could be educated to see the necessity of limiting reproduction. He also hoped that if people saw overpopulation as the source of all problems, they would be less likely to challenge authority.[57]

Malthus' aristocratic and pessimistic ideas encouraged people to think of material progress as impossible or futile and to adopt an attitude of cruelty or indifference toward much of humanity. Malthus attempted to provide natural or biological explanations for

---

[50] Ibid., p. 591.
[51] Ibid., pp. 106, 112-120.
[52] McDonald, 1979, p. 233.
[53] Malthus, 1960, pp. 382-383, 408-412, 415, 419, 442, 455-457, 587.
[54] Ibid., pp. 121, 458, 464.
[55] Ibid., pp. 41, 121-123.
[56] Ibid., pp. 128-131, 136-138, 538.
[57] Ibid., pp. 14, 542-543.

problems of production and distribution. Underlying all of this was an implicit devaluation of human creativity. Malthus relied on a method of argument that was based on the initial assertion of what were no more than plausible premises. Once stated, these plausible, but thoroughly arbitrary and unproven premises could be used to generate a series of logically related conclusions. Such arbitrary assertions included the following: the world is at or near absolute overpopulation; the progress of the past can not continue; population growth always neutralizes improvements in food production; population growth rates tend to be rigid over time; manufacturing labor is less productive than agricultural labor; the city and town are degrading social environments compared to the countryside. Malthus proved none of these premises; most have since been disproven. As we will see later, many contemporary environmental arguments have been constructed along the same lines as Malthus' arguments.

It was not until 1877 that a formal organization was created to promote Malthus' ideas. It was named the Malthusian League. This organization would later become part of the Society of Constructive Birth Control, founded in 1927.[58] His thinking had an impact in other ways. Influential thinkers such as David Ricardo and John Stuart Mill adopted views similar to Malthus.[59] Malthus and his supporters opposed efforts to vaccinate the entire population against small pox in what was probably one of the first large scale, practical applications of Malthus' ideas.

Edward Jenner developed an anti-smallpox vaccine and promoted its use in a 1798 book entitled *An Inquiry into the Causes and Effects of the Variolae Vaccine*. Published the same year as the first version of Malthus' population argument, it had entirely different purposes, i.e., preventing what Malthus thought of as one of the positive checks on population. Reverend Malthus, like his mentor the Reverend Joseph Townsend, saw plagues as a regulator of population. Instead of supporting vaccination, Malthus, logically enough, attacked Dr. Jenner. Followers of Malthus would successfully block the general vaccination of the entire population for decades.[60] Eighty years after Jenner's book was published, people were still dying, unnecessarily, of smallpox in Ireland.[61]

As we will see in later chapters, Malthus and his ideas continue to be a significant influence as part of environmental thinking. One analysis of the rise of the contemporary environmental movement argues that radical environmentalism in particular can be traced back to Malthus and Darwin.[62] This may well be true for environmentalism in general even though Malthusian ideas have been subjected to withering criticism. For example, Fredric Wertham points out that population changes are analyzed by Malthusians as an abstract process separated from actual developments. In his 1967 book, *A Sign For Cain*, Wertham went on to argue that Malthusians typically underestimate natural resources, underestimate human creativity, and arbitrarily substitute biological perspectives for sociological ones, thereby preventing the search for social remedies. In the end, life itself is devalued. Wertham charged that Malthusianism is closely tied to reactionary political

---

[58] Demerath, 1976.
[59] Barnett and Morse, 1963, pp. 51, 56.
[60] Chase, 1982, pp. 55-66.
[61] Ibid., p. 64.
[62] Pepper, 1984, p. 12.

forces, is linked to racism and the protection of privilege, and is a ready made justification for all sorts of overt and indirect violence.[63]

In his 1981 book, *The Ultimate Resource*, Julian Simon refuted contemporary Malthusian arguments, particularly the general pessimism in those ideas. Among other things, Simon pointed out that population growth has been a cause of and consequence of social and economic progress. Simon pointed out that the greatest improvements in history in standard of living took place during the fastest population growth in history. Simon also concluded that there is no evidence showing that population growth inhibits or prevents economic development.[64]

ENGLISH CONSERVATIONISM

A case had been made that England lagged well behind the United States in the development of a distinct and coherent conservation movement. The environmentalist writer and leader Max Nicholson[65] claimed that such a movement existed in the United States by 1908, but not in England until 1963. This may be technically true, but it is also misleading. Many of the themes and views that were part of romantic ecology in Germany and, as we will see later, the more extreme wing of American conservationism became elements of upper-class English culture long before 1908. In a sense, England's upper class was its conservation movement.

What seems to have happened in England is that a persistent and surviving aristocracy combined with certain kinds of newer economic interests to form what one historian has called an aristo-finance elite. This elite inherited the aristocratic disdain for industrial technology and applied science. In addition, this elite merged with interests involved in or itself became involved in foreign economic activity and lost interest in domestic production. We will look first at this anti-industrial culture and then turn to the explanations for the continuing influence of this culture.

WIENER

The most extensive examination of English upper-class hostility toward industrialism is Martin J. Wiener's *English Culture and the Decline of the Industrial Spirit, 1850-1980*. Wiener argues that even though England was one of the important locations for the industrial revolution, the country never came to be economically or politically dominated by industrializing forces, public or private. The aristocracy and its culture survived as a dominant force.

---

[63] Wertham, 1967.
[64] Simon, 1981.
[65] Nicholson, 1970, p. 161.

Aristocracies, titled or not, are made up of people who rule by virtue of inherited position and who define the past and the future in terms of the perpetuation of that rule.[66] Of the titled aristocracies, the English one has been most successful in adapting to the modern world and adapting the modern world to itself. The English aristocracy's success has been due partly to the use of primogeniture, which kept estates intact by making the eldest son the primary inheritor. Probably more important, however, was the British aristocracy's effort to take command of productive and financial enterprises in the early 19th century, in spite of their disdain for production and career.[67] The English aristocracy also demonstrated its adaptiveness by handing out titles to the rising bourgeoisie and by accepting marriages of male aristocrats to untitled heiresses.[68] Many English manufacturers and merchants reciprocated by acting as if the only reason they ever wanted money was to win the approval of aristocracy.[69]

In Wiener's view, the aristocratic tendency, perhaps on the defensive in the late-1700s and early-1800s, reasserted itself by the mid-1800s. Admiration for material progress in England peaked in the 1850s and began to decline.[70] In the second half of the 1800s aristocracy merged with, took over, or absorbed leading business interests and aristocratic values and education won out over scientific-technical education. Intellectuals such as John Stuart Mill, Mathew Arnold, and John Ruskin promoted the stationary or no growth society, decried overpopulation and ugly materialism, and worried about the alienation of people from nature. Stability, ending growth, and control over people became more important, the creation of wealth less.[71]

By the late-1800s a counterrevolution against scientific-technical values was advancing. Rural nostalgia was on the rise and English greatness, then on the decline economically, was said to be rooted in the countryside.[72] A right-wing preservationist movement appeared in the 1870s portraying material prosperity as a menace and even offering to sacrifice property rights to preserve old buildings.[73] A series of early conservation organizations were created. The Commons, Open Spaces and Footpaths Preservation Society was founded in 1865. An Act for the Preservation of Seabirds was passed in 1869 and a Society for the Protection of Birds was started in 1889. The National Trust for Places of Historic Interest or Natural Beauty was established in 1895. In the 1890s the Duke of Bedford committed himself to saving wildlife globally and in 1903 the Society for the Preservation of the Fauna of the Empire was founded.[74] The British Vegetation Committee was formed in 1904 and out of this came the British Ecological Society.[75] The preservationist movement set about undermining confidence in

---

[66] Lacey, 1983, pp. 21-22; Powis, 1984, p. 1.
[67] Perrott, 1968, pp. 131-133; Powis, 1984, pp. 62-72.
[68] Baltzell, 1964, p. 9; Perrott, 1968, pp. 7-8, 72-73.
[69] Lacey, 1983, p. 135.
[70] Weiner, 1981, pp. 8-20, 30.
[71] Ibid., pp. 21, 32-38.
[72] Ibid., pp. 50, 55.
[73] Ibid., pp. 67-71.
[74] Nicholson, 1970, pp. 154-155.
[75] Ibid., p. 155.

the creative powers of people, elevating the past over the present, and criticizing industrial capitalism and materialism. This movement was deeply pessimistic.[76]

As of the beginning of the twentieth century, criticism of industrialism and modernization pervaded all major political tendencies in England.[77] Such criticism existed in the United States but it was limited to small groups and did not then become a widespread rejection of progress.[78] Anti-progress themes were developed in England by Arnold Toynbee and his ideas would influence both English socialists and right-wing Torries.[79] According to Bramwell, the ideas of ecologism became fully developed within "High Tory" circles in the 1930s.[80] Even major English economists expressed a distaste for industrialism, from John Stuart Mill to Alfred Marshall and John Keynes.[81]

Toryism was based on the quasi-feudalist idea that "economic forces should be made to accommodate themselves to the established patterns of social relationships."[82] This produced a hostility toward materialism, commercialism and profiteering where these disrupted the dominance of traditional ruling classes. This sort of view was expressed openly by people at the top of the English social order, such as Viscount Halifax.[83] The Tory poet T.S. Eliot warned in 1939 that unregulated industrialism would lead to the exhaustion of natural resources.[84] Striking an anti-Tory tone in 1969, the conservative Edward Heath described Britain as a "Luddite's paradise...a society dedicated to the prevention of progress and the preservation of the status quo."[85]

Anti-consumption and anti-materialist views also became embedded in Fabian Socialism, providing a leftist version of anti-progress ideas. Some labor leaders, like Ramsey McDonald, shared the Tory disdain for economic policy that was aimed at raising production.[86] In the 1970s the Labor Party, rhetorically favorable to technological progress in the 1960s, mixed calls for nationalization and redistribution with goals of harmony and stability.[87]

Wiener noted that in England and other parts of the industrial world the opposition to technological progress became better organized and more aggressive in the 1970s. Wiener observed that

> A new cultural phenomenon came of age in the 1970s: explicit and organized opposition to the results of technical and material advance. This was of course part of a development embracing the entire industrialized world, where antigrowth and anti-technology

---

[76] Wiener, 1981, pp. 68-69.
[77] Ibid., pp. 42-49, 62, 82-83, 111, 118, 120.
[78] Ibid., pp. ix, 6.
[79] Ibid., pp. 82-84.
[80] Bramwell, 1989, p. 104.
[81] Wiener, 1981, pp. 90-92.
[82] Ibid., pp. 98-99.
[83] Ibid., pp. 102-103.
[84] Ibid., p. 115.
[85] Ibid., p. 163.
[86] Ibid., pp. 120-121.
[87] Ibid., pp. 162-164.

movements had taken root among left-wing university students and had become a force to be reckoned with in public life.[88]

This development was part of the emergence of contemporary environmentalism. In England that "new cultural phenomenon" was openly associated with the Right as well as the Left. As we will see, the image of environmentalism in the U.S. shifted around 1980. It then acquired a leftist or liberal tag. Its substance however did not change nor did the nature of the most important forces backing it.

The lack of commitment to material progress among English elites has been noted by many students of English history. While they are not in total agreement, there is some consensus on the factors which contributed to this reaction against industrialism. Explanation of these things in England also may help us to understand what has happened in the United States. This is made more likely by the close connections between the American and English upper classes.

It is Wiener's contention that even though England was an early leader in the industrial revolution, the industrialists never became the dominant force in the economy and that they were co-opted and absorbed by social and economic forces with little or no commitment to English production or to technological and material progress. Wiener observes that a surviving English aristocracy combined with rentier capitalists and was thereby able to sustain its cultural hegemony.[89] That elite also reshaped the industrial bourgeoisie in its own image. According to Wiener[90] an accommodation took place in the mid-1800s between the most successful businessmen, most of whom no longer participated directly in their businesses, and the aristocracy. He notes that by 1896, 167 noblemen, a fourth of the total peerage, were directors of companies. Over time, England's business leaders usually accommodated themselves to an "elite culture blended of preindustrial aristocratic and religious values and more recent professional and bureaucratic values that inhibited their quest for expansion, productivity, and profit."[91]

Wiener[92] went on to say that British banks pulled away from long-term involvements in industrial activity in the late-1870s. He suggested that though this may have been based partly on economic considerations the "pullback from industrial involvement was made more likely by the social separation that already existed between the worlds of finance and industry, and the contemporaneous entrenchment of anti-industrial sentiments in the financial and professional classes."

According to Wiener,[93] the milieu of finance "was not all that different from the traditional world of the aristocracy." The London based financial class merged more easily with aristocracy than the northern based industrialists. The finance-aristocracy merger became more complete in the twentieth century. As noted above, the top industrialists were absorbed into this aristo-finance elite.

---

[88] Ibid., p. 165.
[89] Ibid., p. 8.
[90] Ibid., p. 12.
[91] Ibid., 127.
[92] Ibid., pp. 128-129.
[93] Ibid., p. 145.

Finance became internationally oriented, thoroughly intertwined with aristocracy, and the dominant force in government.[94] These interconnected interests became a source of anti-industrial ideas and they shaped an economy to be compatible with those ideas.

CAIN AND HOPKINS

In a two part analysis published in 1986 and 1987 P. J. Cain and A. G. Hopkins described and explained the development of what they called "Gentlemanly Capitalism." According to Cain and Hopkins[95] the modern British aristocracy had its origins in the late-1600s decision by feudal aristocrats to embrace a market philosophy. This produced a merger of "pre-capitalist heritage with incomes derived from commercial agriculture." The newly profit oriented class was nevertheless still a landed class oriented to order, authority and status.

As a market economy emerged in England, there were some roles which were more consistent than others with the status of a gentleman. Those roles were rentier, banker, upper level positions in law or the Church, military officer, large merchant, and insurance and brokerage. These activities allowed compromise with capitalism without involvement in the "'vile and mechanical' world of manufacturing."[96] By 1700 the City of London, England's financial center, was already entwined with England's aristocracy.[97] Within this aristocratic capitalism the landed interests were dominant until roughly 1850 and then succeeded by financial and commercial interests.[98]

Agreeing with Wiener, Cain and Hopkins say that industrial capitalism never achieved dominance in Britain. The gentlemen capitalists "derided the technology upon which [their] wealth depended" and were "concerned with managing men rather than machines." The gentlemen capitalists promoted minimal government and free trade, policies adopted by England in the mid-1800s.[99]

After 1850, according to Cain and Hopkins, a new upper class was formed from "an amalgam of rentier money, service employment and the remnants of landed society." This is generally consistent with Wiener's estimate of when the manufacturing tendency peaked and began to decline. By the late-1800s England was dominated by a developed "aristo-financial elite." This elite went about developing an oligopolistic structure for English industry. The directors and managers received their education at "public schools," that is, elite private schools.[100] Landed wealth perpetuated itself by investing abroad through London and by intermarrying with the financial aristocracy.[101] This supports Wiener's[102] observation that English financiers became enamoured with foreign

---

[94] Ibid., p. 145.
[95] Cain and Hopkins, 1986, p. 504.
[96] Ibid., 1986, pp. 506-507.
[97] Ibid., 1986, p. 507.
[98] Ibid., 1986, p. 510.
[99] Ibid., 1986, pp. 508, 515, 524.
[100] Cain and Hopkins, 1987, pp. 6, 10.
[101] Ibid., 1987, p. 6.
[102] Wiener, 1981, pp. 128-129.

markets in the late-1800s, allowing the domestic industrial base to deteriorate. There are, of course, some similarities to this in what has happened with the U.S. since the 1960s. We will look at that later.

England's role in the world, long based on naval power, became dependent on its world financial role in the late-1800s. That began to decline after 1914. The continuing global significance after 1914 of England's aristo-finance elite was based on its merger with the U.S. financial establishment.[103]

WARWICK AND OTHERS

Other students of English history have supported the views of Wiener and of Cain and Hopkins. For example, Paul Warwick observes that in the late-1800s England became increasingly dependent on

earnings from City of London financial services, shipping, and foreign investments, as export growth lagged behind that of her principal competitors.[104]

Industrialists, according to Warwick, sought to be like "civil servants, professional men, and men of landed leisure." They joined these other groups to form the English Establishment.[105]

This set of interests became dominant in the 1870 to 1914 period and displayed an "anti-industrial value system."[106] From the late-1800s onward England was increasingly dominated by the gentlemanly preoccupations: stability, clear class distinctions; democracy dominated by "the myth of government by those born to rule."

According to Warwick,[107] England's aristocratic elite's disdain for industry, science and technology coincided with its inclination to maintain an imperial system based on foreign investments and international financial activities, continuing through the twentieth century. Foreign investments were favored in policy decisions over domestic investments and national efforts and policies were aimed at defending empire.

With some relatively minor differences in chronology, Geoffrey Ingham's work is also consistent with Wiener and with Cain and Hopkins. Ingham[108] observes that

Although land ownership has declined in relative importance as a basis for aristocratic class power, I shall argue that the non-productive forms of capitalism to be found in the City assumed this role, especially after the capital export boom from 1870-1914.

---

[103] Cain and Hopkins, 1987, pp. 11, 14, 16-17.
[104] Warwick, 1985, p. 101.
[105] Ibid., pp. 106-107.
[106] Ibid., pp. 106-107, 117.
[107] Ibid., pp. 116-117, 126.
[108] Ingham, 1984, pp. 134-135.

Ingham went on to say that merchants and then bankers became aristocrats and vice versa. English aristocrats, united in part by their educational background, have dominated banking and commerce and the government civil service, which is to a great degree insulated from parliament.[109] This aristocracy has had little commitment to the use of science and technology and the international commercial and financial interests with which it is intertwined are not dependent on production within England.[110]

Consistent with all of the above is Dilwyn Porter's argument that only in brief periods of modern history, during or immediately following the two world wars, have pro-production forces dominated policy in England. Otherwise, the City of London, the Bank of England and the Treasury have succeeded in giving free trade and sound money a higher priority than "the maintenance and development of the nation's productive capacity."[111]

To summarize, the British aristocracy adapted to capitalism by involving itself in non-industrial sectors of the economy, developing a base of power and influence in finance, commercial farming, rentier activity and insurance. During the mid-1800s financial activities replaced the control of land as the most important basis for the continued dominance of the aristocracy. The British Aristocracy early on had made a successful transition from its feudal role by embracing commercial farming in the 1600s and becoming involved in other nonproductive endeavors during the 1700s and 1800s. There was some merger of the top levels of industry with the aristo-finance elite and that elite became involved in the control of some of the industry. The involvement of aristocrats in finance and the absorption of financiers into the aristocracy became a critical factor in English social, cultural, political and economic life as England's financial center in London became the dominant force in foreign policy and a major power in domestic and political affairs.[112]

Max Nicholson's observation that England lagged well behind the United States in the development of an organized conservation movement may be true, but it is very misleading. Long before such a movement existed in the United States, 1908 according to Nicholson, many of the views held by the more extreme conservationists in the U.S. were already embedded in the upper levels of English society and they were generally associated with politics of a rightist, elitist, and aristocratic flavor.

The aristo-finance elite was itself England's conservation movement. The conservationist ideas were deeply reactionary and they were closely associated with people who were, and are, correctly described as Tory, elitist, reactionary, and Aristocratic. The conservationist ideas in many respects were the views and values of England's Aristocracy, an Aristocracy which survived by adapting to the modern world and by adapting the modern world to its own needs and interests.

Malthus' preoccupation with scarce land and population growth, his criticisms of urbanization and industrialization, and his devaluation of human creativity were all attractive to a class rooted in a non-industrial past and seeking a way to prevent

---

[109] Ibid., pp. 136-137, 141-142.
[110] Ibid., pp. 77, 243.
[111] Newton and Porter, 1988, pp. xiii, 93, 112-113, 117.
[112] Cain and Hopkins, 1987, p. 511; Ingham, 1984, pp. 134-135, 142-143; Warwick, 1985, pp. 121-127.

modernization from eliminating them altogether. Fears about overpopulation, resource depletion, materialism, alienation from nature, loss of stability, endangered wildlife and the countryside were expressions of the socio-political concerns of the upper class.

In Germany an ecology movement developed that embraced many of the same views that were central to the English upper class' resistance to the modern world. Before the twentieth century arrived, German ecologists had developed the ideas that everything is interconnected and that everything is of equal value or significance. They were critical of industrialization and urbanization and were very concerned that modern civilization was destroying nature and eliminating human links to nature. In the early-1900s German ecologists were concerned with the extinction of species, deforestation, wilderness destruction, and the disruption of ecological balance. They were critical of progress and fearful of runaway technology. All of this developed in close association with right-wing and racist politics and much of it would be attractive to important elements within the Nazi party.

In England and in Germany ecology and conservationism developed primarily as concerns of the upper class and the political right. What about the early history of conservationism in the United States?

Chapter Three

AMERICAN CONSERVATIONISM,
A GENTLEMAN'S CONCERN

Many of the views that are part of contemporary environmentalism appeared earlier in the United States as part of an elitist opposition to industrialization and modernization. Unlike in England, these views did not permeate national culture in the period prior to World War Two. An elitist conservationism did appear within segments of the upper class and the upper-middle class in the second half of the nineteenth century. Because the ideas and values espoused by these privileged groups were at odds with the mainstream, it was necessary to create a movement to promote those ideas. In England anti-modernist views were already embedded in the culture in the form of Aristocratic preferences and sensibilities. The English upper class needed to preserve an anti-industrial culture while their American counterparts would have to create one.

There are probably many reasons for the differences between England and the United States. The United States had been created with a conscious opposition to aristocracy and to the aristocratic tendency to oppose change, particularly changes related to the rising tide of industry, the city, and democracy. Also, much of early American history had been an effort to conquer a vast wilderness and create a modern nation. The development of manufacturing had been a central goal of many of the country's early leaders, a tendency personified in Alexander Hamilton. In the late 1800s, American success was very much defined in terms of its advancements in technology and industry. The country's size and sparse population made it unreceptive to Malthusianism. The country, in fact, needed high levels of immigration. Much of the American upper class was or became linked to industry and there was no open and formal aristrocracy to lure them away from industry with titles and tradition, as happened in England. Many people in the United States looked to pro-industrial traditions of continental Europe for ideas about the future. There was a much greater diversity of political culture and tradition in the United States. For these and perhaps other reasons, the part of the U.S. upper class that became interested in conservationism needed an organized movement to promote it. Success would be a while coming.

The early history of this conservationism featured a split between what Stephen Fox has called the utilitarian conservationists and the preservationists.[1] The two were competitors in the effort to define American conservationism; each side had a famous symbolic leader. In the period around 1900 the utilitarians were led by Gifford Pinchot who was not inclined to openly challenge growth oriented businessmen or a prevailing culture which was supportive of industry and applied science. Pinchot once said that the conservation movement "has development for its first principle."[2] Pinchot supported a program of "multiple use" which allowed land and resources to be used for a variety of purposes simultaneously.[3] This meant that land might be used simultaneously for timbering, mining, recreation, and conservation. Pinchot's overall focus, however, was resource conservation and he gave little emphasis to resource development. In that specific but important sense, he was not that far from preservationist John Muir, whom he greatly respected.[4]

The Yale educated Pinchot was a "member of the social and political elite of the Republican party."[5] Like his father and like many prominent figures in the history of American conservationism, he was a member of the upper class Century Club of New York. With founder Teddy Roosevelt's help, he also became a member of the Boone and Crockett Club.[6] Pinchot studied forestry in Europe and got his first job "as forester on George W. Vanderbilt's lavish North Carolina estate, Biltmore."[7]

The preservationist wing of the conservation movement was led, at least symbolically, by John Muir. Within the upper strata of American society, Muir, or preservationism, had a larger following than did Pinchot. However, Muir's more radical brand of anti-urban, anti-industrial conservationism did not have broad support among the general population or among many business and property interests, including ranchers and farmers. It was more obviously at odds with the prevailing pro-development culture. Pinchot's softer and more flexible approach was more easily promoted in the political arena. Teddy Roosevelt, America's first conservation president, was emotionally attracted to Muir's anti-modernist naturism, but sided with Pinchot for practical reasons.[8] It was just not possible to implement Muir's program. Teddy Roosevelt and Pinchot were very close.[9] Roosevelt, while governor, appointed Pinchot to supervise New York state's forests and he acted to get Pinchot appointed in 1898 as Chief Forester of the Department of Agriculture, which had no forests until President Roosevelt later transferred forest land from Interior to the Department of Agriculture.[10]

The sentimental favorite of Roosevelt and other upper-class preservationists was Muir. John Muir was born in 1838 into a well-to-do family in Scotland. He died in 1914.

---

[1] Fox, 1981, p. 115.
[2] Ibid., pp. 129-130.
[3] Tucker, 1982, p. 53.
[4] Pinchot, 1998, pp. 101, 103, 171.
[5] Caulfield, 1989, p. 23.
[6] Pinchot, 1998, pp. 47, 144-145.
[7] Ibid., p. xii.
[8] Fox, 1981, pp. 121-130.
[9] Pinchot, 1998, p. 322.
[10] Tucker, 1982, pp. 52-53.

His father, who is alleged to have been a bully as well as a zealous preacher, brought John to America in 1849. Muir successfully avoided service in the Civil War, spending a couple of years in Canada for that purpose, and had little interest in the issues surrounding those momentous events.[11] Muir consciously rejected Christianity in 1867 and he began a decades long deep interest in nature, involving extended stays in the wilderness.[12] According to William Tucker, "Muir's 'wilderness experience' combined those old American characteristics of a Puritan upbringing and a pagan love of nature." The austere union with nature was frequently interrupted, however, with visits to one or another of Muir's extremely wealthy friends.

Muir reportedly said the following about one of his first wilderness experiences:

> I am lost - absorbed - captivated with divine and unfathomable loveliness and grandeur of Nature. Somehow I feel separated from the mass of mankind, and I do not know whether I can return to the ordinary modes of feeling and thinking or not.[13]

Although not an aristocrat by birth, Muir here expresses the very aristocratic idea that a higher appreciation of nature separates him from and elevates him above "the mass of mankind." It is Nietzschean paganism that Muir was flirting with here, that is, some idea that the masses are an inferior breed incapable of higher level sensitivity.[14] Muir reportedly saw no distinction between animate and inanimate matter and he thought the ranking of creatures from 'lower' to 'higher' was just a human conceit.[15] Muir's extremism would lead to a permanent split with Pinchot, who was himself closely tied to various upper-class interests.[16]

In 1889 Robert Underwood Johnson, associate editor of *Century* magazine, formerly *Scribner's Monthly*, and, like Pinchot, a member of the upper-class Century Club, recruited John Muir to write articles about the Yosemite hinterland.[17] The *Century* was becoming one of the top magazines in the country.[18] These articles contributed to the effort to have Yosemite National Park created, accomplished legally in 1890. At the urging of Johnson, Muir continued this work with the creation in 1892 of the Sierra Club.[19] They used the Appalachian Mountain Club, established in Boston in 1876, as a model.[20] The meeting at which the Sierra Club was created took place in the office of attorney Warren Olney. Olney and Muir would later become adversaries.[21]

The term 'conservation' was apparently first used in the modern sense of the word around the time the Appalachian Mountain Club was created.[22] It was apparently derived

---

[11] Fox, 1981, pp. 42-47.
[12] Ibid., 50-52, 79-80.
[13] Ibid., p. 7.
[14] Carey, 1992, pp. 62-63.
[15] Fox, 1981, p. 13.
[16] Tucker, 1982, pp. 52-55.
[17] Marquis Who' Who, 1910-1911; Wolfe, 1978, p. 244.
[18] Tebbel and Zuckerman, 1991, p. 72.
[19] Wolfe, 1978, p. 254.
[20] Fox, 1981, p. 107.
[21] Wolfe, 1978, p. 254.
[22] Nicholson, 1970, p. 168.

from the word "conservancies" which referred to government controlled forests in British dominated India.[23] Pinchot and an associate committed the Teddy Roosevelt administration to the use of the term.[24] There were conservationist writings before this, in the works of people such as Ralph Waldo Emerson and John Burroughs, and there had already been conflicts over issues of conservationism. For example, in 1852 the cause of saving the sequoias was taken up by James Russell Lowell's *Atlantic Monthly*.[25] The Mountain Club, however, may have been the first real organizational effort of conservationism. The Club was initiated by Edward C. Pickering who was a member of one of Boston's most elite families.[26] Pickering's great-grandfather was a New England federalist who promoted the breakup of the union through the creation of a northern confederacy.[27] Many of the early members of the Mountain Club were part of the faculty of Harvard University and many were members of Boston's most elite social circles, sometimes referred to as Boston Brahmins. Among the better known names associated with the club were Cabot, Lowell, Peabody, Lawrence, Eliot and Higginson.[28] In the decades that followed the creation of the Mountain Club, it was such "old WASP gentry" which provided most of the leadership for conservationism and preservationism.[29]

The Mountain Club's Thomas Wentworth Higginson, who was a radical abolitionist and friend of John Brown, was the grandson of an English army officer.[30] Higginson also became a prominent Mugwump. The Mugwumps were an elitist, anti-industrial movement of the 1870s and 1880s. Mugwumps criticized the crassness of industrialism and the typical Mugwump also was an advocate of laissez faire economics and opposed tariffs. Since tariffs were used to promote industry, there was a consistency in these positions. Mugwumps also were extremely conservative. It was industrialism they were having problems with, not the hierarchy of class and status. To that they were firmly committed.[31] They were free market aristocrats, an amalgamation that existed in England and would become an important feature of American politics and culture as well.

The presence of and the influence of this gentry in conservationism is a primary reason for the charge by some that conservationism was racist and elitist. The anti-urban sentiments of conservationists were tinged with prejudice against the Irish, Italians and Slavs. The city was viewed as less pure than the countryside. William T. Hornaday, a leader of wildlife conservation, said in his 1913 book, *Our Vanishing Wild Life*, that "All members of the lower classes of Southern Europe are a dangerous menace to our wild life." He went on with alarm to warn that the "Italians are spreading, spreading, spreading."[32] Racist views permeated the thinking of Madison Grant, co-founder of the Bronx Zoo and a leader of the Save the Redwoods League and the Boone and Crockett

---

[23] Kline, 1997, p. 59.
[24] Pinchot, 1998, p. 326.
[25] Nicholson, 1970, pp. 164-166.
[26] Birmingham, 1987, p. 137.
[27] American Council of Learned Societies.
[28] Documents provided by the Archivist of the Appalachian Mountain Club, Boston, MA.
[29] Fox, 1981, pp. 345-347.
[30] American Council of Learned Societies.
[31] Hofstadter, 1955. pp. 135-145.
[32] Fox, 1981, p. 347.

Club. Grant's racial ideas were combined with preservationism in his 1916 book *The Passing of the Great Race*. Sounding very much like a Social Darwinist, Grant argued that humans are only marginally different from animals and both are products of heredity.[33] The conservationist-preservationist views of Teddy Roosevelt included elements of racism.[34] The charges against conservationism were well founded.

During the 1890s Muir spent a lot of time with William Keith and a circle of spiritualists led by a Swedenborgian clergyman named Dr. Joseph Worcester. Swedenborg was an eighteenth century mystic claimed by Madame Blavatski as a forerunner to her occultism. Muir and other conservationists may have been attracted to Swedenborg's idea that god, man and nature are part of one unity. Muir had reportedly rejected Christianity because, in part at least, it was inconsistent with this holism. Although neither was German, both Blavatski and Swedenborg influenced the German Volkish movement.[35]

Muir also became closely connected to Robert Underwood Johnson, who he met in California in 1889.[36] Johnson brought Muir into association with two of America's most wealthy and influential families, the Osborns and the Harrimans,[37] and he was a link to such British luminaries as Rudyard Kipling and Lord Curzon.[38] Johnson was also Muir's connection to Teddy Roosevelt.[39] Among Muir's new friends was Henry Fairfield Osborn, an important figure in the development of the conservation movement and a zealous eugenicist. Osborn received much of his education in London at Cambridge University. He was a member of the upper class Boone and Crockett Club and the Century Club. In 1893 Johnson took Muir on a trip up the Hudson River to Osborn's estate, Castle Rock. The encounter with Osborn produced one of Muir's most important friendships.[40]

By the end of the 1890s Muir was a regular traveling companion of Edward Henry Harriman and the entire Harriman family.[41] Mrs. Edward H. Harriman would be one of the primary financial backers of the eugenics movement in the early-1900s.[42] Johnson had also brought Muir into contact with Teddy Roosevelt; Johnson had met Roosevelt when T.R. had earlier walked into the office of the *Century* magazine with Henry Cabot Lodge.[43] Roosevelt, an avid hunter and outdoorsman, took a guided tour of Yosemite with Muir.[44]

When Muir became involved in a conflict over a proposal to dam the Tuolumne River and flood a valley in California, called Hetch Hetchy by the Indians, Muir's allies included Johnson, the Harrimans and Henry Fairfield Osborn, the Appalachian Mountain

---

[33] Ibid., p. 347.
[34] Ibid., pp. 116-121.
[35] Fox, 1981, pp. 50, 52, 79-80, 368; Mosse, 1964, pp. 41-43.
[36] Johnson, 1923, p. 278.
[37] Fox, 1981, p. 127; Wolfe, 1978, pp. 261-261, 331.
[38] Johnson, 1923, pp. 398-399, 503, 524, 528-530.
[39] Wolfe, 1978, pp. 289, 314.
[40] Ibid., pp. 261-262.
[41] Fox, 1981, p. 127; Wolfe, 1978, pp. 261-262, 331. Wolfe
[42] Kennedy, 1970, p. 114.
[43] Johnson, 1923, p. 385.
[44] icholson, 1970, p. 174; Wolfe, 1989, p. 289.

Club, and a good part of the nation's media, including the *Century, Collier's, the New York Times*, and the *Nation*. The supporters of the dam included Gifford Pinchot, Senator George Norris and Warren Olney, a co-founder of the Sierra Club.[45] Johnson was a close friend of Pinchot also, but was disappointed with his stand on this issue.[46]

These connections and associations are part of the basis for Stephen Fox's observation that "Conservation was never more an elitist conspiracy than at its birth." Early conservationists frequently acted behind the scenes and often did not seek public support. Conservation and preservationism were largely the causes of the well-to-do and the rich. Many of its supporters, like Harriman, Osborn and Roosevelt, were politically very conservative and often racist. When the first National Conservation Conference was held near the end of the Roosevelt presidency, one of the conservation speakers called for the conservation of the Anglo-Saxon race.[47]

William Tucker observed in his analysis of contemporary environmentalism that the values and viewpoints of environmentalism are very old, not new as many believe. They are "the values and positions that have ever been espoused by a nation's aristocracy." America's untitled aristocracy, the Osborns, Rockefellers, Harrimans and others, was attracted to the anti-modern ideas of Muir and the preservationist wing of conservationism. One version of these anti-modern, aristocratic ideas appeared in 1930 with the publication of an influential book titled *I'll Take My Stand*. The book was a collection of essays by a group of southern intellectuals clustered around Vanderbilt University and calling themselves the Nashville Fugitives. Relating this to contemporary environmentalism Tucker observed that

> Decades later, the fundamental rejection of industry, progress, and science has proved to be far more popular, when presented in an acceptable context, than even the Nashville Fugitives might have imagined. Environmentalists have essentially rediscovered and in some cases reinvented, the conventions of aristocratic conservatism that were articulated-for one of the few times in American history-by the Nashville Fugitives in 1930. Any understanding of contemporary environmentalism must begin with a rereading of *I'll Take My Stand*.[48]

In the introduction to that book the authors declared themselves to be the enemies of industrialism, applied science, and practical production. They also argued that industrialism leads naturally to state planning and to a system that is not substantially different from communism.[49] This more-or-less repeats Malthus' warning that efforts to increase production will end up violating property rights, i.e., upper-class property rights.

Samuel Hays also has noted the important role played by anti-industrial and anti-materialist views in the early history of conservation. Upper income people brought "the

---

[45] Fox, 1981, pp. 144-145; Wolfe, 1978, p. 338.
[46] Johnson, 1923, pp. 291, 307.
[47] Pinchot, 1998, pp. 345, 347; Tucker, 1982, p. 60.
[48] Tucker, 1982, p. 9.
[49] Twelve Southerners, 1930/1951, pp. ix-xx.

enthusiasm of a religious crusade" to the effort to save America from modernization.[50] Hays:

> Conservation...was oriented toward the countryside, toward nature and the eternal values inherent in nature, rather than toward the more artificial materialistic, and socially unstable cities.[51]

The so-called artificial world is in reality quite natural for a species capable of creating and building, instead of merely adapting. Aristocrats cannot or will not acknowledge this.

Without the support of the Osborns, Harrimans, Johnson, the Appalachian Mountain Club, and much of the nation's press (e.g., *New York Times, Chicago Tribune, Collier's, Century, Nation*),[52] it is unlikely that Muir could have waged the battles that he did. Although broader success was half a century away, these early events indicated the possible influence that highly organized and well financed efforts might have, especially if aided by aggressive use of media.

THE HIGHLY ORGANIZED ROCKEFELLER EFFORTS

Among the upper-class families with an interest in conservation was the Rockefellers. They would become one of the leading forces behind the post-World War Two expansion of conservationism and the emergence of the contemporary environmental movement. John D. Rockefeller, Jr. was the most generous supporter of conservationism in its early years, giving tens of millions of dollars to the cause. He also played the role of activist, as in his efforts in the 1920s to have a park created at Jackson Hole in Wyoming.[53] Two of Junior's sons, John D. Rockefeller III and Laurance, would be major figures in the post-World War Two movement. A third, David, would be a promoter of global environmentalism.

In the pre-World War Two period the Rockefeller interests also became deeply involved in an area that would become increasingly intertwined, both organizationally and ideologically, with conservationism and environmentalism - population. Fox notes that "As social movements, population control and conservation shared parallel histories, intersecting at many points over the years."[54] That probably began with Malthus. John D. Rockefeller III would later be eulogized by the population control establishment and given the informal title of "Mr. Population." In the early decades of the 1900s the focus was on the solution of social problems through population control and eugenics, one of Henry Osborn's areas of specialization.

---

[50] Hays, 1959, pp. 141-142.
[51] Ibid., p. 143.
[52] Fox, 1981, pp. 144-145.
[53] Ibid., pp. 221-223.
[54] Ibid., p. 310.

John D. Rockefeller, Jr. set up the Bureau of Social Hygiene in 1911.[55] The Bureau, the Laura Spelman Rockefeller Memorial, and, less openly, the Rockefeller Foundation would all play a role in the promotion of eugenics. Jennifer Gunn has noted that:

> For them [the Rockefellers and their associates], the science of eugenics, particularly the tool of selective breeding, offered a therapeutic approach to the problems of the social order through the biological and social control of the population... JDR, Jr.'s views were not unusual; they were shared by his peers in the capilatist class who saw their economic and social status as 'natural,' by members of the rising professional classes, by reactionary nativists, and by progressive socialists and social reformers.[56]

The phrase "progressive socialists" refers primarily to a group of elitist eugenicists (e.g., George Bernard Shaw, Harold Laski, J. B. S. Haldane) who were confidant that government could be made to serve their particular cause.[57] The effort by Rockefeller organizations and foundations to affect social policy and popular opinion was part of a general upper-class effort that would only get stronger throughout the twentieth century.

William Buxton[58] quotes Max Mason, President of the Rockefeller Foundation in the 1920s, saying that the purpose of the Rockefeller Foundation's program was "control through understanding." In his book on the Carnegie, Ford and Rockefeller foundations, Edward Berman observed that foundations are

> class institutions that attempt to create a world order supportive of the interests of the class that they represent...The foundations are clearly part of the American ruling class. Their vast wealth enables them to articulate programs, set certain agendas and shape the world order in a manner consonant with the interests of the few associated with them.[59]

As we will see in Chapter Six, foundations have played a critical role in the growth of today's environmentalism. In the field of population, Raymond Fosdick and others at high levels of Rockefeller organizations promoted an agenda of purifying society through the control of reproduction.[60]

One of the Rockefeller family's closest allies in these activities, the aforementioned Henry Fairfield Osborn, was the Honorary Vice President for the Third International Congress of Eugenics, held at the American Museum of Natural History in August of 1932. Osborn, who was a friend too of Robert Underwood Johnson,[61] also contributed one of the "Scientific Papers" published in a 1934 volume entitled *A Decade of Progress in Eugenics.*[62] These Congresses were initiated to promote the "pure science" of eugenics, the founder of which was Sir Francis Galton. Galton also founded the first "modern eugenics society" - "The Eugenics Education Society of Great Britain." Galton's

[55] Collier and Horowitz, 1976, pp. 104-105.
[56] Gunn, 1999, p. 98.
[57] Kevles, 1985, pp. 85-87, 184-186.
[58] Buxton, 1999, p. 179.
[59] Richardson and Fisher, 1999, p. 8.
[60] Gunn, 1999, pp. 102-103.
[61] Jones, 1965, p. 163.
[62] Rosenberg, 1984.

successor as head of that Society, Major Leonard Darwin, organized the First International Congress of Eugenics, held in London in 1912.[63] Leonard was a son of Charles Darwin. Havelock Ellis' influential book promoting eugenics, *The Task of Social Hygiene*, was published in the same year.[64] The Second International Congress was held at the American Museum of Natural History in 1921. Henry Fairfield Osborn, whose son and nephew would play equally important roles in post-World War Two conservationism, served as president for that Second Congress. A committee formed by Osborn at that Congress would become the American Eugenics Society.[65]

The year of the Second Congress, 1921, was also the year that a student of Havelock Ellis, Margaret Sanger, started the American Birth Control League. Sanger, not from a privileged background, became a significant figure in the birth control and eugenics movements. Some know her from her famous or infamous comments. In 1919 she announced her goal by saying "More children from the fit, less from the unfit - that is the chief issue of birth control." The "unfit" in her mind were those who were retarded or physically deformed. She also believed that the intellectual potential of 70 percent of the American people was that of a 15 year old. Her politics were a mixture of individualism, elitism and antistatism.[66]

In the "scientific paper," entitled "Birth Selection versus Birth Control," given at the Third International Congress held in New York in 1932, Osborn began by asserting that[67]

> Eugenics is not a human invention by Francis Galton or any of his predecessors or successors. It is a long known and universal law, namely the survival of the fittest and elimination of the unfittest

Osborn went on to argue that people are being forced to pay attention to this natural law by the crisis of "over-population" and the crisis of the over-multiplication of the unfit and unintelligent, of the reign of terror of the criminal, of the tragedy of unemployment. The solution to these crises is "prolonged and intelligent and humane birth selection aided by humane birth control." About three years into the Great Depression Osborn thought that unemployment was caused by excessive reproduction, especially by those with low intelligence. It appears that he should have been out of a job.

Osborn briefly described his recent world travels and then summarized what he had learned from those travels in what he called the "six overs."

> Over-destruction of natural resources, now actually world-wide;
> Over-mechanization, in the subsitition of the machine for animal and human labor, rapidly becoming world-wide;
> Over-construction of warehouses, ships, railroads, wharves and other means of transport, replacing primitive transportation;

---

[63] Ibid., p. 1.
[64] Gunn, 1999, p. 102.
[65] Rosenberg, 1984, pp. 3-5.
[66] Kennedy, 1970, pp. 1-2, 115-117.
[67] Rosenberg, 1984, pp. 29-41.

Over-production both of the food and of the mechanical wants of mankind, chiefly during the post-war speculative period;

Over-confidence in future demand and supply, resulting in the too rapid extension of natural resources both in food and in mechanical equipment;

Over-population beyond the land areas, or the capacity of the natural and scientific resources of the world, with consequent permanent unemployment of the least fitted.[68]

Many of the central themes of contemporary environmentalism are laid out here, almost forty years before the first Earth Day. There are too many people consuming too much, too much production, too much use of technology and over-use of resources. In Osborn's view it is these kinds of things that are the causes of depression level unemployment. Concentration of wealth, speculation, low wages, growing inequality and credit crunches are not worth mentioning. Osborn's "scientific paper" provides a clear link between the Malthusian and Social Darwinist tradition and environmentalism.

Sounding much like population control advocate Margaret Sanger, Osborn recommended that ways be found to encourage the fit to reproduce and discourage the unfit from reproducing. He preferred this to generalized birth control efforts that he feared would lead to greater reductions among the fit than the unfit. Birth selection, he thought, should be primary, birth control secondary or subject to further study.

Even the generally kind entry for Osborn in *American National Biography* had to take note of his racist and aristocratic tendencies. They said the following about the "distinguished Aryan enthusiast."

Osborn's evolutionary interpretation also upheld conservative poltical and social values. His early evolutionary studies were conducted in the religious context at Princeton. In later years, as he solidified his ties with New York elites, he condemned twentieth-century social developments. Repelled by the nations's growing urbanization and ethnic pluralism, he adopted conservationist objectives, becoming a leader in the Audubon Society, the American Bison Society, and the Save the Redwoods League. His concern for the preservation of flora and fauna led Osborn to glorify the outdoor activities of the field biologist and condemn the experimental biologist who worked indoors in urban laboratories. Only the scientist who did firsthand work in the field could understand nature and nature's laws. Osborn's concern for the preservation of nature also extended to the white Anglo-Saxon Protestant elite to which he belonged. A proponent of eugenics, he viewed unrestricted immigration as a threat to public health and human survival. In *Men of the Old Stone Age* (1915) he claimed that humanity had declined after Cro-Magnon because of the onset of civilization and racial mixing. Based on his studies of fossils, which indicated that heredity controlled evolution, Osborn maintained that only those of a particular ancestry should guide evolution. He termed his evolutionary theory aristogenesis.[69]

The entry went on to note that Osborn created exhibits at the American Museum of Natural History which were intended to engender fear over unrestricted immigration.

---

[68] Ibid., pp. 30-31.
[69] Garrity and Carns, 1999.

Osborn's "scientific paper" was by no means clearly the most vicious of the contributions offered at the Congress. He had stiff competition. For example, one of the papers started out with the following:

The various dysgenic classes which are so rapidly increasing in the United States constitute our vast 'aristocracy of the unfit.' They are an undesirable group of citizens which the more thrifty, intelligent, and superior stocks willingly tax themselves to support and perpetuate. This increasing horde will ultimately overrun and destroy the diminishing posterity of the better classes unless a practical program of restrictive eugenics is adopted and effectively executed.[70]

This burden on society, according to the author, was made up of "defectives" such as the insane, idiots, criminals, and paupers and other "undesirables" such as the blind, the deaf, feebleminded, and epileptics. This argument is virtually identical to the propaganda of the Nazi movement.[71] In such company Osborn did not stand out.

Not apparently a speaker at the conference, but long associated with the Rockefeller interests, Dr. Alexis Carrel wrote the following in his 1935 book.

There remains the unsloved problem of the immense number of defectives and criminals. They are an enormous burden for the part of the population that has remained normal. As already pointed out, gigantic sums are now required to maintain prisons and insane asylums and protect the public against gangsters and lunatics. Why do we preserve these useless and harmful beings? The abnormal prevent the development of the normal. This fact must be squarely faced. Why should society not dispose of the criminals and the insane in a more economical manner? We cannot go on trying to separate the responsible from the irresponsible, punish the guilty, spare those who, although having committed a crime, are thought to be morally innocent. We are not capable of judging men. However, the community must be protected against troublesome and dangerous elements. How can this be done? Certainly not by building larger and more comfortable prisons, just as real health will not be promoted by larger and more scientific hospitals. Criminality and insanity can be prevented only by a better knowledge of man, by eugenics, by changes in education and in social conditons. Meanwhile, criminals have to be dealt with effectively. Perhaps prisons should be abolished. They could be replaced by smaller and less expensive institutions. The conditioning of petty criminals with the whip, or some more scientific procedure, followed by a short stay in a hospital, would probably suffice to insure order. Those who have murdered, robbed while armed with automatic pistol or machine gun, kidnapped children, despoiled the poor of their savings, misled the public in important matters, should be humanely and economically disposed of in small euthanasic institutions supplied with proper gases. A similar treatment could be advantageously applied to the insane, guilty of criminal acts. Modern society should not hesitate to organize itself with reference to the normal individual. Philosophical systems and sentimental prejudices must give way before such a necessity. The development of human personality is the ultimate purpose of civilization.[72]

---

[70] Rosenberg, 1984, p. 193.
[71] Wertham, 1980.
[72] Carrel, 1935, pp. 318-319.

From 1906 to 1939, and on an emeritus basis afterward, Carrell was on the staff at the Rockefeller Institute for Medical Research. He co-authored a 1938 book with Charles Lindbergh after Lindbergh had become fascinated with the occult and conservationism. Lindbergh claimed that it was Carrell who got him interested in the occult.[73]

The preservationist wing of the conservation movement, the emerging population control effort, and the eugenics movement were all dominated by upper-class interests. The network of people around the Rockefellers and the Osborns provided links among the three groups. As was the case in Germany and, in a more directly relevant way, England, ecological ideas and concerns about population were directly linked to reactionary and elitist political views. This aristocratic tendency in no way receded after World War Two. In the period leading up to the birth of environmentalism in the 1960s, the leading voices of conservationism became, if anything, more Malthusian in their views on reproduction and more extreme in their criticisms of industrial society. Among the most important and the most extreme were Henry Fairfield Osborn's son Fairfield and his nephew Frederick Osborn. These extremists were the mainstream of conservationism.

---

[73] Fox, 1981, pp. 233-239, 370; Marquis Who's Who, 1940-41.

Chapter Four

PREPARING THE WAY - THE POST-WAR YEARS

The activities of leading conservationists and developments in the organization of population control and conservation efforts in the post-World War Two period lay the foundation for the emergence of environmentalism. This period, in terms of ideas and people, is also a link between the pre-war preservationists, along with the related eugenics and population control groups, and the rise of the contemporary environmental movement. There is no single day, month or even year that is clearly a dividing point between the post-World War Two preparations and actual birth of contemporary environmentalism. One might argue, for example, for the year 1970, the year of the first Earth Day, as the birth of environmentalism. Or, a case might be made for 1968 when important parts of the media began aggressive coverage of environmental issues. I think, however, that a good case can be made for the year 1964. As we will see, President Johnson announced the arrival of a new conservationism in 1964 and he very quickly made a partial commitment to the population issue. President Johnson's actions were closely tied to other events that led up to the 1970 Earth Day. So, we will treat the period from roughly the end of World War Two to 1964 as a time during which the ground work was laid for the emergence of environmentalism, which occurred roughly between 1964 and 1970.

In the years between World War Two and 1964, the most influential writers on conservation and population control issues probably were the Osborn cousins, Frederick and Fairfield, and William Vogt. We will examine some of their ideas and this will lead us to some of the important events of this period.

One of the most famous books of the modern conservation movement is William Vogt's *Road to Survival*. Until Rachel Carson's *Silent Spring* appeared in 1962, it was the best selling conservation book ever. Published in 1948, it featured an introduction by financier Bernard M. Baruch. Baruch was for many years closely associated with many of Wall Street's leading interests, including Morgan and Guggenheim.[1] Vogt was involved in conservation and population issues for over thirty years. He worked with the Audubon Society in the 1930s, was chief of the conservation section of the Pan American Union from 1943 to 1950, and was the national director of the Planned Parenthood

---

[1] Lundberg, 1937, pp. 190-193.

Federation of America from 1951 to 1961. Planned Parenthood had been created in 1939 out of a merger of the American Birth Control Federation and the Clinical Research Bureau and got its name in 1942.[2] One of the co-founders was the aforementioned Margaret Sanger. In the 1960s Vogt served as secretary for the Conservation Foundation. The self-described ecologist was a member of the upper class Century Association or Club and the Cosmos Club.[3] Vogt was a descendant of the first Episcopal rector in New Amsterdam.[4]

In his book Vogt sounds at times like an English aristocrat railing against the industrial era and expressing disdain for much of the human race. He calls for "high-minded leadership,"[5] by which he apparently meant leadership which is willing to deny the possibility of progress for much of the people of the world.

Although resources and destruction of the environment are mentioned by Vogt,[6] the primary threat in his view is population growth. Sounding much like Malthus[7] a century and a half earlier and like Paul Ehrlich two decades later, Vogt sounded the alarm.

> There are too many people in the world for its limited resources to provide a high standard of living. By use of the machine, by exploitation of the world's resources on a purely extractive basis, we have postponed the meeting at the ecological judgment seat. The handwriting on the wall of five continents now tells us that the Day of Judgment is at hand.[8]

Vogt discourages us from thinking that progress is still possible. He went on to declare that all but three or four Latin American countries were overpopulated and that only Brazil and Argentina had any chance of reaching a standard of living near that of the United States.[9] At the time he said this, the population density for South America was well below that of the United States which was, in turn, a small fraction of the densities for successful countries or soon to be successful countries like France, Japan and Germany.[10]

Vogt said that Japan with its near 80 million people was over-populated, could not feed itself, and had a dismal economic future. He even suggested that past improvements in sanitation and production had been a mistake, allowing people to live who now cannot be provided for.[11] Fifty years later the population of Japan had grown to more than 120 million people and Japan was one of the most successful nations in the world.

Vogt noted that some experts predicted that China's population would rise from its then 430 million to 950 million by the year 2000. Vogt asserted that China faced

---

[2] Piotrow, 1973, pp. 15-16.
[3] Who Was Who In America, Vol. V.
[4] New York Times, 1968d, p. 31.
[5] Vogt, 1948, p. 80.
[6] Vogt, 1948, pp. ix, 44, 67, 115.
[7] Malthus, 1960, pp. 51-52, 370, 537.
[8] Vogt, 1948, 78.
[9] Ibid., pp. 152, 166.
[10] New York World-Telegram, 1959.
[11] Vogt, 1948, pp. 216-218, 238.

immediate disaster and it would be impossible for her population to grow much without outside help.[12] China's population in 2000 exceeded the prediction by about 300 million.

Along with wildly inaccurate prognostications, Vogt arbitrarily and without any evidence linked population growth to problems such as the quality of hospitals and the educational system.[13] Twenty years later in *The Population Bomb*, Paul Ehrlich would link overpopulation to everything except the gravitational effects of the moon.

Barely concealed in all of this discussion was that type of "high mindedness" which reeks of aristocratic elitism. Vogt's tendency to make completely unsupported claims that have ugly implications is demonstrated in the following "high-minded" comment:

> The rising living standard, as material progress is called, is almost universally assumed to be to the advantage of the human race. Yet its toll, in terms of erosion of the human nervous system, has given the United States one of the highest insanity rates in the world.[14]

The tone of this is similar to the English upper class' view of industry and progress. They don't see any need for it and don't want to believe that it produces any real benefits.

This antagonism toward industry and rising levels of material consumption even leads Vogt, like his English counterparts, to attack certain aspects of capitalism.

> One of the most ruinous limiting factors is the capitalistic system-and this is one of the gravest criticisms that can be leveled against it. The methods of free competition and the application of the profit motive have been disastrous to the land....Business has been turned loose to poison thousands of streams and rivers with industrial wastes; and hundreds of cities are spending millions of dollars so that they may safely drink the waste dumped into the rivers upstream.[15]

Vogt's most consistent concern however is with the mass consumption of the majority of people. There is never any mention of the consumption of the rich, either in terms of its impact or as a bad example. That is always the case in environmental writings. Vogt[16] says, for example, that one of the reasons that land in the U.S. has been overused is that farmers wish to make money in order to have a car, radio, and bathroom. Vogt clearly sees these as illegitimate wants. Vogt went on to express other similar concerns.

> By using up our real capital of natural resources, especially soil, we reduce the possiblity of ever paying off the debt. To me it seems impossible to escape the conclusion that the relatively high material living standard we have set for our farmers cannot be realized in the long pull; and it is even more fantastic to seek it for the millions of nonproducers who are, in a very real sense, parasitic on the land.[17]

---

[12] Ibid., p. 219.
[13] Ibid., pp. 79-80.
[14] Ibid., pp. 37-38.
[15] Ibid., p. 34.
[16] Ibid., pp. 41-43.
[17] Ibid., p. 44.

That Vogt does in fact think of much of humanity as little more than parasites is further demonstrated when he attacks the medical profession for its 2000 year old commitment "to keep alive as many people as possible."[18] These feelings are reflected in chapter titles and in subheadings. Chapter 4 is titled "Industrial Man - the Great Illusion" and subsections include "The Parasite" and "More Hungry Mouths."

Vogt specifically asserted that we must abandon the commitment made by President Franklin Roosevelt to aid in the economic progress of other countries.

> Americans of good will have advocated an American standard of living, or something approaching it, for the entire world. 'Freedom from want' was the carrot held before the noses of less prosperous peoples, to enlist their support during the war. What a monstrous deception this was, of ourselves and them, should be clear to anyone who thinks in terms of the carrying capacities of the world's lands.[19]

Instead of seeking an alliance for progress Vogt wanted a global effort to limit the reproduction of those "parasites." Vogt's dim view of humanity was also expressed in more subtle ways. Like Malthus, Vogt discussed the productivity of land as if human activity and creativity were irrelevant. In an expression that has a very contemporary, globalist ring to it, Vogt declared that "few of our leaders have begun to understand that we live in one world in an ecological-an environmental-sense."[20]

The same year that Vogt's *Road to Survival* appeared, Fairfield Osborn published his book, *Our Plundered Planet*. Osborn's book reportedly drew heavily on the "insights" of the racist German ecologist Ernst Haeckel,[21] discussed in Chapter Two. These two books were ideological bridges between the earlier preservationist conservationism and the environmentalism that emerged in the 1960s. Also, the *New York Times* editorialized in 1953 that these two books were largely responsible for an ongoing revival of the Malthusian doctrine.[22] Marshall Robinson, who was in the 1970s vice-president of Resources and Environment of the Ford Foundation, later wrote that Osborn's book was a "bible" for those already committed to the idea that human activities were undermining the quality of the environment.[23] It was translated into thirteen languages.[24] Osborn, a product of Groton, Princeton and Cambridge, was president of the New York Zoological Society from 1940 to 1968 and was a founder with Laurance Rockefeller of the Conservation Foundation. Osborn was president of the Conservation Foundation for many years and he was affiliated with the following groups: Save the Redwoods League, Audubon Society, Boone and Crockett Club, American Committee for International Wildlife Protection, International Committee for Bird Preservation, Zoological Society of London. He was a member of the Century Club.[25] Upon his death, the *New York Times*

---

[18] Ibid., pp. 48, 167.
[19] Ibid., p. 44
[20] Ibid., pp. 14-15.
[21] Winks, 1997, pp. 42-43.
[22] New York Times, 1953a, p. 14.
[23] Robinson, 1993, p. 12.
[24] Winks, 1997, p. 42.
[25] Marquis Who's Who, 1962-63.

described him as "one of the world's foremost conservationists."[26] Several years after Osborn's death, Laurance Rockefeller, who succeeded Fairfield as president of the New York Zoological Society, wrote an article about Osborn for Reader's Digest entitled "My Most Unforgettable Character."[27] Laurance met Osborn at his father's home and they worked together from 1939 onward.[28]

Compared to much of what was written after the mid-1960s, Osborn's book seems moderate. However, much of the radical environmentalist rhetoric and ideology is foreshadowed in this book. Osborn's interest in the English Malthusian doctrine was natural. Beside the fact that the Osborns were related by marriage to the famous British-American banking family, the Morgans,[29] the senior Osborn, Henry Fairfield, had studied in England under such luminaries as T.H. Huxley and was personally acquainted with Charles Darwin who had been heavily influenced by Malthus.[30]

Great emphasis is given in *Our Plundered Planet* to overpopulation and the exhaustion of soil. Osborn asserted, for example, that population growth is "the major cause of the world-wide depletion of the natural living resources of the earth."[31] Other issues raised by Osborn included deforestation and the adverse effects of DDT, fourteen years before Rachel Carson made this one of the first issues of the emerging environmental movement.

Osborn treated human creativity with disdain. Osborn[32] observed that man "has seemingly 'discovered' the secrets of the universe" and now acts as if he does not have to "live by its principles." Further on, Osborn[33] referred positively to a new concept of man, one that views humans as a "large scale geological force" that is capable of reeking havoc on nature. He recommended that we abandon what he portrayed as an excessive faith in the "marvels of modern technology" and recognize that there are limits to our abilities to get "subsistence from the earth."[34]

These kinds of remarks are very important. They show that what Osborn wanted was something much broader and deeper than solutions to specific problems. He wanted a change in underlying values and goals, a change in worldview. Sounding much like the German ecologist Moritz Arndt, Osborn[35] suggested that the future is hopeless unless we accept "the concept that man, like all other living things, is a part of one great biological scheme." Osborn[36] proposed "world-wide planning" to protect and repair nature.

This sort of talk has very little to do with addressing and solving problems. It is instead an attempt to redirect human purpose, away from the idea of the material progress and toward some goal of adaptation to nature, that is acceptance of things as they are.

---

[26] New York Times, 1969, p. 47.
[27] Rockefeller, 1972.
[28] Winks, 1997, pp. 42-43.
[29] Strouse, 1999, pp. 78, 80, 495.
[30] Ibid., p. 272.
[31] Osborn, 1948, p. 41.
[32] Ibid., p. 31.
[33] Ibid., p 176.
[34] Ibid., p. 199.
[35] Ibid., pp. 196.
[36] Ibid., pp. 37-38.

Humanity, said Osborn,[37] "must recognize the necessity of cooperation with nature." Osborn knew that a cultural shift of this magnitude could only be achieved after intense study and preparation and only if private and government resources were committed to it. A full commitment on the part of the educational system would be needed.[38]

The essentially political nature of Osborn's views is indicated by his low regard for facts. In fact, Osborn, like his more recent successors, displays a stunning disregard for facts. Also, like Malthus before him, he shows little or no appreciation for the advances that made it possible for the world's population to grow. Instead, he treats population growth as a threat, or what Paul Ehrlich and others later would call a population bomb, instead of a consequence of rising productivity.

That much of the world's poverty existed, and still exists, in its most sparsely populated regions did not interest Osborn for one sentence or one word in his book. Instead, he wanted to talk abut the overpopulation crisis overtaking China as it made a "desperate effort to feed its crowding millions."[39] That the population density of China was well below many European countries and many states of the U.S. was not even worth mentioning.[40]

The year of the book's publication was also an important year in the development of the modern conservation movement. Here too Fairfield played a role. In April of 1948 Fairfield announced the formation of the Conservation Foundation at a meeting held at the University Club in New York. The New York Zoological Society, of which Osborn was the first president, was also involved in the creation of the Conservation Foundation. Osborn also served as the first president of the Foundation. He was joined on the Foundation's board of trustees by Laurance S. Rockefeller, one of the most important backers of post-World War Two conservationism and of environmentalism, and by Sir John Boyd-Orr.[41] According to Collier and Horowitz,[42] Rockefeller helped Osborn to create the Foundation. In the early-1960s Boyd-Orr wrote what is in part a benign book, entitled *The White Man's Dilemma*. Boyd-Orr appears committed to real efforts to increase global food production.[43] On the other hand, he describes Malthus as "a pioneer in economics and a man of sincerity and ability."[44] Also, in his arguments for a world government he sounds very much like his aristocratic friend and associate, Lord Bertrand Russell.[45]

Osborn delivered an unabashed Malthusian message at a Washington symposium in 1948, a message carried live over the ABC network. Osborn:

> The cultivatable lands of our world...are estimated at approximately 4,000,000,000 acres. It is computed that 2 ½ acres of land of average productivity are required to

---

[37] Ibid., p. 201.
[38] Ibid., p. 200.
[39] Ibid., pp. 90-91, 98-99.
[40] U.S. Bureau of the Census, 1984.
[41] New York Times, 1948, Apr 6, p. 25.
[42] Collier and Horowitz, 1976, p. 399.
[43] Boyd-Orr, 1964, pp. 23, 43-48, 57.
[44] Ibid., p. 41.
[45] Boyd-Orr, 1964, pp. 12-15; New York Times, 1961b, p. 18.

provide a minimum adequate diet for each person. Therefore it is evident that there is today available an average of less than two acres per individual and that this productive land reserve for each person is constantly diminishing due to population increases.

Some countries have less than an acre of productive land per capita. No wonder there are worldwide shortages and that hundreds of millions of people are either undernourished or actually on the brink of starvation.

Hope for the future of man rests primarily, therefore, upon whether he realizes before it is too late that the maintenance of the earth's fertility is essential to his survival; further, that there is a limitation to the number of people that the earth is capable of supporting.

As matters stand today, these two stark truths, never too clearly recognized in the course of human history, have been almost totally obscured by the dazzling triumphs of materialism and industrialization.[46]

Osborn apparently did not even mention that the poverty and economic problems of much of the world had nothing to do with population or population growth. He does not even hint at the fact that most poor nations had low population densities. In this reproduction of the Reverend Malthus' distinctly unChristian sermons, Osborn seemed to think that agricultural limits represent some higher force which will overcome "materialism and industrialization." This is a very strange mode of thinking indeed. What possibly can Osborn be thinking when he makes materialism in its broadest sense an evil? It is clearly not greed he has in mind; it is the material needs of people that he conceives of as an evil. The only readily apparent way in which those needs would be evil is that their fulfillment, in Osborn's view, will require changes or policies that will threaten the status and power of the Osborns and his peers. The Nashville Fugitives had said as much. Malthus said as much.

The contemporary linkage between globalism and environmentalism was foreshadowed in the next year in another speech by Fairfield. He reportedly asserted that the world was waiting for a higher level of international political cooperation and that the cause of conservation could bring that about.[47]

In 1950 the world was only five years out of the war against Nazism and fascism. Given the association between Nazism and ideas about eliminating handicapped people,[48] it might surprise at least some people that something close to this would be proposed in public in that year. Margaret Sanger, as noted earlier a co-founder of Planned Parenthood and a leader of the American Birth Control League, proposed that the government sponsor a program to sterilize the feeble-minded and those carrying transmissible, congenital diseases. Sanger, repeating views she had held for three decades, called for quality, not quantity in reproduction. She also reportedly represented Africa, Asia, and South America as being overpopulated.[49] Such an image for Africa and South America is ludicrous, in 1950 or today.

William Vogt, who was, as noted before, the national director of the Planned Parenthood Federation, gave a speech in the following year in which he proclaimed that

---

[46] Loftus, 1948, pp. 1, 34.
[47] Teltsch, 1949, p. 15.
[48] Wertham, 1967; 1980.
[49] New York Times, 1950, p. 26.

overpopulation was a deadlier killer than the atomic bomb. Like Sanger, he referred to overpopulation as a problem of Asia, Latin America, and Africa, and he called for a national and an international policy to limit population.[50] In 1955 Vogt claimed that technology had not improved life in North America and he warned that population growth and improvements for those already alive in backward countries will mean less access to natural wealth for the people of the United States.[51] Fairfield Osborn's cousin, Frederick, gave a similar speech around this time. He was at the time secretary of the American Eugenics Society.[52]

Other, perhaps even more famous, people made similar remarks. Dr. Julian Huxley, brother of drug-use advocate, population control advocate, and novelist Aldous Huxley, sounded the alarm about population growth. Along with one of these alarms, he speculated that ten percent of UFO sightings were valid.[53] As we will see below, the Osborns were apparently impressed with the quality of Huxley's thinking. As noted before, Henry Fairfield Osborn, Sr., had been a student of T. H. Huxley, Julian's grandfather. Aldous Huxley praised Osborn's *Our Plundered Planet* and wrote the following in 1948 to Fairfield.

> I have been trying to put this question . . for the last year or two even succeeding in planting it in the *Bulletin of the Atomic Scientists* this summer, pointing out that while mankind could do very well without atomic energy, it cannot dispense with bread. But hitherto I have had no audible response from any quarter. I hope very much that you, with your scientific authority and your beautifully organized collection of facts, will be able to make some impression in influential quarters. . .
>
> . . .I see this problem of man's relation to Naure as not only an immediate practical problem, but also as a problem of ethics and religion. It is significant that neither Christianity nor Judaism has ever thought of Nature as having rights in relation to man . . You will find orthodox Catholic moralists asserting . . . that animals may be treated as things. (As though things didn't deserve to be treated ethically!) The vulgar boast of the modern technologist . . that man has conquered Nature has roots in the Western religious tradition, which affirms that God installed man as the boss, to whom Nature was to bring tribute. The Greeks knew better than the Jews and Christians. They knew [about] hubris towards nature ...Xerxes is punished, not only for having attacked the Greeks, but also for having outraged Nature in the affair of bridging the Hellespont.
>
> But for an ethical system that includes animate and inanimate Nature as well as man, one must go to Chinese Taoism, with its concept of an Order of Things, whose state of..balance must be preserved...Whitman comes very close to the Taoist position. And because of Whitman and Wordsworth and the other 'Nature Mystics' of the West, I feel that it might not be too difficult for modern Europeans and Americans to accept some kind of Taoist philosophy of life, with an ethical system comprehensive enough to take in Nature as well as man. People have got to understand that the commandment, 'Do unto others as you would that they should do unto you' applies to animals, plants and things, as

---

[50] New York Times, 1951, p. 42.
[51] Long, 1955, p. 16.
[52] New York Times, 1953, p. 22.
[53] Bracker, 1955, p. 21; New York Times, 1954, p. 13.

well as to people; and that if it is regarded as applying to people..then the animals, plants and things will, in one way or another, do as badly by man as man has done by them...[54]

Huxley warned that our commitment to technology was creating a "modern, scientific dictatorship."[55]

In 1953 Fairfield Osborn followed up his earlier book with the publication of *The Limits of the Earth*. The essentials of the argument presented later in the 1972 *Limits to Growth* are offered here. As has been commonplace, Africa and South America are portrayed as having a population problem. Osborn voices his pessimism about the potentials of modern agricultural methods and predicts that the world will not be able to feed four billion people.[56]

Osborn did something that later environmental writers almost never do; that is, he acknowledged that a rising standard of living might be the best birth control.[57] Nevertheless, he offered up a modification of Malthus which still contains all of Malthus' vicious pessimism. As noted earlier, Malthus saw land as the essential resource problem. In Osborn's updated version, it is resources in general rather than the population to land ratio. This is the neo-Malthusian argument which will emerge as a central theme of contemporary environmentalism, particularly in the 1970s. Osborn warned that the numerator, the resources of the earth, is "relatively fixed." The denominator, population is changeable and controllable. He described this as a "law" that we cannot ignore if we are to avoid crisis.[58] In this new version, any shortage, real or alleged, of any important resource can become a substitute for the agricultural limits in Malthus' polemic.

The year Osborn's book came out, 1953, was the first year of operation for a new population control organization, The Population Council. Both Fairfield and Frederick Osborn were involved in this new effort.

The Osborns were part of old money. They were descendants of Cornelius Vanderbilt and John Jay. J.P. Morgan, an American Founder of the Morgan banking dynasty, was uncle to the Osborns' fathers.[59] The Osborns were also closely associated with the other major American financial power, the Rockefellers. Frederick Osborn worked with John D. Rockefeller III on the creation in 1952 of the Population Council.

In 1952, John D. Rockefeller III called a conference on population problems to be held in Williamsburg, Virginia. (The Rockefeller Foundation has been active in population control research since the middle 1930s.) Frederick Osborn was a prominent member of the Williamsburg conference and became a charter board member and first vice-president of the Population Council, the organization which grew out of the conference. Rockefeller himself served as the first president of the Council and was succeeded by Frederick Osborn in 1957. According to the Population Council's 1965 progress report, Frederick Osborn set up the first offices, organized the Council into the demographic and

---

[54] Bedford, 1973, pp. 484-485.
[55] Ibid., pp. 688-689.
[56] Osborn, 1953, pp. 212-213, 223-224.
[57] Ibid., pp. 208-211.
[58] Ibid., pp. 207, 224-225.
[59] Strouse, 1999, pp. 78, 80, 96, 272.

medical programs, recruited the first staff members, and served as the chief executive officer during the first six years. In 1959 he became chairman of the executive committee, a position he held until 1968. Meanwhile, cousin Fairfield was active in Planned Parenthood-World Population and Frederick helped found the Population Association of America.[60]

Frederick Osborn was born in 1889. He was a partner at the banking firm of Grayson M.-P. Murphy and Company from 1921 to 1938.[61] Grayson M.-P. Murphy gained some notoriety as a result of allegations that he was involved in a high level plot against President Franklin Roosevelt.[62] Osborn became over time more and more involved in population issues and eugenics. The entrance for Frederick in *Biographical Memoirs* includes the following.

> He served as a trustee of the Carnegie Corporation, the Social Science Research Council, the Milbank Memorial Fund, Princeton University, the American Museum of Natural History, the Rockefeller Institute for Medical Research, the Frick Collection, and International House, and was a member of the Interstate Palisades Park Commission. He was mainly responsible for persuading the Milbank Memorial Fund and Princeton University to establish the University's Office of Population Research, and succesfully assisted in interesting a variety of foundations in supporting research projects in a number of universities. Notable among these was an inter-university group studying the social and psychological factors affecting fertility, which later became known as the Indianapolis Study and was published by the Milbank Fund. This was the forerunner of surveys that were taken up after World War II, and have now been taken over as a regular governmental operation. Osborn was a founding member and director of the Population Association of America and a key participant at the Paris meeting of the International Union for the Scientific Study of Population in 1936. He transformed the American Eugenics Society from an organization mainly devoted to the advocacy of racial improvements by sterilization into a society that fostered scientific studies of the transmission of human traits.[63]

Osborn worked for three years after the war with the United Nations Energy Commission before assuming his position with the Population Council.[64]

Frederick would often strike a moderate tone compared to his openly racist uncle, Henry Fairfield Osborn. However, he could also suggest sterilization as a global population control strategy and he complained in 1968 that improvements in medicine and public health were allowing more and more people with inferior genes to survive and spread those genes.[65]

The population cause was given a boost by the generosity of a number of foundations, much of which was money provided to start population research programs at

[60] Barclay, Enright, and Reynolds, 1970, p. 3.

[61] Marquis Who's Who, 1962-63.

[62] Archer, 1973.

[63] Biographical Memoirs; Document on file at Seeley G. Mudd Manuscript Library, Princeton University. Provide to the author by Steve Jones.

[64] New York Times, 1964a.

[65] Osborn, 1960, p. 105; 1968, pp. 19-20, 79-82.

universities. Money came from the Rockefeller Foundation, Rockefeller Brothers Fund, the Ford Foundation and also from the Population Council, itself a recipient of foundation support. Around this period of time, 1957, Laurance Rockefeller added to the family's involvement in conservation by creating the American Conservation Association.[66] In 1962 the Ford Foundation announced that it would intensify its efforts in the areas of conservation and population control. The following year Ford announced that it was creating a special department to deal with birth control and the Rockefeller Foundation said that population control was now going to be one of its top priorities.[67]

All of this was laying the groundwork for the emergence of a more aggressive environmentalist-population control movement in the 1964 to 1970 period. The atmosphere was heating up around 1960. A variety of notables were out sounding the alarm over the destructive consequences of population growth. Sir Julian Huxley, for example, was still at it. In 1959 he proposed a new global effort to combat overpopulation, a worse threat in his view than nuclear war. Speaking at the annual luncheon of the Planned Parenthood Federation of America, Huxley warned that population growth would exhaust the earth's resources and undermine civilization. He urged that we reject the quantity oriented goals that are part of population increase, mass production, and industrialization. This, of course, substantially replays the aristocratic outlook rooted in England's earlier history. Huxley was quoted[68] as saying that we need to place "meaningful quality," probably referring consciously or unconsciously to people such as himself, above "meaningless quantity," probably referring consciously or unconsciously to the majority of people in the world.

Retired general and investment banker William H. Draper, Jr., was out speaking to the public about overpopulation and foreign policy. Draper, a partner at Dillon, Read & Co., had recently worked to produce the Draper Committee Report given to President Eisenhower in July of 1959. The Report recommended that the U.S. government initiate a policy of supporting population control efforts. Draper was soon to become a vice-chairman of the World Population Emergency Campaign led by Lammot du Pont Copeland.[69]

Copeland and Draper also became involved in the related efforts of retired Dixie Cup Corporation head Hugh Moore.[70] As we will see below, Hugh Moore was one of the links between the so-called moderates in the population control establishment and the extremists. Also out speaking to the well-to-do about the dangers of overpopulation, and thereby winning the praise of Frederick Osborn, was John D. Rockefeller III. Rockefeller was arguing for government action in this area at the beginning of the 1960s.[71] William Vogt came out with a new book in 1960 entitled *People! Challenge to Survival*. He warned that a flood of humanity was ravaging the earth and devastating the biosphere.

---

[66] Bachrach and Bergman, 1973; Caldwell and Caldwell, 1986; Collier and Horowtiz, 1976.

[67] Fowle, 1963, pp. 1, 12; Kihss, 1962, pp. 1, 32; New York Times, 1963, p. 2.

[68] Petersen, 1959, p. 32.

[69] Bachrach and Bergman, 1973, pp. 43-48; Demerath, 1976, pp. 38-44; New York Times, 1959, p. 4; 1960, p. 45.

[70] Eder, 1960, p. 32; 1960a, p. 8.

[71] Cortesi, 1961, pp. 1, 17; New York Times, 1960a, p. 11; 1961a, p. 17.

Alan Gregg, medical director of the Rockefeller Foundation, likened population growth to a cancer.[72]

According to Piotrow, John D. Rockefeller III, Hugh Moore, and William H Draper, Jr., made the government's adoption of birth control their mission. None of this, however, had any apparent effect on the policies of President Dwight Eisenhower, who consistently refused to involve the government in these areas.[73] Years later and out of office, Eisenhower reportedly changed his mind and became more supportive of the population establishment. Having failed with President Eisenhower, the population control leaders turned their attention to one of Eisenhower's potential successors, John Kennedy.

At least twice in 1959 Kennedy was interviewed for the public record and asked about his views on population. The first transpired on November 27; the interviewer was one of the most famous and influential journalists of that era, James Reston. Reston was also one of a handful of journalists with extensive and strong ties to the upper levels of the Establishment. Reston was close to such Establishment luminaries as Dean Acheson and John J. McCloy.[74]

The title of Reston's article was "Kennedy Opposes Advocacy By U.S. Of Birth Control."[75] It was a page one story. Reston reported that Kennedy was opposed to any U.S. government policy advocating birth control in other countries. Kennedy's views reportedly prompted Margaret Sanger to declare that she would leave the country if Kennedy was elected.[76] Kennedy went on to say in the interview that we had not advocated birth control for our own country or for Western Europe and we shouldn't be doing so for black, brown or yellow people. Kennedy expressed his optimism that resources could be developed to provide for a growing population. Reston attempted to get Kennedy to say that his views were the views of the Catholic Church. Reston was unsuccessful in this and it does appear that Kennedy's views were steeped in secular argument, not in any simple way a reflection of church doctrine.

Ten days later Kennedy would again be questioned about his views on population, resources, and birth control, this time by the editor-in-chief of Harper's magazine, John Fischer.

Fischer: In these underdeveloped countries, do you think they can ever solve their economic problems as long as their population keeps rising at the rate of about 3 percent a year, doubling every forty years?

Kennedy: Well, I would think it was a population increase closer to 2 percent. But then you have to have an annual rate of increase of at least 6 percent in your gross national product, so that you have a 2 percent increase to take care of the population increase, another 2 percent to provide increased standard of living of the population, and another 2 percent to provide increased momentum in the years ahead. In terms of food, at least, if you provided for the kind of agricultural production increases necessary, if you provided for the calorie output per acre in India that you have in Japan or even in Western Europe--which is not impossible with

[72] Bates, 1960, p. 3; Poore, 1960, p. 45.
[73] New York Times, 1961, p. 41.
[74] Bird, 1992, pp. 125, 313; Fischer and Fischer, 1994, pp. 160, 241; Reston, 1991, pp. 140-156, 163.
[75] Reston, 1959, pp. 1, 12.
[76] Piotrow, 1973, p. 50.

new fertilizers, the control of water and education of the farmers--you could increase that production faster than the population. We've had a population increase in the United States which was as great as any place in the world, but our food production increases faster. Those with whom I've talked at the experimental stations of the Department of Agriculture point out what the Dutch and the Japanese produce per acre; and would indicate that increased productivity in the UnitedStates, which is really a technological explosion in the United States in food production (which is the heart of our agricutural problem), is going to continue; and that, with a concentrated technological effort, it can be done, and that must be our goal.

Fischer: Am I right, however, in thinking that no nation, except possibly Communist Russia and Communist China, has ever achieved annual growth rates of 6 percent a year for a considerable period? It's much greater than we ever achieved.

Kennedy:I would think that since the war the countries of Western Europe and Japan, which started at a rather low level--I'd have to recall their exact growth rate, but I would think that their growth rate was in several instances bigger than that. Economists such as Professor Rostow and others believe that the Indians could do it, in their third five-year plan, if they receive sufficient foreign assistance. What is the alternative? I think we must do it. Otherwise you just say you're going to ration poverty among an increased number of people.

Fischer: Do you see any hope at all of slowing up the rate of population increase?

Kennedy: You mean through birth control?

Fischer: By any method whatever.

Kennedy: Of course, the population increase is a matter of more children surviving and adults living to an older age, which gives us an immediate problem now. I'm not sure that the mathematical predictions of doubling the population every forty years will be fulfilled. Once the average person around the world can hope to reach three score and ten, once nine out of ten children live through the first year rather than two or three out of ten, I don't think you're going to get the arithmetical, geometrical doubling every forty or fifty years. Now, on the question of limiting population: as you know the Japanese have been doing it very vigorously, through abortion, which I think would be repugnant to all Americans. Some other countries have instituted programs of birth control, including the Indians. Their success has been rather limited. Most people consider their families to be their families, and that it is other people's families that provide the population explosion. The techniques are rather imperfect, and it should be remembered that in the experience of the countries which have used them, these techniques have not had a significant effect on the population expected. As you know, the Chinese were pushing it for a while, but are not now.

Fischer: They have appeared to abandon it.

Kennedy: So have the Russians, who believe this policy would indicate the inability of the Communist system to solve its problems. I believe it is a judgment which the countries and the people involved must make as to whether they wish to limit their population. Since it involves so personal a decision I think it would be unwise for the United States to intervene.[77]

---

[77] Kennedy, 1961, pp. 265-67.

Fischer invited Kennedy to adopt a pessimistic outlook on population, to embrace population control, and/or to say that Communism might be the only way to achieve an adequate rate of economic growth. Kennedy was having none of it. Instead, he recommended that everyone concerned with population growth support a program of economic development, which he suggested would over the long term bring down population growth rates. Fischer was not a mere journalist. He was in many ways connected to Establishment interests. He had been a Rhodes Scholar, was a trustee of the Brookings Institution and a member of the Council on Foreign Relations. He was also a member of the upper-class Century Association or Club.[78]

Shortly after Kennedy was elected, William H. Draper, Jr., a close associate of such Establishment luminaries as John J. McCloy, publicly advised the President to commit the government to population control, especially in underdeveloped countries.[79] The President was not taking orders from Draper or anyone else. He did not commit the country to population control.

Eight months later, James Reston would attack Kennedy for failing to support the effort to get Latin American countries to adopt population control measures. Citing predictions of rapid population growth for that region, but failing to note of course that most South American countries had relatively low population densities, Reston went on to say:

> Yet the President is saying that (1) vast outlays of aid to Latin America are essential, but (2) what happens to the population of Latin America is none of our business. He does not take the same attitude about other aspects of Latin American life. He does not tell them what to do with their economies, but he does say that unless they control their economies, and use U. S. aid to lift the standard of living of all the people and not just some of the people, they cannot have that aid.
>
> This raises a fundamental question: How can they control their economies or raise the standard of living of all their people if they do not control their populations? This is the root of the problem, and nothing is surer than that there will be a decisive revolt against foreign aid one day if the population problem is not faced.[80]

Kennedy was being consistent. He was saying that countries generally had a right to decide how to run their economies and he was saying they had a right to arrive at their own population policies. The only condition Kennedy was imposing was that nations getting aid had to adopt policies to develop their economies and spread the benefits beyond the upper classes. Reston, himself a member of the Council on Foreign Relations and one of the journalists in the country with the strongest ties to the intelligence and foreign policy networks, was telling Kennedy that Latin American countries had a right to decide neither. The interests Reston was tied to demanded that Latin American countries open up their economies to foreign interests.[81] Reston also claimed that population growth was a "menace to world peace" and to national security. Ten years

---

[78] Council on Foreign Relations, 1963; Marquis Who's Who, 1978-1979.
[79] New York Times, 1960b, p. 23.
[80] Reston, 1961, p. 22.
[81] Gibson, 1994, pp. 35-76.

later, Reston listed too many people and machines as two of the three top problems facing the world.[82]

Three days after Reston attacked Kennedy, another of the country's leading journalists, Arthur Krock, criticized Kennedy along similar lines.[83] Krock was also quoted that month in the upper class dominated Council on Foreign Relations' journal, *Foreign Affairs*. Krock was criticizing both Eisenhower and Kennedy for their failure to support population control. The author of this article, Jack Zlotnick, went on to bemoan the fact that both communism and democracy featured ideas that were hostile to Malthusian arguments. The core global problem, in Zlotnick's view, was the drop in the death rate in poor countries; this was fueling a rapid population growth.[84]

Kennedy's positions on just about everything were diametrically opposed to the views of the Anglo-American Establishment. He rejected the resources scarcity argument, did not believe the world was overpopulated, and he was completely committed to a program of national and international development through increased use of advanced production technologies. He also rejected another upper class argument, one that often is presented as the alternative to the Malthusian doctrine. That is, he did not believe that the future of the United States or of the world could be left entirely up to the partially open and partially manipulated market place.[85] Kennedy was opposed to the kind of free market economics and free trade policies that became the official dogma in the 1980s and 1990s, promoted by Clinton as well as Bush and Reagan.[86]

The effort to influence the climate of opinion and ideas continued in 1962 with the publication of Rachel Carson's *Silent Spring*, originally entitled *Man Against Nature*. David Brower and other conservation leaders embraced Carson's argument about biological diversity and her attack on DDT.[87] Also published in 1962 was a collection of essays by Anglo-American notables, edited by Fairfield Osborn. Although many of the contributors to the Osborn book did strike a moderate tone, many did not. For example, Sir Charles Darwin, the grandson of the renowned student of Reverend Malthus, likened people to rats who were cast ashore of an island and proceeded to overpopulate it.[88] Arnold Toynbee offered that the only way to solve the population problem was through the creation of a world government.[89] A third contributor, Lord Boyd Orr, mixed cautious remarks with an assertion that the population explosion is one of the dangers created by modern science and it is a threat to "our civilization."[90]

Among the most consistently strident contributions was the one by Julian Huxley.[91] According to Huxley, overpopulation is a "cancer" that overrides all other problems. Huxley complained that many groups found reasons to oppose global population control.

---

[82] Reston, 1971, Sec. VII, p. 11.
[83] Krock, 1961, Sec. IV, p. 9.
[84] Zlotnick, 1961, pp. 683-694.
[85] Gibson, 1994, pp. 19-76.
[86] Frank, 2000; MacArthur, 2000.
[87] Fox, 1981, pp. 295-300.
[88] Osborn, 1962, pp. 29-35.
[89] Ibid., pp. 135-141.
[90] Ibid., pp. 103-107.
[91] Ibid., pp. 223-233.

Communists attack it on ideological grounds, the Catholic Church for religious reasons, the Chinese because population represents strength, and Africans because they suspected racist motives. Like Reston and Krock, Huxley went against Eisenhower and Kennedy, saying that loans and aid should be contingent on recipient countries' willingness to adopt population control policies. Huxley:

> No grants or loans for development should be made unless the country was willing to frame and stand by a rational population policy aimed at limiting the growth of its population, and some of the aid would be allocated to help it implement any such policy.[92]

Huxley, sounding a theme that would become constant in the environmentalist literature, linked population growth to pollution and to resource depletion.

> Man has been overexploiting the natural resources of this planet. He has been misusing its soils and polluting its waters. He has wasted enormous amounts of resources which he ought to have conserved. Almost everywhere (though mainly in underdeveloped and overpopulated countries), more and more marginal land is being taken into cultivation, more forests are being cut down, more soil erosion is taking place. Everywhere (but in this case especially in the most 'developed' countries) high-grade raw materials are being used up at a frightening rate, and lower grade sources are having to be used. Almost everywhere the supplies of water are becoming insufficient. We are well on the way to ruining our habitat.[93]

In 1969 Huxley would invert Vogt's warning that progress causes mental illness. Huxley reportedly warned that human mental instability would prevent man from handling the technology he has created. He went on to refer to the creation of technology as our Frankenstein problem.[94] Mary Shelley's novel, *Frankenstein Or, The Modern Prometheus*, contains many warnings about and admonitions against science and human curiosity.[95] American statesman and scientist Benjamin Franklin was called the modern Prometheus by philosopher Emmanuel Kant.[96] Shelley was probably making a play on Franklin's name.

The editor of the book, Fairfield Osborn, and his cousin Frederick also contributed pieces. Frederick's article discussed the implications of population growth for trends in genetic inheritance. Frederick Osborn suggested that population growth and the pressures it created would force us to take a closer look at who is having the children.[97] Osborn asserted that genetics are major determinants of intelligence and of personality and that it would be dangerous to allow more "defective persons" to be born. Without defining that term, he suggested that about two percent of the population fit in that category and that it

---

[92] Ibid., p, 231.
[93] Ibid., p. 225.
[94] New York Times, 1969, p. 11. Oct 12
[95] Shelley, 1975, pp. 13, 35-38, 43, 49, 52.
[96] Van Doren, 1991, p. 171.
[97] Osborn, 1962, pp. 51, 66.

might become necessary to go beyond voluntary measures to limit the increase of defective persons.[98]

Fairfield, the book's editor, also wrote the introduction. He argued that rapid population growth was the most important problem facing the world.[99] Obviously that view would not have been shared by most people in poor countries, many of which were still under colonial rule or had just recently achieved independence. Colonialism and neo-colonialism were apparently just trifling matters in the minds of Osborn and his friends. It was not worth mentioning or getting into. Fairfield[100] chastised the human race for believing that its achievements in science and technology and its ability to create cities allowed humanity to escape the laws of nature. Around this time Osborn was working with Prince Philip and Prince Bernhard to save endangered species.[101] The Princes were also at this time the leaders of the World Wildlife Fund. One must suspect that the leading 'endangered species' was the Anglo-American upper class.

Early in 1963 Reston again attacked Kennedy for his refusal to back the population control movement. He quoted the former president of the World Bank and Rockefeller associate, Eugene R. Black, who warned that population growth will frustrate all efforts to raise the standard of living of poorer countries. In fact, he said, it will be difficult to even maintain current standards.[102] A few weeks later *Fortune* magazine would be citing Black for his objections to Kennedy's practice of using American business self-interest as a way to get their support for the industrialization of Latin economies.[103] That is, aid dollars were being used to make purchases from American business; this in *Fortune's* eye coopted them. Black warned Kennedy that his efforts would fail and then objected to the efforts themselves.

In June of 1963 a host of upper class luminaries published an open appeal to President Kennedy. The gist of this appeal, entitled "Population Explosion Nullifies Foreign Aid," was that population growth was undermining the attempts to assist poor countries.[104] The list of signatories included members of the some of the wealthiest and most influential families in the United States, including Aldrich, Cabot, Chase, Lamont, Scripps, Rockefeller, and Vanderbilt. It also included Fairfield Osborn, William H. Draper, Jr., and others directly involved in the growing conservation-population control movement. In a bit of double talk, they claimed to agree with Kennedy that the "U.S. should not impose birth control on other nations" but then recommended the withholding of foreign aid as a possible sanction against those countries whose efforts to control population were judged unsatisfactory.

In a 1973 book, which included a forward written by future President George H. W. Bush, Phyllis Piotrow[105] claimed that Kennedy was creating a straw man in 1959 when he said he was against any coercive effort to make other countries adopt birth control

---

[98] Ibid., pp. 63-66.
[99] Ibid., p. 7.
[100] Ibid., p. 10.
[101] Devlin, 1963, p. 1.
[102] Collier and Horowitz, 1976, p. 416; Lundberg, 1975, p. 40; Reston, 1963, p. 6.
[103] Gibson, 1994, pp. 61-62; Murphy, 1963.
[104] Hugh Moore Fund, 1963.
[105] Piotrow, 1973, p. 44.

policies. She pointed to the Draper Committee's work as an example of the fact that no one was trying to use coercion. The 1963 proposal to withhold aid from countries that refused to adopt population control policies, a proposal that had very broad backing in the American upper class, shows that JFK was not conjuring up any straw man.

This "appeal" to Kennedy, perhaps better described as an admonition, was paid for by the Hugh Moore Fund. Hugh Moore, the founder of the Dixie Cup Company, was a director of the Campaign to Check the Population Explosion and co-founder, with Draper, of the Population Crisis Committee, formed in 1965.[106]

In the two decades following World War Two, the more extreme and anti-modernist tendencies of the earlier period survived and developed within the conservation establishment. Increasingly, there was added emphasis on issues such as resource depletion and pollution. Consistent with major elements of the earlier movements in Germany, England and the United States, the conservation movement displayed an aristocratic conservatism and elitism. Kennedy, like Franklin Roosevelt, had a primarily human use and resource development orientation to conservation. Kennedy was opposed to the population control movement, making only tiny concessions to it, like agreeing to share information on birth control with other countries. The whole thrust of the Kennedy Presidency was to expand production, support scientific progress, and develop resources for human use. In the six years following Kennedy's death the environmental movement, with a strong preservationist and Malthusian tone, would burst upon the national scene, putting its imprint on both major political parties and on most of the political spectrum.

The anti-growth, pessimistic message of the new conservationism made the Democrats far more conservative and calls for government protection of nature gave the Republicans an area in which they could be "liberals."[107] Within six months of Kennedy's death, President Lyndon Johnson announced the new conservationism and shortly thereafter the federal government was committed to the cause of population control. By the end of the decade the contemporary environmentalist movement was hatched. By the beginning of the eighties, environmentalism was coming to be associated in the minds of many with "liberalism." As we will see, it was and is in most important ways the same old wolf.

---

[106] Barclay, Enright and Reynolds, 1970.
[107] Tucker, 1982.

Chapter Five

ENVIRONMENTALISM ARRIVES

In the 1960s and 1970s environmentalism emerged as a major force in the U.S. and the world. It would enlist support, at least superficially, from a majority of Americans. Few politicians wanted to be seen as opponents of the new creed. Conservatives and Republican Presidents would declare themselves as supporters or even leaders of the cause. In debates about environmentalism in the late-1970s and early-1980s, however, it was increasingly associated with liberalism and big government. This image apparently crystallized around the beginning of the Reagan Presidency. This would prove to be of great advantage to the forces behind the environmental movement, many of whom could, when necessary, quickly doff their environmental hat and replace it with their free market, anti-government hat, and vice versa. In the international arena conservative, free-trade economics would be openly combined with environmentalism. Today's environmentalism was announced as the "new conservationism" in 1965 and it picked up its current name in the late 1960s in the enthusiastic coverage of the mass media. The term "environmental" had been used in its current sense in a 1959 textbook,[1] but it did not begin to catch on until the end of the 1960s. It's coming out party was Earth Day, 1970.

Although he did not use the term until the following February, LBJ announced the coming of the "new conservationism" in a speech given in 1964, six months after he had taken office.[2] In England the cause was being taken up by the Duke of Edinburgh, i.e., Prince Philip. The English and American activities were linked directly through the person of England's Max Nicholson, who was involved on both sides of the ocean.[3]

The 1964 "Great Society" speech given at the University of Michigan and the messages on conservation sent to Congress the following February committed the President, at least rhetorically, to the more extreme, preservationist elements of conservationism. Those views always had been dominant within conservationism, but were in the past impractical in national politics. Around this time, *Time* magazine declared that the preservationist John Muir was actually the "real father of

---

[1] Schoenfeld, Meier, and Griffin, 1979.
[2] Johnson, 1965; 1965a.
[3] Nicholson, 1970, pp. 161, 269-270.

conservationism." This was a clear message that the previously elitist and marginal ideas of a Muir or an Osborn were about to become mainstream.

Although LBJ's 1964 speech included the goal of abundance for all, it also featured many comments that could be called "Green" in the environmentalist vernacular of the 1990s. LBJ warned against unbridled growth and proposed that his Great Society would be a "place where men can renew contact with nature." He warned that the expansion of cities was eroding the time-honored value of "communion with nature" and that people were in danger of being "condemned to a soulless wealth."[4] LBJ also made the following unexplained and, therefore, strange remark, coming in the middle of a major political speech.

> Within your lifetime powerful forces, already loose, will take us toward a way of life beyond the realm of our experience, almost beyond the bounds of our imagination.

Johnson defined neither the "powerful forces" nor the "way of life." These were puzzling if not troubling remarks coming from the President of the United States. Later President George H. W. Bush would make similarly puzzling use of the concept of "new world order." Bush never explained that term.

LBJ followed up his Great Society speech with two 1965 conservation messages to congress, one of which quoted Ralph Waldo Emerson's observation that "In the woods we return to reason and faith."[5] On February 8, 1965, President Johnson[6] submitted two messages to Congress, one on natural beauty and the other concerned with the preservation of wilderness. In those messages, Johnson embraced what he referred to as the "new conservation." Although President Kennedy had indicated a concern with pollution,[7] his primary emphasis had been on economic and resource development. President Johnson's statements represented a qualitative shift in focus.[8]

In his message on natural beauty, President Johnson[9] announced that he would call a White House Conference on Natural Beauty which would "serve as a focal point for the large campaign of public education" concerning the threats to our natural heritage. Johnson also announced that the Chairman of this Conference would be Laurance Rockefeller. The language and overall thrust of Johnson's messages to Congress and of his 1964 speech are similar to the report of the Outdoor Recreation Resources Review Commission (ORRRC) which was also chaired by Rockefeller, who was called the "nation's most prominent individual conservationist" by *Time* magazine.[10] The ORRRC had been appointed by President Eisenhower, but it did not complete its work until Kennedy was in office.

The ORRRC submitted its report to the Congress and the President in 1962. While Kennedy accepted some of its specific recommendations concerning government

---

[4] Johnson, 1967 (1964).
[5] Johnson, 1965a, p. 13.
[6] Johnson, 1965, 1965a.
[7] Krier and Ursin, 1977, pp. 170, 172.
[8] Caulfield, 1989.
[9] Johnson, 1965, p. 11.
[10] Time, 1965b, p. 71.

organization and funding related to recreation,[11] it was Johnson who gave voice to the broader goals and values expressed in the report. After referring to what Johnson called the "darker side" of technology and industry, Johnson said that the "new conservation" must be concerned with the "total relation between man and the world."[12] Johnson's emphasis on a growing pollution problem was joined to a stated concern with the importance of nature for man's spiritual well-being and an assertion that only nature is unambiguously beautiful.[13] In these and other comments he seems to be relying directly on the ORRRC report, or something similar to it.[14] President Johnson's focus on environmental problems and Laurance Rockefeller's leadership in this area were the subjects of a number of *Time* magazine articles in 1964 and 1965.[15]

In their history of the Rockefeller family, Collier and Horowitz suggest that in his work with the ORRRC "Laurance transformed himself from a gentleman conservationist into a statesman in the emerging environmental movement."[16] The American Conservation Association, led by Laurance, spent 800,000 dollars between 1962 and 1964 promoting the ideas of the ORRRC and created a Citizen's Committee for the ORRRC Report made up of 150 leaders from business, labor and public affairs. Rockefeller went on to also head up the Citizen's Advisory Committee on Recreation and Natural Beauty which advised LBJ on environmental issues. Laurance remained the chairman of this group after President Nixon renamed it the Citizen's Committee on Environmental Quality.[17]

In his State of the Union messages for 1965 and 1966, Johnson referred to "the explosion in world population and the growing scarcity in world resources,"[18] and he emphasized that the U.S. was embarking on a new foreign aid policy that made the control of population a primary goal.[19] The Establishment had been pushing Johnson to adopt the population cause from the beginning. For example, just nine weeks after LBJ assumed the office, the *New York Times* admonished Johnson for not focusing enough on population. They asserted, incorrectly, that "unneeded poverty and unwanted population are inseparable."[20] LBJ's commitment, such as it was, to population control was, according to Peter Bachrach and Elihu Bergman, a "watershed" development in the emergence of the contemporary population control efforts.[21] LBJ was the first American president to publicly support birth control. He was apparently unenthusiastic about it,[22] as was his Republican successor, Richard Nixon.[23] LBJ's public endorsement of conservation and population control, however, would provide an example of the

---

[11] Kennedy, 1962.

[12] Johnson, 1965, p. 2.

[13] Ibid., pp. 2-3.

[14] Outdoor Recreation Resources Review Commission, 1962, pp. iii, 1, 6, 13-14, 22-24.

[15] Time, 1964; 1965, 1965a, 1965b.

[16] Collier and Horowitz, 1976, p. 382.

[17] Collier and Horowitz, 1976.

[18] Reston, 1965, p. 28.

[19] Johnson, 1966.

[20] New York Times, 1964, p. 28.

[21] Bachrach and Bergman, 1973.

[22] Piotrow, 1973, pp. 161, 227-228.

[23] New York Times, 1971a, p. 30.

liberalism-environmentalism connection that free enterprise conservatives would later latch onto. They would choose to ignore the previous hundred years in which there was no such linkage and during which the cause of preservation and population control was overwhelmingly the property of the rich and aristocratic conservatives. Conservative critics of environmentalism would similarly ignore the evidence for upper class backing of the environmental movement in the last third of the twentieth century.[24]

In that 1965 *Time* magazine article that declared John Muir the "real father of conservation,"[25] *Time* also observed that

> From sea to shining sea, the inevitable growth of U.S. humanity and industry has crushed grass, leveled trees, blasted out mountains and damned off rivers.

The battle to change this, according to *Time*, was led by Laurance Rockefeller, who inherited the interest from his father, John D. Rockefeller, Jr. Among Rockefeller's opponents at the time was Pope Paul VI, who told the United Nations that same year that we should focus on improving production rather than limiting population. Along the way Paul VI referred to JFK as the "great, departed" President Kennedy.[26] A careful reading of Paul VI's 1967 encyclical, "Populorum Progressio," will show how close in outlook JFK and the Pope were, and how much at odds that Pope was with the Osborns and other neo-Malthusians. [27]

In 1965 Laurance was chairman of the White House Conference on Natural Beauty. Laurance had become involved in conservation by 1947 when he took over the Jackson Hole Preserve, Inc., from his father. In that same year, as noted earlier, he worked with Fairfield Osborn to create the Conservation Foundation. He considered Osborn to be one of the major influences on his life.[28]

In 1952 a report, commissioned by President Truman, linked America's national security to access to resources around the world and Laurance and Osborn latched onto the issue.[29] The following year, the Ford Foundation decided to create an organization, Resources for the Future, to monitor world resources. Laurance joined its board in 1958. By this time Laurance was a commissioner of the Palisades Park, director of the Hudson River Conservation Foundation and of the New York Zoological Society. He was about to head up the Outdoor Recreation Resources and Review Commission. [30] In the related area of population control, the efforts of the Osborns, Laurance's brother John D. Rockefeller III, and their allies were paying off. In 1966 a Population Office was established within the Agency for International Development. Funding for that program grew from 10 million dollars in 1966 to 125 million in 1971. Also in 1966 the Office of Economic Opportunity was authorized to make birth control part of its community action program. In 1967 the position of Special Assistant to the Secretary of State for Population

---

[24] Sadler, 1996.
[25] Time, 1965b, p. 62.
[26] Middleton, 1965, pp. 1, 2.
[27] Paul VI, 1967.
[28] Collier and Horowitz, 1976, p. 302; Time, 1965, p. 54-55; 1965b, p. 71.
[29] Collier and Horowitz, 1976, p. 303.
[30] Ibid., p. 307.

Matters was created. In 1968 President Johnson appointed a President's Committee on Population and Family Planning which led to the establishment in 1970 of the Commission on Population Growth and the American Future. In these events the media helped in two ways. They covered the population issues beginning in 1959 in a way that increased public receptivity to population control. This included the presentation of facts in such a way as to mislead readers, e.g., creating an impression that malnutrition in Latin America was due to overpopulation. The media also failed to report legislative developments in this area while they were underway, making it harder for the opposition to activate their potential supporters.[31] John D. Rockefeller III's contribution to all of this earned him the Margaret Sanger award in 1967 from Planned Parenthood-World Population. The award had been established the previous year "to mark the 50th anniversary of the family planning movement in the United States."[32]

In 1970 an article appeared in the *NACLA Newsletter* (North American Congress on Latin America Newsletter) charging that the population control establishment was part of the imperialist schemes of America's upper class families. The article was entitled "Population Control in the Third World." The authors were William Barclay, Joseph Enright, and Reid T. Reynolds.

As noted earlier, those basing their views on demographic transition theory, like President Kennedy, looked to economic development to both slow down or end population growth and to produce a better life. The idea being, among other things, that a rising standard of living, with a reduction in infant and child mortality, combined with movement of people from the countryside to the city would reduce both the need for and the desire for large families. To put the latter in crass terms, children are transformed from a low cost source of labor in backward agriculture to an economic responsibility in urban-industrial society. These and other changes associated with modernization produce a natural transition in which people decide to have fewer children. The population control establishment argued that population growth had to be stopped first, before economic development could occur. In the 1970s the same interests would argued that both population growth and development had to be stopped.

In the *NACLA* article, Barclay, Enright and Reynolds described the upper class dominance of population control organizations. They briefly described some of the activities of the Osborns and Rockefellers, dating back to at least the 1930s, and went on to discuss other population control notables such as William H. Draper, Hugh Moore and John J. McCloy. Draper's views impressed a future president, George H. W. Bush, while Bush was serving as chairman of the Republican Task Force on Population and Earth Resources. When in the House of Representatives in the late-1960s, Bush was a leading advocate for birth control initiatives in the U.S. and abroad.[33] Moore was one of the Establishment's more extreme voices on population control and John J. McCloy was the

---

[31] Bachrach and Bergman, 1973, pp. 50-54; Piotrow, 1973, pp. 222-223; Reston, 1966, p. 44

[32] New York Times, 1967, p. 42.

[33] Piotrow, 1973, pp. viii, 103, 141, 164.

most prominent spokesman for that Establishment on many different types of issues,[34] so much so that McCloy acquired the unofficial title of "Chairman of the Establishment."[35]

The article also argued that the population control establishment was made up of five key organizations which were extensively interconnected with such upper-class institutions as the Council on Foreign Relations and with foundations associated with, inter alia, the Rockefeller, Mellon, and duPont interests. The five population organizations were the Population Council, Population Reference Bureau, Planned Parenthood-World Population, Population Crisis Committee, and the Campaign to Check the Population Explosion. They pointed out that the last organization was viewed by many as being extremist, but that it was nevertheless extensively intertwined with the allegedly more moderate groups.

Whatever the exact nature of those connections, it is clear that by the late-1960s the Establishment had constructed a well organized network of organizations to press the new Malthusianism.

Meanwhile, the new conservationism was gathering steam heading for the first Earth Day. The conservationist and population control efforts, long interconnected, became totally intertwined in terms of organization, leadership, backing and ideology. Among the organizations producing the new conservationism was the Aspen Institute.

The Aspen Institute was formed following a 1949 conference organized by Paul Paepcke, founder and head of Container Corporation of America, and two University of Chicago professors, Guiseppe Borgese, son-in-law of Thomas Mann, and Robert M. Hutchins, later Vice President of the Ford Foundation and President of the University of Chicago. During the 1960s Aspen conducted seminars for high school teachers to promote an interest in environmentalism. This may have played a role in generating support for environmentalism in the 1970s. Aspen also played a role in developing and advocating a post-industrial strategy for the U.S. economy, i.e., a shift from an industrial, energy intensive economy to one based more on services or, for some, information processing. Beginning in 1963, Aspen held a series of conferences involving deans of leading business schools and representatives of industry and the business press in order to promote the idea that education in business and economics has to be brought in line with the coming shift to post-industrial society.[36]

In the mid-1960s, a new program was initiated by Aspen to promote national discussion of the population problem in the Western Hemisphere and environmentalism was a continuing focus for Aspen's seminars for business executives. Aspen's Chairman, Robert O. Anderson, also Chairman of Atlantic Richfield, helped to finance the 1970 Earth Day and provided seed money for the creation of Friends of the Earth. He also financed the organization in 1970 of the International Institute for Environmental Affairs, later renamed the International Institute for Environment and Development. In addition, Aspen conducted international workshops entitled 'Environment and the Quality of Life'

---

[34] Bird, 1992.
[35] Ibid.
[36] Hyman, 1975, pp. 3, 81-82, 162, 168-70.

and it had direct and indirect influence on United Nations conferences on food and population.[37]

In the mid-1960s, when *Time* magazine was declaring the anti-modernist John Muir the true father of conservationism, there were prominent figures still defending modernism and offering a more optimistic view on science and its applications. For example, in a 1965 speech Robert Kennedy offered the following defense of production oriented science and technology:

> Although we do make mistakes in the application of our technology, mistakes that effective public policy combined with technological knowledge can avoid, the promise of science and technology offers the only hope that man will live and prosper in our physical environment.
>
> It offers the promise of sufficient food for all the people of the world.
>
> It offers the promise of detection and prevention of destruction by natural phenomena.
>
> It offers the promise of adequate housing and clothing for all mankind.
>
> It offers the promise of a standard of living in which all mankind can live in dignity and civilization, freed of the brutalization of a daily scramble for animal existence.
>
> It is these applications of science rather than science itself which is the promise of science to the man on the street and the citizen of a newly developed country. It is science and its application through technology that has created a revolution in expectations in the developing sectors between modern man and his physical environment.[38]

This view was implicitly and explicitly rejected by many spokespersons for environmentalism, before and after Kennedy's time. That same year, for example, William Paddock and Paul Paddock came out with a book, entitled *Famine - 1975*, that recommended we cut off all aid to countries designated as hopeless.[39] The optimistic view expressed by Kennedy was frequently attacked in a savage way.

In 1967, England succeeded in getting the Council of Europe to declare 1970 a European Conservation Year.[40] This would give a global character to the emerging cause. In the U.S. another environmental group was created in 1967 - the Environmental Defense Fund. This was part of a rapid build-up in the organizational structure. The following organizations were created between 1968 and 1971: Zero Population Growth, Club of Rome, Friends of the Earth, Union of Concerned Scientists, Natural Resources Defense Council, League of Conservation Voters, International Institute for Environmental Affairs, Greenpeace.[41] A supporter of Friends of the Earth, Atlantic Richfield's board chairman Robert O. Anderson, helped to finance the creation of the John Muir Institute in 1969. David Brower was the leading conservationist in this organization and in the internationally oriented Friends of the Earth, based initially in England, Switzerland and the

---

[37] Hyman, 1975, pp. 100-102, 212, 229-238, 252, 272-297, 353-376; Sale, 1993, pp. 40-42.
[38] Ross, 1968, p. 335.
[39] Tucker, 1982, pp. 98-105.
[40] Nicholson, 1970, pp. 206-207.
[41] Carmin, 1999, pp. 101-121; Gibson, 1992; New York Times, 1971, p. 52 (Jan 10); Sale, 1993.

United States.[42] Brower also was the founder of Earth Island Institute. It is Brower who asked Paul Ehrlich to write the best-selling book, *The Population Bomb*. Ehrlich and others in the Sierra Club started Zero Population Growth in 1968.[43]

Another type of activity got under way in 1967. At one of the country's top think tanks, a group began an examination of future educational needs in relation to what the group called the "World Macroproblem," by which they meant "uncontrolled technology, application, and industrial development."[44] This work was led by Willis Harman, who was director of the U.S. Office of Education's Educational Policy Research Center, a research unit at the Stanford Research Institute in Palo Alto, California. Harman is also known for his research in the area of drug use.[45]

The Harman group claimed that U.S. civilization in general was based on what they called pathogenic premises, i.e., ideas about the world that lead to "diseases." The "diseases" they had in mind were primarily damage to nature and humans allegedly caused by applied technology and industry.[46]

These think tankers consequently decided that the problems of the world were primarily things like too much commitment to technology, positive attitudes toward population growth, the independent nation-state, and the idea that humans are different from the rest of nature.[47] This activity led to the publication of a number of books, the best known of which is probably Marilyn Ferguson's *The Aquarian Conspiracy*. Another of these was Willis Harman's 1976 book *An Incomplete Guide to the Future*. Therein he recommended a transition away from industrial society to what he called transindustrial society. This transition will require that we reduce our use of modern technology and industry and achieve greater harmony with the ecology.[48] Theodore Rozak, an author that Laurance Rockefeller claimed had a deep impact on him,[49] was warning against the dangers of "technocratic totalitarianism" in his widely read book, *The Making of a Counter Culture*.[50] Rozak developed some of this further in his 1975 book entitled *Unfinished Animal: The Aquarian Frontier and the Evolution of Consciousness*. In this book, Rozak argued for the environmental superiority of paganism over Christianity.[51]

President Johnson led the Democratic Party in its embrace of the new conservationism. He did this with a lack of consistency and, at times at least, with little enthusiasm. It appears that he did this in the same manner that he committed the country to the war in Vietnam. That is, it was substantially a matter of compliance with and submission to pressure. In fact, the same forces asking him to escalate the war in Vietnam[52] were also promoting the new conservationism. The most obvious example of

---

[42] Becher, 2000, p. 112; Davies, 1969, p. 21.
[43] Fox, 1981, pp. 309-313.
[44] Dickson, 1971, p. 335.
[45] Anderson, 1983, pp. 68, 142; Lee and Shlain, 1985, 197-199, 293.
[46] Dickson, 1971, p. 336.
[47] Ibid., pp. 337-338.
[48] Harman, 1976, pp. 21-49.
[49] Collier and Horowitz, 1976, p. 401.
[50] Rozak, 1969, pp. xii, 50-51, 265.
[51] Ibid., 1975, p. 165.
[52] Shoup and Minter, 1977.

that would be the Rockefeller interests, leaders in both areas. Another example would be McGeorge Bundy, a Vietnam hawk, who left his position as a national security advisor to LBJ and took over the Ford Foundation which was one of the primary funders of the new conservationism and of population control activities.[53] Bundy was Ford's president from 1966 to 1979; he is credited with making the Ford Foundation a force in setting the national agenda.[54]

Around this time an article appeared which would help to create that future association of "left" or "liberal" politics with environmentalism. The supposedly left-wing publication, *The Nation*, adopted views virtually identical to people such as the Osborns, ideas long associated with right-wing and Aristocratic groups. This crossover, which is reminiscent of the penetration of almost all parts of the English political spectrum by Malthusian and preservationist ideas, appeared in a 1968 article by Robert and Leona Rienow, entitled "Conservation for Survival." The Rienows, sounding more than just a little bit like English Aristocrats, sounded the alarm on population growth and the alleged destruction of nature brought on by mass consumption. The Rienows:

> On November 20, 1967, an unthinking, if not an ignorant, crowd stood in the foyer of the Commerce Department and applauded wildly as the census clock registered the 200 millionth inhabitant. In thirty-five years, perhaps even in twenty-five, if bullish tendencies prevail, another 100 million Americans will appear on the scene. These are the increased hordes who will inundate the parks, blight the landscape, crowd the beaches, destroy the air and make life unbearable for one another.
>
> They are also compounded of an individual and collective appetite that is driving society to dyspepsia. Every '7 1/2 seconds a new American is born,' begins our *Moment in the Sun.* "He is a disarming little thing, but he begins to scream loudly in a voice that can be heard for seventy years. He is screaming for 26,000,000 gallons of water, 21,000 gallons of gasoline, 10,150 pounds of meat, 28,000 pounds of milk and cream, 9,000 pounds of wheat, and great storehouses of all other foods, drinks, and tobacco..."
>
> "He is requisitioning a private endowment of $5,000 to $8,000 for school building materials, $6,300 worth of clothing, $7,000 worth of furniture--and 210 pounds of peanuts to pass through his hot, grasping little hand. He is yelping for a Paul Bunyan chunk, in his own right, of the nation's pulpwood, paper, steel, zinc, magnesium, aluminum, and tin..."
>
> This infant will grow into the world's most prodigious consumer, citizen of a nation that accounts for one-fifteenth of earth's people but consumes one-half of its total product (and aspires, by the year 2000, to consume 83 percent of it). We wallow in statistics projecting a gross national product by the turn of the century that will be more than double our present GNP--and appear charmed by the vision of 244 million cars on the road in that same year. We plan on a building pace of five times present experience. It is this double threat of more people demanding per capita production that makes the modern conservationist run scared.

---

[53] Gibson, 1994.
[54] Nagai, Lerner and Rothman, 1994, p. 27.

Nor can he muster much hope to save the beauty and balance of man's surroundings when he considers the relentless, savage power of the forces of predation. The exploiters are armed with an artillery of modern machinery as to make the universe quake.[55]

If this is "liberalism" it is the liberalism of Thomas Robert Malthus and John Locke, not FDR and JFK.

Matching the rhetoric of Paul Ehrlich's *The Population Bomb*, also published in 1968, and focusing on the theme popularized by the Club of Rome's 1972 book, *The Limits to Growth*, the Rienows[56] warned that the world's resources were being exhausted by human "gluttony." Not to be out done, Ehrlich would propose in the following year that we should consider having the government put sterility drugs in reservoirs and in food shipped to foreign countries to reduce the number of gluttons.[57] Like Harman and the Stanford Research Institute group, the Rienows[58] called for "revolutionary shifts in values and social goals." The core of that revolution would be a rejection of the "expansionist doctrine."

Near the end of the article the Rienows looked to England for solutions, referring to a suggestion made by the Scenic Hudson Preservation Conference that we create in the U.S. a version of the British National Trust which would review all economic projects in "light of historical as well as environmental damage."

This type of article could later be quoted to show that environmentalism was a cause of the left or of "liberalism." This would provide grist for a very misleading debate in the 1980s and 1990s. In that debate environmentalism came under attack for its alleged connections to big government rather than for its reactionary, aristocratic values and goals. This has happened in the face of the clear historical record showing that extreme conservationism has long been the cause of old, private wealth and the clear evidence that contemporary environmentalism is the offspring of private, upper class interests.

The new conservationism was getting a major boost from the media. While the *Nation* was preaching to affluent liberals, *Sports Illustrated*, part of Henry Luce's Time, Inc., was targeting other sectors of American society. The *New York Times* reported that the magazine had highlighted man's pillaging of the environment and concluded that "the engineer's tyranny over the environment must be ended." The *Times* emphatically agreed with this and editorialized that:

Beyond the immediate detailed issues of the ecological crisis, one fact stands out: Earth's capacity to support human life is finite. If that limit is exceeded vast disasters could result--and some of those disasters may be not far off. What is implied in these discussions is a direct challenge to popular ideas about 'progress.' The issues involved are too important to be ignored simply because the conclusions are unpleasant. Humanity can survive only if the natural environment that has produced and supported it is protected

---

[55] Rienow and Rienow, 1968, pp. 138-139.
[56] Ibid., p. 140.
[57] Hill, 1969, p. 19.
[58] Rienow and Rienow, 1968, p. 141.

against the powerful threats that now impinge as man uses godlike powers with much less than godlike wisdom.[59]

This viewpoint is profoundly Malthusian. There is no finite "earth's capacity" in any straightforward or simple way. In fact, the earth has very little capacity to support human life without the addition of human creativity. The natural environment produces very little of the end products we consume. The *Times'* views are ideological, not objective or scientific, ways of looking at the human relationship to nature. They do in fact reproduce Malthus' own logic and assumptions. The suggestion that there will be "unpleasant" conclusions about humanity's future is also completely in keeping with the Reverend Malthus. A few months later, the *Times* added to this, warning that the "reckless, unheeding misuse of technology and the refusal to respect ecological values may make earth an uninhabitable environment."[60]

Also in 1968, major foundations announced new initiatives in the area of ecology and population. Secretary of State Dean Rusk, who had earlier in the year identified nuclear weapons and the population explosion as the two primary threats facing the world, announced that he was rejoining the Rockefeller Foundation to oversee a study of global population.[61] The Ford Foundation announced a multimillion dollar program to fund ecology programs at seven universities. The largest grant went to Yale University.[62] Other notables were speaking out on ecology. The Conservative party candidate for Senator from New York, James Buckley, announced that protection of the environment was the one area in which he supported government intrusion into private affairs.[63] Lord Ritchie-Calder, president of England's Conservation Society, was speaking out about the dangers of population growth, pollution, and atomic waste.[64] Three years later, the Lord joined Lester Brown, president of Worldwatch Institute, and other notables such as Planned Parenthood Federation president Alan Guttmacher and civil liberties activist Corliss Lamont as a signer of the Humanist Manifesto II. Among the "rights" promoted in the Manifesto were birth control, abortion, divorce, sexual freedom and euthanasia. The Manifesto also called for worldwide ecological planning.[65]

The importance of the Anglo-American connection in the development of an international ecology movement was again demonstrated in the following year, 1969, in the publication of a book entitled *Wildlife in Danger*. The book was produced by English officials involved in conservation and parks and by members of the International Union for Conservation of Nature and Natural Resources.[66] The preface was written by one of America's most important conservationists, Joseph Wood Krutch. Over the course of his life Krutch became a neopagan critic of modern industrial society.[67] In that preface he

---

[59] New York Times, 1968, p. 14.
[60] New York Times, 1968b, p. 42.
[61] New York Times, 1968a, p. 2; 1968e, p. 23.
[62] New York Times, 1968c, p. 29.
[63] Tolchin, 1968, p. 25.
[64] Shuster, 1968, p. 25.
[65] Blau, 1973, pp. 1, 51.
[66] Fisher, Simon and Vincent, 1969.
[67] Fox, 1981, pp. 229-233.

quoted Harrison Brown's warning that mankind would not be satisfied "until the earth is covered completely to a considerable depth with a writhing mass of human beings, much as a dead cow is covered with a pulsating mass of maggots."[68]

These were the sentiments of some leaders of the new conservationism on the eve of the environmental revolution. That revolution would be hailed not on the streets, but in the Establishment media.

EARTH DAY AND THE ENVIRONMENTAL REVOLUTION

In 1970 a book written by the English conservationism leader, Max Nicholson, was published; it had a rather assertive title - *The Environmental Revolution: A Guide for the New Masters of the World*. Nicholson was involved in promoting the Countryside in 1970 Conference in England. This coincided with America's first Earth Day, the White House Conference on Natural Beauty, and the formation of the Population Commission led by John D. Rockefeller III. As noted above, 1970 was also declared European Conservation Year.[69]

In his book, Nicholson observed that since the world had been subjected to a "preliminary softening-up campaign" over the preceding two decades, it was ready to be convinced that it must "finally and unequivocally renounce all claims to be above ecological laws."[70] Although Nicholson[71] worried that Christianity and Judaism, with their positive views of human productive and reproductive tendencies, would obstruct the achievement of harmony with nature, he was optimistic that by the mid-1970s the effort to educate people to want that harmony would begin to have an impact.

Nicholson went on to say that

If the ultimate goal is to be full harmony between man and nature all those influences and vested interests which lead mankind into postures and situations inconsistent with that goal must in turn be converted or otherwise brought into line, or in extreme cases neutralised. This process cannot be left to chance. Being above all concerned with the ends the conservation movement must be untiring in devising and applying the means to achieve them as fully and as swiftly as possible.[72]

One of "the interests" that Nicholson felt had to be "brought into line" or "neutralised" was applied modern science. Taking a position completely opposite to the earlier quoted view of Robert Kennedy, Nicholson recommended the following:

Modern science in its origins was closely linked with natural history, and even with activities which we would now include in conservation. This remained true right up to the

---

[68] Fisher, Simon and Vincent, 1969, p. 7
[69] Nicholson, 1970, pp. 266-267; Piotrow, 1973, p. 194.
[70] Nicholson, 1970, pp. 263-264.
[71] Ibid., pp. 264-265, 267.
[72] Ibid., p. 278.

days of Darwin, a mere century ago. More recently however the lavish patronage of armed forces, of certain industries and of the State have swung its emphasis away from general biology and from studies basically concerned with the environment, and have led to disproportionate artificially induced expansion in physics, chemistry and certain other branches, including recently the competitive exploration of outer space. This distortion has had not only quantitative but qualitative effects, through offering greater opportunities and prizes, and conferring better status and experience of public affairs on scientists remote from the mainstream of studies related to the earth and its living creatures. Such studies have thus not only been relatively starved of resources, but have been very thinly served by outstanding scientists capable of providing statesmanlike leadership for their integration and further development.[73]

This amounts to a declaration of political war against all attempts to employ human creativity in the reshaping of the world and to improve the material conditions of life. It was also a direct attack on Kennedy's priorities and goals.

Nicholson seemed quite assured of success. Perhaps that was because of the wealth and power of the leaders of this effort. In 1970, Prince Philip, Prince Bernhard and other prominent individuals like Joseph Slater of the Aspen Institute and Aurelio Pecci of the Olivetti company were out promoting the revolution.[74] Of course the Rockefeller-Osborn interests were still at work. Another reason for Nicholson's confidence may have been that the mass media was supporting the environmental revolution. Nicholson observed that "the mass media are spreading the message all the time with significant results."[75] Kirkpatrick Sale in his 1993 book *The Green Revolution* noted that the major media gave big coverage to environmental issues in 1970.[76] Actually, that began before 1970. Months before the initial Earth Day (April 22), major print media such as *Time, Life* and *Newsweek*, carried cover stories on the environment. In time and in tone they were leading rather than following and they were going well beyond just covering things; they were spreading the message. The media helped the environmental movement to create fears about pollution and other issues.[77]

Time's February 2, 1970, cover story featured a picture of the allegedly left-wing ecologist Barry Commoner. The upper-class conservative and publisher of *Time*, Henry Luce, had introduced a regular section on the environment about six months earlier. The ideological slant in *Time's* coverage was readily apparent. In an article entitled "Fighting to Save the Earth from Man" Time quoted arch-Malthusian Paul Ehrlich and it referred positively to ecologist Lamont Cole's fears that the urban environment was one that selected the wrong genes. But the most prominent ecologist in this story was Barry Commoner.

One might wonder what a magazine that was usually vehemently opposed to communism and socialism and to anyone else who wanted to intervene in the private

---

[73] Ibid., pp. 228-229.
[74] Lewis, 1970, p. 3; Pace, 1970, p. 8; Raymont, 1970, p. 37.
[75] Nicholson, 1970, p. 272.
[76] Sale, 1993, p. 23.
[77] Petulla, 1987, p. 121.

enterprise economy was doing promoting a left-wing ecologist. Well, in the higher circles, political labels can have many meanings and many uses.

Time liked Commoner's warnings about technology's destructive impact on the environment, dubbing him the "Paul Revere of Ecology". They politely dissociated themselves from Commoner's argument that material security was needed to end population growth.[78] In other words what they liked about this left-wing ecologist was his criticism of technology. His other possible sins could be forgiven, although not embraced.

Sounding very much like the Harman group at the Stanford Research Institute, *Time* criticized Christianity and Judaism for promoting the idea that nature exists for humans. *Time* suggested that we replace this with the "ecological truth." They went on to emphasize that we must reconsider our commitment to economic growth.[79] In April of 1970, twenty theologians met at the School of Theology at Claremont College in California to discuss the role of Christianity in the environmental crisis. Most of these clergymen were in agreement that Christianity "had given sanction to exploitation of the environment by science and technology and thus contributed to air and water pollution, overpopulation and other ecological threats."[80]

Time's sister publication, *Life,* also devoted that week's cover story to ecology. Their story was entitled "Ecology Becomes Everybody's Issue."[81] Life criticized President Kennedy because he had never embraced conservationism and noted that none of the candidates in the 1968 presidential campaign was willing to emphasize the issue. Nevertheless, they said that conservation issues might dominate the coming decade because the press was printing stories about ecology on a daily basis. They also observed that 13,000 law students, 20 percent of the total, would take a course in environmental law in 1970. The first Earth Day had not even occurred yet, but both the media and the nation's legal profession were already committed to environmentalism as one of the issues, if not "the" issue, of the coming decades.

Life offered that:

> The tide of information about pollution has left us no excuse for not knowing what we have been doing to ourselves. For the first time in history we are being forced to recognize that the earth is a finite resource, and the public response to this tremendous fact promises to shake American society. 'The politics of environment' says Social Anthropoligist Luther Gerlach, 'will be the biggest mass movement in the history of this country.' The movement has begun.[82]

Life's apparent enthusiasm for the prospects of an environmentalist mass movement, one that will "shake American society," is somewhat unusual given Henry Luce's and Time, Inc.'s "conservative" image. However, it is not that unusual if we recognize that what is to be shaken is the majority's expectation of or hope for a better life, not the wealth,

---

[78] Time 1970, pp. 58-59.
[79] Ibid., pp. 62-63.
[80] Fiske, 1970, p. 12.
[81] Life, 1970, pp. 22-30.

privilege and power of the upper class. It is not unusual in that light and, of course, not unusual in light of the history of ecology and conservationism.

Time and *Life* were not the only publications pumping environmentalism in the pre-Earth Day period. About a week earlier, *Newsweek's* cover story was entitled "Ravaged Environment." The description of this cover story, appearing above the issue's index, began with the following:

> America, a nation profligate with its resources, contempuous of its natural environment, is suddenly waking up. Its citizens are beginning to ask why they must put up with the world they helped create. Ecology, environment, pollution are the stuff of daily headlines. The qualtiy of life is becoming a central political issue of the 1970s - reaching into the White House itself.[83]

Like Time, Inc., *Newsweek* anticipated with approval that ecology and environment would become major issues of the 1970s. They all seemed very confident of this. As legal historians James Krier and Edmund Ursin, both strong supporters of environmentalism, pointed out in 1977, there were no specific events that triggered the crisis. Rather, what occurred was a change in thinking.[84] The media was a leader of this change.

Newsweek's young General Editor, Kenneth Auchincloss, struck a pretty radical tone. His father-in-law, Malcolm Muir, had been chairman of the board and editor-in-chief of *Newsweek* and was associated with many important upper-class groups, including the Council on Foreign Relations, Conference Board, Committee on Economic Development, and the Ditchley Foundation.[85]

Like Time-Life and the Stanford Research Institute group, Auchincloss thought that much of the problem was in our religious beliefs. Auchincloss:

> What explains man's extraordinary brutality toward his environment?
> Perhaps the fundamental problem, ecologists believe, has been man's own view of himself. Outside of primitive societies, he has rarely regarded himself as part of nature, as one cog in a giant system that controls him as much as he controls it. 'Civilized' man has liked to think of himself as a bit above that. For those raised in the Judeo-Christian tradition, the Book of Genesis taught that man was created in the image of God, who gave him 'dominion over the fish of the sea, and over the fowl of the air, and the cattle, and over all the earth, and over every creeping thing that creepeth upon the earth.' Man was the lord and nature was his subject; all too often life seemed a struggle of man against nature, not a joint venture between the two.[86]

He went on to quote favorably a warning that "economic growth may well have to be eliminated altogether" and he concluded that the real villains in all of this are consumers who want too much and have too little concern with the ecological costs of their

---

[82] Ibid., p. 23.
[83] Newsweek, 1970, p. 3.
[84] Efron, 1984, pp. 56-57; Krier and Ursin, 1977, pp. 299-300.
[85] Marquis Who's Who, 1962-1963.
[86] Newsweek, 1970, p. 32.

consumption. This sort of talk, appearing in one of the country's two leading weekly news magazines in 1970, would leave little for the latter day eco-radicals to say.

Another part of the cover story was written by *Newsweek* General Editor George Sokolov. Sokolov reported that those familiar with national politics agree that no other issue had ever moved so quickly from "the grass roots" to public policymaking. Sokolov noted that no recent president had played any role in this; it happened in spite of them. He left this unexplained, saying that one had to go back to Teddy Roosevelt to find a president who was also "a great environmentalist." This comment reflects the environmentalist movement's views of Nixon, Kennedy, and even Johnson. The environmental movement was a pretty unusual mass movement in other ways. Its "grass roots" was people such as the Osborns and Rockefellers and institutions such as the Ford Foundation. This sort of thing led at least one theorist of mass movements to observe that social movements were more and more frequently created from above. More about this later.

The editors of *Newsweek* ended their lengthy coverage, pages 31 through 47, with an editorial entitled "Needed: A Rebirth of Community." This piece was a replay of the Standard Research Institute's proposals. Newsweek called for the Age of Conservation to begin, for the time of expansion to end, and for a global effort to reduce pollution. They also quoted Rockefeller University's Rene Dubos, who said that we need something like a new religion, one based on the idea of harmony with nature and each other.

The idea that environmentalism needed to be a kind of religion appears frequently, often in the context of attacks on the Judeo-Christian tradition. One of the, if not the, most referenced versions of this was published by Lynn White in 1967.

White argued that the Judeo-Christian tradition encouraged scientific-technical progress directly and indirectly. It did so directly through its ideas about man's relationship with nature and indirectly by supporting democracy through the assertion that every person has a soul and is created in the image of god. It was this democratic impulse, according to White, that led to the education and elevation of the non-elites and to the idea that science should serve the practical needs of the vast majority of people. That is, the Judeo-Christian teachings include a belief in progress and an idea that humans were given dominion over nature.[87] As sources of scientific-industrial society, Judeo-Christian values and democracy were, in White's view, impediments to the environmental movement.

These kinds of ideas were given a boost by the nation's leading newspaper, the *New York Times*. On January 4, 1970, again months before the first Earth Day, the *Times* carried an article by Edward B. Fiske entitled "The Link Between Faith and Ecology," which began with the following:

> Over the centuries the growth of Western science and technology has been closely tied to Judeo-Christian religious values. Isaac Newton and other early scientific giants explained their activities and findings in religious terms. The fundamental teaching of

---

[87] White, 1967.

Genesis that man is created in God's image and intended to have 'dominion' over the rest of creation gave ultimate significance to the scientific method.

As men become increasingly concerned with polluted streams, foul air and other evidence that technological advances do not necessarily constitute progress, it is not surprising that some of these fundamental religious assumptions are also coming to be questioned. The result is what may prove to be the most far-reaching new religious issue of the 1970's - the theology of ecology, or man's relationship to his environment.

This fall the National Council of Churches established an Environmental Stewardship Action Team that hopes to put theologians, scientists and others to work on the problem. Several conferences have already been held by an association of 75 religious thinkers known as the Faith-Man-Nature Group. Another is scheduled this month at St. Xavier College in Chicago.

The fundamental assumption of these groups - one that is shared by ecologists outside the church - is that the current environmental crisis is not simply scientific and political in nature. 'Since the roots of our trouble are so largely religious,' wrote Lynn White, Jr., a historian, in *Science Magazine*, 'the remedy must also be essentially religious, whether we call it that or not.'

Fiske went on to say that

Most work in the field begins with the recognition that despite the fundamental Biblical affirmation of the goodness of creation, Christian thought has entertained ideas that have, as Julian Hartt, a Yale theologian, put it last week, 'legitimized man's total exploitation of his environment.'

Fiske concluded:

Thus far the new interest in ecology has been largely academic, but church leaders hope that local congregations - like elements of the new left on college campuses - will soon make issues such as air pollution part of their social action program.

This may not be as uncontroversial as it sounds. Ecologists now recognize that fighting for clean air and water is not like supporting motherhood but involves fundamental shifts in national values and priorities.

'If we are serious about increasing the quality of life for all men,' said the Rev. Norden C. Murphy of the N.C.C., for instance, 'we may have to declare a moratorium on how much we consume. We may have to reject the assumption that a gross national product that goes up each year is a good thing.'[88]

Three years later the *Times* published an editorial by one of England's leading intellectuals making the same kind of argument. The writer was Arnold J. Toynbee; the article was cleverly titled "The Genesis of Pollution."[89] A lengthier version of this appeared in the Summer, 1973, issue of *Horizon*.

---

[88] Fiske, 1970, p. 5.
[89] Toynbee, 1973, p. 15.

Our ancestors became human in the act of inventing tools, and within the last two centuries we have discovered how to increase the potency of our tools enormously. We have achieved this by harnessing one after another of the physical forces of inanimate nature, from water power to atomic energy. Here, manifestly, we have the immediate cause of both the genocide at Hiroshima and Nagasaki and the worlwide pollution that threatens to bring comparable catastrophes to human life, on an even broader scale.

Some of the major maladies of the present-day world - in particular the recklessly extravagant consumption of nature's irreplaceable treasures and the pollution of those of them that man has not already devoured - can be traced back to a religious cause, and that this cause is the rise of monotheism.

If one has been brought up as a Christian, Jew or Moslem, one has been conditioned to take monotheism and its mundane implications for granted...

For premonotheistic man nature was not just a treasure-trove of 'natural resources.' Nature was, for him, a goddess, 'Mother Earth,' and the vegetation that sprang from the earth, the animals that roamed, like man himself, over the earth's surface, and the minerals hiding in the earth's bowels all partook of nature's divinity. The whole of his environment was divine, and his sense of nature's divinity outlasted his technological feats of cultivating plants and domesticating animals: wheat and rice were not just 'cereals,' they were Ceres herself, the goddess who had allowed man to cultivate these life-giving plants and had taught him the art.

My observation of the living religion of eastern Asia, and my book knowledge of the extinquished Greek and Roman religion, have made me aware of a startling and disturbing truth: that monotheism, as enunciated in the Book of Genesis, has removed the age-old restraint that was once placed on man's greed by his awe. Man's greedy impulse to exploit nature used to be held in check by his pious worship of nature. This primitive inhibition has been removed by the rise and spread of monotheism. Moreover, the monotheistic disrespect for nature has survived the weakening of the belief in monotheism in the exmonotheistic part of the world, and it has invaded that major portion of the world in which monotheism has never been established.

This, then, is the nemesis that modern Western man, together with his imitators in countries like Japan, has brought upon himself by following the directive given in the first chapter of the Book of Genesis. That directive has turned out to be bad advice and we are beginning, wisely, to recoil from it.

This amounted to a rejection of most of what people had come to think of as the progress of Western civilization. We will examine this more closely later. It was the activities of the Osborns, Rockefellers, Toynbee, and others that constituted the real birth of contemporary environmentalism. In that sense, Earth Day, 1970, was neither the beginning nor the apex of the environmental movement. During the time leading up to that first Earth Day, the reactionary and aristocratic quality of environmental thought was clear. This was not so much a "liberal" or a "conservative" movement, but, rather, an aristocratic movement of the world's richest and most influential people.

In many ways, however, the political nature of the emerging environmentalism probably remained unclear to most people. In the early-70s conservatives such as Ronald Reagan, Barry Goldwater, and James Buckley were speaking out on behalf of the environment while the "liberal" *New Republic* referred to it as "the Ecology Craze" and radical journalist I. F. Stone called Earth Day a "gigantic snowjob." Writing from a leftist perspective, both Murray Bookchin and James Ridgeway claimed that big business created the ecology movement[90] and Ridgeway charged that the ecology crusade was "a cover for the energy game."[91] Many on the left called it a distraction from the problems of poverty, racism and the Vietnam war.[92] Although Democrats in the U.S. House were more likely than Republicans to back environmentalist views, a 1981 national poll indicated only slight differences in the country between "liberals" and "conservatives" on environmental issues.[93] Writing for *Esquire* magazine, Jon Margolis noted in 1970 that

> The militant preservationist is a radical. Well about nature he's a radical; about people he may be quite conservative. This is not a new irony. Since the movement began before the turn of the century, it has been a split between those who wanted to save and manage nature for people--all the people--and those who wanted to leave it just as it was for nobody at all, or perhaps for those with the time, money, and culture to appreciate true wilderness. At the beginning, this schism was personified by Gifford Pinchot, head of the Forest Service under Teddy Roosevelt, and a populist, and John Muir, founder of the Sierra Club, and a mystic. They were friends for a while, camping out together in the Grand Canyon, but they became estranged, first over the Hetch Hetchy Dam, which violated Yosemite National Park but brought low-cost public power to San Francisco. The preservationists fought the dam bitterly, making common cause with the private-utility industry. Then or later, they seemed not at all embarrassed about the bedfellow.[94]

The President of the United States, Richard Nixon, made concessions to the environmental movement, but he was not willing to support the Rockefeller Population Commission's conclusion that the U.S. should move toward zero population growth, nor would he support the Commission's pro-abortion position nor would he support their recommendation that birth control services be made generally available to minors.[95] The *New York Times* would editorialize in May of 1972 that President Nixon gave the "thoughtful" Rockefeller report "the back of his hand" and that the President had failed to give a "reasoned and positive response."[96]

Anti-war clergyman Richard Neuhaus came away from the first Earth Day with more than just misgivings. Soon after, he wrote the following:

> The [ecology] movement's organizers called radicals to the barricades, only to find most of the choice places already taken by the executives of the corporate giants. There they stood together at the barricade, bold and unflinching in the face of - nobody.
>   According to the trade paper *Advertising Age*, companies rushing to buy prime time for Earth Day included Proctor and Gamble, General Electric, Goodrich, Standard Oil of New Jersey [Exxon], Dupont, International Paper, Phillips Petroleum, Chevron Oil, General Motors, and Atlantic Richfield. It might be thought that these companies had

---

[90] Neuhaus, 1971, p. 83.
[91] Ridgeway, 1970, pp. 16-17.
[92] Hayward, 2000.
[93] New York Times, 1978, p. B10; Shabecoff, 1981, p. 30.
[94] Margolis, 1970, p. 173.
[95] Piotrow, 1973, pp. 194, 197.
[96] New York Times, 1972, p. 44.

been put on the defensive by Earth Day and were rushing to defend themselves. But even a cursory examination of the content of the advertising quickly disabuses one of that notion. They are the positive champions of the war against pollution.[97]

The upper-class interests that owned and controlled these and other giant corporations had been promoting a war against "pollution" for a very long time. They also had been making the case that population growth was the primary danger facing the world, that is, people were the real problem.

For example, a full page ad published in the *New York Times* in 1964 as an open letter to President Johnson warned him that the Great Society was threatened by the population explosion. The giant corporations and wealthy families represented among the signatories included the Standard Oil of New Jersey, Goodyear, Morgan Guaranty Trust, Gulf Oil and Sears and families such as Aldrich, Cabot, Chase, Draper, Fosdick, Lamont, Loeb, Scaife, Osborn, Prentice, Reid, Rosenwald, and Wriston. In other words, what bothered Neuhaus on the first Earth Day was simply a continuation of the involvement of upper-class interests in conservation and population control, now being called environmentalism.

In the early-70s the upper class backed Club of Rome attempted to scare the public into accepting less growth with warnings that the world's resources were almost exhausted and the environment was being destroyed by growth in population, industrial production and consumption. The Club of Rome, formed with the support of Fiat Chairman Giovanni Agnelli, promoted this argument in 1972 with the release of and aggressive promotion of a "study" entitled *The Limits to Growth*. Their computer generated predictions of imminent resource scarcity and ecological breakdown, outlined in the book, were given a feeling of reality by the 1973-74 and 1979-80 oil crises.[98] Not everybody recognized these crises as artificial.

The authors of *The Limits to Growth* (Donella Meadows, Dennis Meadows, Jorgen Randers and William W. Behrens) were offering a new version of a very old argument. Ideas of resource scarcity had appeared more than a century earlier in the writings of David Ricardo, John Stuart Mill, and, of course, Malthus. These three Englishmen had focused on land as the scarce resource. A different line of argument appeared with Gifford Pinchot, who warned in the early 1900s that some raw materials (e.g., coal and iron) were running out. Both Vogt and Osborn linked population growth to the general issue of natural resource scarcity.[99]

The new limits to growth argument presented the same essential viewpoint dressed up with tables, graphs and computer modeling. This stands as one of the most famous examples of the GIGO problem, i.e., garbage in, garbage out. The resource figures fed into the computer were invalid. The study assumed no future technological progress. There were other problems. The study was roundly criticized by a large number of

---

[97] Neuhaus, 1971, p. 84.
[98] Golub and Townsend, 1977.
[99] Barnet and Morse, 1963, pp. 27, 51, 76-82.

experts, but it was widely disseminated and it was widely quoted long after it had been discredited.[100]

Between 1965 and 1970 the percentage of people who indicated a concern about pollution problems increased dramatically.[101] Sometime between 1967 and 1970 this appears to have reached a majority of the U.S. population. The same is probably true of overpopulation fears. Then U.S. Representative to the United Nations and later President, George H. W. Bush observed in a 1973 foreward to Phyllis Piotrow's *World Population Crisis* that

> Few issues in the world have undergone such a rapid shift in public attitudes and government policies over the last decade as the problems of population growth and fertility control.[102]

A similar observation has been made about ecological issues. Writing in *Public Opinion Quarterly*, Hazel Erskine referred to changes in public opinion about ecology as a "miracle of public opinion." She went on to sat that "alarm about the environment sprang from nowhere to major proportions in a few short years."[103] It sprang from "nowhere" because other than "a few oil spills," there were no obvious reasons for it.[104] Such a rapid shift required the aid of the media.[105]

Bush, who associated himself with the views and efforts of William H. Draper, Jr., and John D. Rockefeller III and praised the Population Crisis Committee and others, was pointing out, accurately, that it had been only since the end of the Kennedy Presidency that overpopulation and the idea of a population crisis had taken hold. Bush did not stop to note that people were also much more pessimistic in 1973 than they were in 1963.

There were few more aggressive purveyors of that pessimism in the early 1970s than biologist turned ecologist Garret Hardin. Writing in the midst of the first major oil crisis of the 1970s, Hardin took advantage of what was essentially an artificial and created shortage[106] to try to convince people that progress was over and we had only two options. Hardin asserted that we could either create a world government to control reproduction and ration resources or we could adopt a vicious life boat ethics.

This 1974 article by Hardin was entitled "Lifeboat Ethics, The Case Against Helping the Poor." It appeared in the September issue of *Psychology Today*. Hardin suggested that we think of the nation as a lifeboat that has a limited amount of resources to support people. Hardin[107] then said that "the current energy crisis" shows that we have already exceeded in some ways that carrying capacity. Hardin thus became simultaneously a Malthusian of the first rank and a propagandist for the major oil companies.

---

[100] Cole et al., 1973; Simon, 1981; Walker, 1981.
[101] Davies, 1970; Erskine, 1972; Gibson, 1992; Humphrey and Buttel, 1982.
[102] Piotrow, 1973, p. ix.
[103] Erskine, 1972, p. 120.
[104] Krier and Ursin, 1977, p. 299; Petulla, 1988, p. 274.
[105] Dunlap, 1989, p. 95; Petulla, 1987, p. 121.
[106] Blair, 1976; Sampson, 1975; Sherrill, 1983.
[107] Hardin, 1974, p. 40.

Unfortunately, many did not apparently notice this or they decided to chalk up the connection to coincidence, just an oddity.

In a world of dwindling resources and growing inequality, Hardin went on, we will have to adopt a tough policy which will force the rest of the world to accept limits on its population. Encouraging population growth by providing economic aid, in Hardin's view, only leads to a greater and greater number of people living off fixed resources. The spread of humanity is like cancer.

Hardin concluded by saying that until we have "a true world government," we have to reject the sharing ethic and we have to keep people out of the lifeboat. This he said was harsh but necessary. Environmentalism even in its "liberal" reincarnation was a very ugly thing. The successful promotion of something as ugly as this, in the absence of clear evidence to demonstrate its necessity, requires a major insitutional effort. Such an effort was made.

Chapter Six

MISANTHROPIC GIVING

In an important essay discussing social movements in general, John D. McCarthy and Mayer N. Zald pointed out that some movements had been in the past and are in recent periods created in a top down fashion rather than emerging spontaneously from the shared experiences or grievances of a certain part of the population. They noted that while top down creation had existed for a long time, it seemed to be getting more common. This has generally been ignored, even as a possibility, in most research on social movements.[1]

In the top down process, elites make use of large financial resources, particularly foundation money, and control over media to essentially create supporters for a cause.[2] McCarthy and Zald suggest that the functions that were previously carried out by grassroots members of social movements are now performed by paid functionaries and full-time, professional employees.[3] In recent years, the professional training of street level activists has reached new levels with the appearance in 1995 of the well financed, California based Ruckus Society. Among the Society's focal points are environmentalist and anarchist protests against globalization.[4] As we will see, global environmental initiatives and promotion of global "free trade" both come from the same groups.

As we have seen, the media gave a big boost to the emergence of environmentalism. This, of course, was not a case of creating something out of nothing. Those promoting environmentalism in the media and those involved in organizing the movement had the conservation and population control organizations to build from. What the organizers did was to vastly expand an already existing network of organizations and give it a much larger number of supporters. They also vastly increased the amount of money that was available to environmentalists. Much of this was provided through foundations,[5]

---

[1] For examples see the following: Banks, 1972; Blumer, 1974; Herberle, 1951; Killian, 1973; Lauer, 1976; Lewy, 1980; Perry and Pugh, 1978; Touraine, 1981; Wilkinson, 1971.

[2] McCarthy and Zald, 1987, pp. 340-341, 358-359, 368-375, 383-385.

[3] Ibid., pp. 340-341.

[4] http//ruckus.org/about.htm

[5] Ingram and Mann, 1989, pp. 135-137.

something that McCarthy and Zald pointed out was typical of the top down type of social movement.[6]

There are thousands of private foundations in the United States. Most of them have relatively small assets and there is a considerable concentration of total assets in the wealthiest foundations. Within the 3,138 foundations large enough to be listed in the Foundation Directory in 1980, the top six controlled twenty percent of total assets and the top twenty-five controlled thirty-five percent.[7] Twenty years later there were over 6,200 foundations, but only twenty had endowments over one billion dollars.[8]

Most of the large foundations were created by wealthy families and they are controlled by members of the upper class and representatives of large banks, insurance companies and corporations. The remainder of the wealthy foundations are corporate foundations, operated by officers of corporations. Power over the distribution of foundation money gives the upper class a significant role in shaping cultural, political and economic trends and provides a means of influencing public opinion. The control over media is probably even more important. Foundations also shelter money from taxes while allowing the upper class to maintain control over the assets and profits.[9]

At the beginning of the 1960s, grants for population control activity and for what was then called 'conservation' were so small that they did not merit mention in the annual reports of the Foundation Center, which gathers information on such activity. They also were not significant enough to appear in the index of the Foundation Center's Grants Index. By the beginning of the 1970s this would change dramatically. In 1963, a total of 957,000 dollars was given to various conservation groups by eight foundations. For the two years 1970 and 1971, 34.2 million dollars in grants are listed under the heading of 'Recreation and Conservation' and 14.9 million for 'Environmental Studies.' In 1984 the Grants Index reports 89.1 million dollars given for 'Environmental Law, Protection and Environmental Education,' 25.9 million for 'Abortion, Birth Control and Family Planning' and 27.5 million for 'Energy.'[10] The vast majority, if not all, of the grants promoted activities or ideas which are antagonistic to industrial production, economic growth and population growth. What was favored was population control, conservation, labor intensive production and less material consumption. The growth in foundation support parallels and is partly responsible for the growth of the environmental movement. Marcy Darnovsky notes that in 1965 the ten largest conservation groups had less than 500,000 members and a combined budget of less than ten million dollars. In 1990 the top ten had over seven million members and a budget of 514 million dollars.[11]

Two of the leading supporters of environmentalist and over-population causes have been the Ford Foundation and the Rockefeller Brothers Fund. In a five year period in the 1970s (1974 through 1978) the Ford Foundation contributed over fourteen million dollars to environmentalist and population control organizations (e.g., Conservation Foundation,

---

[6] McCarthy and Zald, 1987, pp. 340-341.
[7] Dye, 1983, pp. 142-145.
[8] Domhoff, 1998, pp. 128-129.
[9] Domhoff, 1983, pp. 82-95; Dye, 1983, pp. 142-143.
[10] The Foundation Center, various years.
[11] Darnovsky, 1992, p. 41.

Environmental Defense Fund, Natural Resources Defense Council, Sierra Club). In addition to these contributions, the Ford Foundation also donated close to two million dollars to the Aspen Institute between 1974 and 1982. The Rockefeller Brothers Fund joined the Ford Foundation in contributing to Aspen, giving 715,000 dollars in the same period. The Brothers Fund also contributed over seven million dollars to environmentalist and population control organizations between 1974 and 1978.[12]

Perhaps the most blatant and direct expression of the Rockefeller Brothers Fund's Malthusianism is contained in its 1977 task force report published in book form as *The Unfinished Agenda*. The task force was made up of representatives of the following environmentalist organizations: Environmental Defense Fund, Friends of the Earth, Izaak Walton League of America, Massachusetts Audubon Society, National Audubon Society, National Parks and Conservation Association, National Wildlife Federation, Natural Resources Defense Council, Nature Conservancy, Sierra Club, Wilderness Society, Zero Population Growth. The task force was headed up by Gerald O. Barney, a Brothers Fund staff member, who also edited the book.

The Brothers Fund's book called for a declared national goal of zero population growth or population decrease. In this area it recommended the following: reduction of legal and illegal immigration; promotion of contraception, abortion and sterilization in the U.S. and abroad; promotion of non-marriage and childlessness; sex education for teenagers and pre-teens; elimination of tax deductions for children after the second child; and linking international agricultural assistance to the adoption of policies to stop population growth. The book also proposed that greater controls be established over existing and new technologies. The report recommended the elimination of nuclear power plants and the restriction of research on fusion energy. Logically, it also contained recommendations to reduce energy use and to satisfy remaining needs increasingly through solar energy, coal gasification, fuel-alcohol production and end-use conservation. It suggested reductions in the use of fertilizers and in the consumption of grain-fed meat. Labor intensive forms of agricultural production were recommended for the U.S. and the world. General policies of conservation, resource self- sufficiency and protection of wildlife and wilderness were supported. The Fund's task force also made several recommendations concerning the beliefs and values of the people of the United States. They suggested that education in environmentalism be expanded and that appreciation of nature be promoted. Finally, the report advocated studies of TV programming and commercials to determine their role in educating people about environmental issues, resource consumption, pollution and lifestyles.[13]

During the mid-1970s when this report was produced, the Rockefeller Brothers Fund had six family members on its board, including Laurance Rockefeller who served as chairman. The board also included Henry Kissinger, a long time associate of the family.

The Ford Foundation was not then and is not a family dominated institution. It is though a thoroughly upper-class institution. Its board of trustees in the 1970s included individuals who were members of upper-class organizations (Council on Foreign

---

[12] Foundation Grants Index, various years.
[13] Barney, 1977, pp. 12-22, 29-33, 40, 44, 65-67, 75, 139-142, 159-160.

Relations and the Trilateral Commission) and/or were officers of important private and public organizations (Brookings Institution, Bank of America, Citicorp, CBS, World Bank, Federal Reserve Board, etc.).[14]

Listing the major funders of global population control activities for the period 1965 through 1976, Julian Simon had the Ford Foundation in second place, behind the United States government and ahead of Sweden. The Rockefeller Foundation was in fifth place, just behind Norway. The two foundations donated over 246 million dollars in this period.[15] Simon went on to observe, partly based on the work of Bachrach and Bergman, that the Population Council, Ford Foundation and Planned Parenthood along with several public organizations (Agency for International Development, National Institutes of Health, H.E.W., Bureau of the Census, National Academy of Sciences) constituted a tightly interconnected network of population control organizations.[16]

G. William Domhoff has described the important role played by foundations in the development of environmentalism, none playing a more prominent role than Ford.

> The Ford Foundation also has played a major role in creating and sustaining the environmental movement. Its conference on resource management in 1953 and subsequent start-up funding led to the establishment of the first and most prominent environmental think tank, Resources for the Future, which broke new ground by incorporating market economics into thinking about conservation. In the early 1960s the Ford Foundation spent $7 million over a three-year period developing ecology programs at seventeen universities around the country, thereby providing the informational base and personnel infrastructure for efforts to control pesticides and industrial waste products. At the same time, the foundation put large sums into the land-purchase programs of the Nature Conservancy and the Audubon Society and encouraged environmental education and citizen action through grants to municipal conservation commissions and the nation-wide Conservation Foundation-the latter founded by the Rockefeller family as a combined think tank and policy-discussion group.
>
> The Ford Foundation aided environmentalists further in 1970 by backing a new environmental law firm under the leadership of corporate lawyers, the Natural Resources Defense Council, which received grants from 52 other foundations as well. It also gave $78,000 to the Nature Conservancy, which had 128 other grants from foundations for the same time period, including $1 million from the David and Lucille Packard Foundation in California and $500,000 from the ultraconservative Lilly Endowment in Indiana.[17]

The scientists and lawyers working for the Natural Resources Defense Council at its inception have been described as "the elite shock troops of the environmental struggles under way in the United States and the world." Most of the lawyers were products of the Yale law school.[18]

In fact, the idea for the Natural Resources Defense Council (NRDC) was reportedly brought to the Ford Foundation by two members of one of Wall Street's elite law firms.

---

[14] Taft Corporation, 1978; Marquis Who's Who, 1978-79.
[15] Simon, 1981, p. 292.
[16] Ibid., p. 305.
[17] Domhoff, 1998, pp. 132-133.
[18] Robinson, 1993, p. 39.

The two were Whitney North Seymour and Stephen P. Duggan. Duggan, a product of Phillips Exeter, Harvard and Columbia, and Seymour, also Columbia, were partners at the law firm of Simpson, Thacher and Barlett. Both were members of the upper class Century Club. Seymour was from 1955 to 1970 the chairman of the board of trustees of the Carnegie Endowment.[19] Seymour and Duggan brought an associate of Seymour's, John Adams, with them to head the NRDC. Thirty years later Adams was still there. He was one of the fifteen members of the board of directors for Earth Day 2000.

During the 1970s, when the organizational network of environmentalism was growing rapidly, the Ford Foundation made large contributions to dozens of population control and environmental organizations. The following is a list of the primary recipients for the 1975 through 1978 period and the amounts given to them by the Ford Foundation.

Conservation Foundation	$700,000
Environmental Defense Fund	$529,000
Environmental Law Institute	$654,210
Family Planning Foundation, India	$300,000
Human Ecology Research Foundation	$258,000
Latin American Demographic Center, Santiago, Chile	$286,000
Natural Resources Defense Council	$680,000
Population Center Foundation, Philippines	$390,480
Population Council	$8,661,000
Regional Population Center, Bogota, Columbia	$700,000

The board of trustees of the Ford Foundation in this period included the following people:

- McGeorge Bundy, President of Ford Foundation; member of the Council on Foreign Relations; special assistant to the President for national security, 1961-1966.
- Andrew F. Brimmer; member - Council on Foreign Relations, Trilateral Commission; director - Bank of America, International Harvester, United Airlines, Du Pont Co.; member - Federal Reserve Board, 1966-1974.
- Hedley Donovan; member - Council on Foreign Relations; Editor-in-Chief, Time, Inc.
- Walter A. Haas; director - Bank of America; trustee - Levi Strauss Foundation.
- Robert S. McNamara; President of World Bank; member- Council on Foreign Relations; director - Brookings Institution; President, Ford Motor Co., 1960-61; Secretary of Defense, 1961-1968.
- J. Irwin Miller; member - Council on Foreign Relations; director - A.T. & T., Equitable Life Assurance Society; Chairman of the Board, Union Bank and Trust co.

---

[19] Dye, 1983, p. 137; Marquis Who' Who, 1978-79; Robinson, 1993, p. 39.

- Franklin A. Thomas; director - Citicorp, CBS, Inc., Aluminum Company of America.

The president of the Foundation from 1966 to 1979, McGeorge Bundy, was a member of one of America's most influential families. He went to the Ford Foundation straight from his position as national security advisor to Presidents Kennedy and Johnson. That is, he went from being an administrator of the Vietnam war, and one of its most important supporters, to being a leading promoter of environmentalism.[20] McNamara was, of course, Secretary of Defense during the build-up for and many of the years of the war in Vietnam. This is not at all discordant given the real history of ecology and environmentalism. It is if one uncritically accepts the post-1970s use of the term "liberal" to describe environmentalism. The trustees of the Ford Foundation were carrying on the long tradition of upper class support for ecology.

Most of the published academic research on the environmental movement overlooks entirely the history of upper class leadership in this area and fails to examine such activity today. This is made all the more important by the total silence of the mass media on these facts and the reluctance of almost all politicians to even mention it. A good example of the failure of academia is in the research and writing on the anti-nuclear movement where the involvement of upper-class interests is too often either completely unexplored or is given brief and superficial attention.[21]

During the period in which the long term growth of nuclear energy in the United States was brought to an end, upper-class foundations were supportive of the anti-nuclear movement. They supported that movement in ways that went beyond financial support. They did provide money to leading forces in the anti-nuclear movement. For example, between 1974 and 1982, the heyday of the anti-nuclear movement, the Ford Foundation, Rockefeller Brothers Fund, and Rockefeller Family Fund collectively gave almost seven million dollars to four of the most active anti-nuclear groups - the Natural Resources Defense Council, Sierra Club, Union of Concerned Scientists, Environmental Defense Fund.[22] The Ford Foundation and Robert O. Anderson, Chairman of Atlantic Richfield and of the Aspen Institute, supported the creation of another antinuclear group, the Friends of the Earth.[23] In addition to its financial support for the antinuclear cause, the Rockefeller Brothers Fund, as noted above, committed itself against nuclear energy, calling for its complete elimination in its 1977 task force report.[24]

The whole idea of energy scarcity was given a boost at the Ford Foundation. The Foundation began in the early-1970s to focus on "the United States' appetite for abundant and cheap energy."[25] Ten years earlier, President Kennedy discussed cheap and abundant

---

[20] Robinson, 1993, p. 38.
[21] See the following examples: Barkan, 1979; Bicherstaffe and Pearce, 1980; Camilleri, 1984; Campbell, 1988; Ebin and Kasper, 1974; Falk, 1982; Gormley, 1983; Inglehart, 1981; McCracken, 1982; Mitchel, 1981; Pector, 1978; Price, 1982; Pringle and Spigelman, 1981; Wasserman, 1979.
[22] Gibson, 1990.
[23] Barkley and Weissman, 1970; Domhoff, 1978; Falk, 1982; Gibson, 1990; Nelkin and Pollak, 1981; Neuhaus, 1971; Price, 1982.
[24] Barney, 1977; Gibson, 1990, p. 329.
[25] Robinson, 1993, p. 40.

energy as a necessary and desired basis for economic progress;[26] to those at the Ford Foundation it merely fed an excessive "appetite." Under the direction of Edward Ames, a member of Ford's Resources and Environment group, the Foundation initiated in 1971 its Energy Policy Project. The Foundation spent four million dollars on this project, which produced twenty-two volumes and received a lot of media attention leading up to 1973. When the oil crisis hit, Ford was ready with recommendations for lower levels of energy use.[27] Energy thereby became a central theme of the environmental movement. All of this was quite odd, since energy scarcity was never demonstrated. It was merely asserted. In fact, around the time that the Ford Foundation was deciding that energy was scarce, a study ordered by Standard Oil of California (SoCal/Chevron) stated that there was an abundance of oil in the world.[28] What the Ford Foundation did between 1971 and 1973 appears to have been preparation of the ideology of energy scarcity. There was no real shortage during the 1973-74 oil crisis, only the one orchestrated by the major oil companies.[29]

This upper class foundation support for environmentalism has continued up to the present. At the end of the 1990s major foundations were still pouring large sums of money into environmentalist organizations, many of them directly involved in promoting Earth Day 2000. The following is a list of grants made by the Ford Foundation which appeared in the Foundation Grants Index, 2000. Most of the gifts were formalized in the year 1998. I have excluded recipients that got less than $75,000.

Aforda Private Limited, Kathmandu	$75,000
Africa Resources Trust	$175,000
African Wildlife Foundation	$150,000
Alternatives and Social Participation Processes, Mexico	$50,000
Appalachian Mountain Club	$200,000
Arizona-Sonora Desert Museum	$150,000
Bethel New Life	$290,000
Casa de la Paz, Chile	$100,000
Cebu Uniting for Sustainable Water Foundation, Philippines	$130,000
Center of Alternative Technologies for the Atlantic Forest, Brazil	$200,000
Central Himalayan Environment Association, India	$250,000
Center for Science and Environment, India	$125,000
Certified Forest Products Council	$200,000
Collins Center for Public Policy	$250,000
Community Resource Group	$500,000
Cross River Forestry Development Department, Nigeria	$80,000
Ecotech Services, India	$77,700
Eduardo Mondlane University	$90,000
Environmental and Natural Resources Law Center, Costa Rica	$100,000
Environmental Defense Fund	$100,000

[26] Gibson, 1994, pp. 24-25; Kennedy, 1962, p. 8.
[27] Robinson, 1993, p. 40.
[28] Sherrill, 1983, pp. 4, 103.
[29] Blair, 1976, p. 275; Sherrill, 1983, pp. 226-227.

Environmental Law Alliance Worldwide	$100,000
Environmental Working Group	$275,000
Federal University of Acre Foundation, Brazil	$350,000
Federal University of Rio de Janeiro, Brazil	$250,000
Federation of Agencies of Social and Educational Assistance, Brazil	$90,000
First Nations Development Institute	$310,000
Forest Stewardship Council, Mexico	$250,000
Fundacion para la Promocion del Desarrollo Sustentable	$100,000
Greater Yellowstone Coalition	$325,000
Group for Environmental Monitoring, South Africa	$233,000
Hanoi Agricultural University, Vietnam	$162,200
Haribon Foundation, Philippines	$80,000
Henrys Fork Foundation	$200,000
High Country Foundation	$100,000
Indian Institute of Bio-Social Research and Development, India	$330,000
Indian Institute of Science, India	$94,700
Indonesian Center for Environmental Law	$150,000
Indonesian Tropical Institute	$635,000
Institute for Management and Certification of Agriculture and Forestry, Brazil	$190,000
Institute of Environmental Science for Social Change, Philippines	$390,000
International Bank for Reconstruction and Development	$75,000
International Institute for Sustainable Development	$170,000
International Union for Conservation of Nature and Natural Resources	$725,000
Jefferson Center for Education and Research	$160,000
Kahublagan Sang Panimalay, Philippines	$95,000
Kasetsart University, Thailand	$254,075
Kenya Forest Research Institute, Kenya	$150,000
Lawyers Environmental Action Team, Tanzania	$80,000
Legal Resources Trust, South Africa	$150,000
Legal Rights and Natural Resources Center, Philippines	$280,000
Local Development Foundation, Thailand	$190,000
Louisiana State University and A & M College	$275,000
Mafisa Planning and Research, South Africa	$100,000
Makerere University, Uganda	$180,000
Mexican Council for Sustainable Forestry	$150,000
Mozambique, Republic of	$579,000
Museum Trustees of Kenya	$275,000
National Environment Trust	$200,000
National Wildlife Federation	$300,000
Natural Resources Defense Council	$75,000
New England Environmental Policy Center	$330,000
Northern New Mexico Legal Services	$368,280
On Purpose Associates	$150,000
Oregon State University	$233,000
Pennsylvania, Commonwealth of	$80,000
Pinchot Institute for Conservation	$300,000

Portland State University Foundation	$150,000
Positive Futures Network	$375,000
Pronatura Chiapas, Mexico	$110,000
Rainforest Alliance	$1,500,000
Save Our Cumberland Mountains Resource Project	$150,000
Sichuan Forestry College, China	$108,500
Sichuan Provincial Forestry Department, China	$374,000
Social and Environmental Reference Center, Brazil	$100,000
Sociedad Peruana de Derecho Ambiental, Peru	$100,000
Society of Hill Resource Management School, India	$220,000
Socio-Environmental Institute for South Bahia, Brazil	$190,000
Stephen Nielson Anderson and Company, Chile	$100,000
Sustainable Development Forum, Mexico	$100,000
Technical Assistance in Alternative Agriculture, Brazil	$180,000
Texas Center for Policy Studies	$225,000
Universidad Autonoma de Chapingo, Mexico	$150,000
Universidad Nacional Autonoma de Mexico	$290,000
University of California, Berkeley	$1,200,000
University of California, Santa Barbara	$150,000
University of Colorado Foundation	$75,000
University of Gadjah Mada, Indonesia	$183,600
University of Montana	$100,000
University of San Paulo, Brazil	$260,000
University of Victoria, Canada	$92,000
University of Yucatan, Mexico	$154,000
Vietnam National University, Vietnam	$81,675
Vitoria Amazonica Foundation, Brazil	$195,000
Watershed Research and Training Center	$300,000
Wilderness Society	$225,000
Yayasan Konphalind, Indonesia	$200,000
Yunan Institute of Geography, China	$196,119
Yunan Provincial Forestry Bureau	$146,800

Perhaps the most impressive thing about this list, beside the number of and size of the grants, is the fully international scope of the giving. That is different from what one would have seen in the 1970s or early-1980s. It would appear that the same sort of organizational mobilization that took place in the United States in the 1960s and 1970s is taking place now on a global scale. An example of this is the Rockefeller Foundation's announcement in 1990 that it would spend 50 million dollars to help form an international network of environmentalists.[30]

The trustees of the Ford Foundation may not be as illustrious as in earlier periods, but there are still strong connections to institutions that play prominent roles within the Establishment. For example, the chairman of the board of trustees is Henry B. Schacht, the former CEO of Lucent Technologies. Schacht is a graduate of Yale University who serves on the boards of directors of the Chase Manhattan Corporation, AT&T, and Alcoa. He is a member of the Council on Foreign Relations, the Conference Board and the Business Council. He had also been a member of the Committee on Economic Development and an honorary trustee of the Brookings Institution.[31] Those are impressive credentials.

Another of the trustees is Paul A. Allaire who is the CEO and chairman of the board of the Xerox Corporation. Allaire is also a director of J. P. Morgan, Lucent Technologies, SmithKline Beecham, and the Sara Lee Corporation. Like Schacht, Allaire is a member of the Council on Foreign Relations. He is a director, since 1993, of that organization.[32]

A third trustee, Kathryn Fuller, is president and CEO of the World Wildlife Fund and is a member of the World Bank's Advisory Committee on Sustainable Development. Another, Frances D. Fergusson is president of Vassar College and serves on the board of the Marine Midland Bank.[33] The Ford Foundation and some of the other major foundations are sometimes described as "liberal."[34] The meaning of the term in that context is different from what many would have meant when they used the term to describe JFK or FDR.

As the century ended, the involvement of the Rockefeller interests in ecology was still evident. The following grants for environmentalist activities of 75,000 dollars or more made by the Rockefeller Brothers Fund were listed in the 2000 Foundation Grants Index. Although it is a significant foundation, the Fund does not have anything close to the assets of the Ford Foundation. The Brothers Fund claims assets of 463 million dollars; Ford has assets of nearly 10 billion dollars.

Alaska Marine Conservation Council	$100,000
American Lands Alliance	$100,000
American Oceans Campaign	$120,000
Cee Bankwatch Network Foundation, Poland	$180,000
Center for Marine Conservation	$80,000
Conservation Law Foundation	$75,000
Czech Eco-Counseling Network	$75,000
David Suzuki Foundation, Canada	$380,000
Earth Council, Costa Rica	$129,500
Earth Island Institute	$253,000
Ecologists Linked for Organizing Grassroots Initiatives and Action	$116,000
Environmental Legal Assistance Center, Philippines	$150,000
Environmental Management and Law Association, Hungary	$150,000
Environmental Partnership for Central Europe, Czech Republic	$90,000
European Natural Heritage Fund, Germany	$80,000

---

[30] Teltsch, 1990, p. C10.
[31] Marquis Who's Who, 2000.
[32] Ibid.
[33] Ibid.
[34] Nagai, Lerner and Rothman, 1994, pp. 149-150.

Forest Stewardship Council	$200,000
Friends of the Earth, Netherlands	$150,000
Friends of the Earth, Japan	$120,000
Hong Kong Baptist University, Hong Kong	$80,000
Institute for Agriculture and Trade Policy	$200,000
Institute for Sustainable Development	$225,000
International Institute of Rural Reconstruction	$80,000
Land and Water Fund of the Rockies	$75,000
National Wildlife Federation	$90,000
Natural Resources Defense Council	$180,000
Ozone Action	$100,000
Pacific Environment and Resources Center	$300,000
Parks Council	$150,000
Pratt Institute	$125,000
Silva Forest Foundation	$75,000
Surface Transportation Policy Project	$100,000
Tri-State Transportation Campaign	$100,000
United States Public Interest Research Group Education Fund	$100,000

Five of the twenty trustees of the Rockefeller Brothers Fund are family members. This includes the Fund's chairman, Steven Rockefeller, whose ideas we will look at in Chapter Eight. Eight other trustees appear in the 2000 edition of Who's Who in America. Among those are the following notables.

- Lewis Hunter; director - World Wildlife Fund; chairman of finance committee and trustee - Pierpont Morgan Library; former chairman of Worldwatch Institute and former director of Worldwide Fund for Nature; member - University Club, Knickerbocker Club, Metropolitan Club.
- David J. Callard; president of Wand Partners; former vice-president with Morgan Guaranty Trust; member - Knickerbocker Club, Union Club.
- Frank G. Wisner; vice-chairman of American International Group; U.S. ambassador to Egypt, 1986-91 and to Philippines, 1991-92 and to India, 1994-97; director - Exxon Oil and Gas; member - Council on Foreign Relations; member - Metropolitan Club, Knickerbocker Club.
- Richard D. Parsons; president of Time-Warner, Inc.; director - Philip Morris Companies; Time-Warner, Inc., Federal National Mortgage Association; trustee - Metropolitan Museum of Art.
- Colin G. Campbell; director - Pitney Bowes, HSB Group, Sysco Corporation, Rockefeller Financial Services, Winrock International; trustee - Charles E. Culpeper Foundation, Colonial Williamsburg Foundation; member - Council on Foreign Relations; member - Century Association.
- Russell E. Train; chairman emeritus of World Wildlife Fund; former chairman of Conservation Foundation; trustee emeritus of African Wildlife

Foundation; chairman of National Commission on the Environment, 1991-93; member - Council on Foreign Relations, Atlantic Council.

Along with the five Rockefeller family members, this board of trustees links the support for environmentalism to global banking and oil, to the high level Council on Foreign Relations and to the exclusive world of upper class clubs.

Many other foundations make major contributions to environmental organizations and causes. The Charles Stewart Mott Foundation, for example, reported in 2000 the following large contributions, along with many smaller ones: $220,000 to the Environmental Defense Fund; $300,000 to the Environmental Working Group; $251,225 to Friends of the Earth, Washington, D.C.; $201,600 to Friends of the Earth International; $525,000 to National Wildlife Federation; over $350,000 to various Sierra Club organizations. The son of the foundation's founder, Stewart Rawlings Mott, has been extensively involved with Planned Parenthood when he wasn't taking care of his investments. The Mott fortune came primarily from General Motors and the United States Sugar Corporation.[35]

The John D. and Catherine T. MacArthur Foundation made over one hundred contributions to environmental organizations and activities. Among the larger ones were the following: $1,000,000 to Columbia University's Center for Environmental Research and Conservation; $475,000 to the Conservation International Foundation; $1,530,000 to the Environmental Defense Fund; $485,000 to the Environmental Law Alliance Worldwide; $312,000 to the International Union for Conservation of Nature and Natural Resources; $1,200,000 to the Natural Resources Defense Council; $1,250,000 to the Union of Concerned Scientists; $2,500,000 to World Resources Institute; $1,265,000 jointly to the World Wildlife Fund and Conservation Foundation.

Among the trustees of the MacArthur Foundation are the following:

- Thomas C. Theobald; former vice-chairman of Citicorp and former CEO and Chairman of Continental Bank of Chicago; partner Blair Capital Partners; director - Xerox Corp., Anixter International, Stein Roe Funds, MONY Group, Jones, Lang Lasalle.
- Murray Gell-Mann; member of President's Advisory Committee on Science and Technology; co-chairman science board of Santa Fe Institute; chairman of board of trustees Aspen Center for Physics, 1973-1979; member - Council on Foreign Relations; member - Cosmos Club, Century Association.
- John P. Holdren; John Heinz professor of environmental policy, Harvard University; chairman of executive committee of Pugwash Conferences on Science and World Affairs; member of President's Advisory Committee on Science and Technology.
- Elizabeth J. McCormack; philanthropic advisor Rockefeller Family & Associates; former assistant to president of Rockefeller Brothers Fund;

---

[35] Marquis Who's Who, 2000; Allen, 1987, pp. 362-363.

overseer Memorial Sloan-Kettering Cancer Center; director - Conservation
International; member -Council on Foreign Relations; member - Century
Association.

- Margaret E. Mahoney; former president of Commonwealth Fund, 1980-
1994; former governor American Stock Exchange, 1987-1992; member -
Overseas Development Council; member Council on Foreign Relations.

- Shirley M. Hufstedler; senior of counsel Morrison & Foerster; director -
Harman International Industries; trustee - Aspen Institute, Colonial
Williamsburg, 1976-1993; Carnegie Endowment for International Peace,
1983-1994; member - Council on Foreign Relations.

The world of high finance, private clubs, global interests, etc. is plainly evident on this
board as well. Through organizations such as the Council on Foreign Relations and clubs
such as the Century, these foundations are interlocked with each other.

The boards of trustees of the environmental organizations are themselves places
where the various elements of the Establishment meet. Elaine Dewar describes this using
the Environmental Defense Fund as an example.

> Founded in the late 1960s by scientists concerned enough about preserving a wetland to
> sue its polluters, its board had long since become dominated by persons at the apex of
> U.S. public; life where economic and political power meet. For example, William Parson,
> consulting partner in the Rockefeller-associated law firm of Milbank, Tweed, Hadley &
> McCloy, was on the board. That law firm had once been the preserve of John J. McCloy,
> a man generally referred to until his death as the chairman of the board of the American
> Establishment. Ted Turner, the founder of CNN and Turner Broadcasting System, joined
> the EDF board in 1991. Investment bankers--people with a profound interest in
> international banking, debt restructuring, terms of trade, and the behavior of the World
> Bank--were well represented.[36]

Earth Day 2000 was produced by groups and people associated with organizations
supported by major upper-class foundations. The organizations and individuals involved
in creating Earth Day 2000 were also much the same as the leading environmentalist
groups and activists from the 1960s and 1970s. Some of the leading figures of the 2000
events were long term agents of upper class environmental interests.

Among those, for example, would be Amory Lovins of the Rocky Mountain Institute.
Lovins was a member of the U.S. Council for Earth Day 2000.[37] He was the author of a
1977 environmentalist book entitled *Soft Energy Paths: Toward a Durable Peace* and
had been a leader of Friends of the Earth, spending much of his time in London. Part of
the book had been discussed at sessions at the Aspen Institute and part of it had appeared
in the Council on Foreign Relation's *Foreign Affairs*. There Lovins got editorial
assistance from William Putnam Bundy, formerly of the Central Intelligence Agency and
brother of the Ford Foundation's McGeorge Bundy. According to Lovins, Gerald Barney

---

[36] Dewar, 1995, pp. 115-116.
[37] http://www.earthday.net/about/board.stm

of the Rockefeller Brothers Fund suggested the basic ideas for the book. Lovins also indicated his debt to the staff of the Appalachian Mountain Club's Pinkham Notch Camp and to the International Institute for Applied Systems Analysis.

Another Earth Day 2000 notable is Lester Brown, president of the Worldwatch Institute since 1974. Brown has been affiliated with Aspen Institute, Zero Population Growth, Common Cause, the World Future Society and he is a long-term member of the Council on Foreign Relations.[38] Julian Simon, in his challenge to the rising pessimism over resources and population, argued that Lester Brown and the Worldwatch Institute were more interested in propagandizing people than in the truth.[39]

Canadian Maurice Strong, like Lester Brown, was a member of the International Council for Earth Day. Strong has been an important figure in international environmentalism for a long time. A 1971 New York Times article, entitled "Planner of Global Talks, Maurice Frederick Strong," noted this role.

> Nine months hence what many consider a small micracle in international relations will occur: Representatives of most of the world's nations will meet at Sockholm to take collective action on global environmental problems.
>
> International conferences are no rarity, but this one will materialize scarcely three years after the very word 'environment' first attracted widespread interest, and in a time when any concerted international action is still hard to contrive.
>
> The architect of this prospective coup is Maurice Frederick Strong.[40]

This former energy company executive became the chairman of the International Union for the Conservation of Nature and Natural Resources and chairman of the Geneva based International Energy Development Corporation and he worked with the World Bank. Strong was chairman of the World Economic Forum. He has had close ties to the U.S. Establishment. He has been a trustee of the Rockefeller Foundation and a director of the Aspen Institute. Elaine Dewar described Strong as "a Rockefeller man" in her book, *Cloak of Green*. Strong became a member of two of the most elite private clubs in the U.S. - Century and Metropolitan.[41] As noted before, many of the people associated with environmentalism have been members of the Century Club. Included are several Osborns, Rockefellers, Arnold Toynbee, and James Reston.[42]

Strong served as secretary general for the 1992 United Nations Conference on Environment and Development (UNCED). In 1991 he had said that

> It is clear that current lifestyles and consumption patterns of the affluent middle class--involving high meat intake, consumption of large amounts of frozen and convenience foods, use of fossil fuels, ownership of motor vehicles and small electrical appliances, home and workplace air-conditioning, and suburban housing--are not sustainable. A shift

---

[38] Marquis Who's Who, 1988-89.
[39] Simon, 1981, pp. 7, 147, 169-170, 303, 316.
[40] New York Times, 1971, p. 22.
[41] Dewar, 1995, p. 284; Who's Who In Canada.
[42] Lundberg, 1968, pp. 340-341.

is necessary toward lifestyles less geared to environmental damaging consumption patterns.[43]

In an interview given in 1992 Strong said that he would like to write a novel with an environmental plot. Strong:

> What if a small group of world leaders were to conclude that the prinicpal risk to the Earth comes from the actions of the rich countries? And if the world is to survive, those rich countries would have to sign an agreement reducing their impact on the environment. Will they do it? The group's conclusion is 'no.' The rich countries won't do it. They won't change. So, in order to save the planet, the group decides: Isn't the only hope for the planet that the industrialized civilizations collapse? Isn't it our responsibility to bring that about? This group of world leaders form a secret society to bring about an economic collapse.[44]

I don't think there is much doubt about the kind of "world leaders" that Strong is fantasizing about. It would be the likes of Prince Philip, the Osborns, Rockefellers and himself. These are, of course, stunning remarks coming from one of the most central figures of contemporary global environmentalism.

Many of the Earth Day 2000 organizations received money in the late-1990s from leading upper-class foundations. Most of the organizations that were sponsors for Earth Day were recipients of foundation grants.[45] Given the history of ecology, this is thoroughly unremarkable. It should, however, raise questions about the meaning and purpose of environmentalism as a system of ideas and values. It is a system of thought better understood as aristocratic politics and ideology than as an attempt to keep our air and water safe.

---

[43] Ray, 1993, p. 4.
[44] Ibid., p. 11.
[45] Foundation Grants Index 2000; http://www.earthday.net/about/sponsors.stm

Chapter Seven

The Aristocratic Nature of
Environmentalism: Marx on Malthus

One of the earliest attempts to analyze the connection of Aristocratic views to environmentalism was a critique of Malthus' resource scarcity and overpopulation arguments. That critique came from the left, from Karl Marx.

Writing in the 1860s, Marx attacked Malthus as an apologist for aristocracy. Marx:

> Malthus also wishes to see the freest possible development of capitalist production, however only insofar as the condition of this development is the poverty of its main basis, the working classes, but at the same time he wants it to adapt itself to the 'consumption needs' of the aristocracy and its branches in State and Church, to serve as the material basis for the antiquated claims of the representatives of interests inherited from feudalism and the absolute monarchy. Malthus wants bourgeois production as long as it is not revolutionary, constitutes no historical factor of development but merely creates a broader and more comfortable material basis for the 'old' society.[1]

A capitalist system dominated by Malthus' ideas is one which suppresses the standard of living of the working classes, limits the forces of production if they are disruptive, and generally adapts itself to the interests left over from feudalism, that is, adapts itself to the needs and goals of aristocracy.

Elsewhere, Marx argued that Malthus favored production only as long as "it maintains or extends the status quo, and serves the interests of the ruling classes."[2] According to Marx, Malthus sided with the aristocracy against the bourgeoisie and with both against the working class. He was, in Marx's view, a servant of the most reactionary segments of the ruling class.[3] Marx observed that Malthus' ideas were "greeted with jubilance by the English oligarchy as the great destroyer of all hankerings after human development."[4] Over the last two decades of his life, Marx did not develop these insights,

---

[1] Marx, 1972, p. 52.
[2] Marx, 1969, p. 118.
[3] Marx, 1969, pp. 119-120; 1972, pp. 61-62; Meek, 1971, pp. 129, 135-137, 176.
[4] Meek, 1971, p. 88.

perhaps in keeping with his assumption that aristocracy would eventually be completely eliminated. He clearly underestimated the staying power of the English aristocracy. Over a hundred years later, William Tucker, an American journalist who is not a Marxist, picked up on these themes and developed a contemporary version of them.

WILLIAM TUCKER

The most extensive analysis of the aristocratic nature of environmentalism has been William Tucker's *Progress and Privilege*. It was Tucker's view that even though it has positive elements, environmentalism represents the "Values and positions that have ever been espoused by a nation's aristocracy."[5] Although the political traditions of the United States inhibit the development of a titled aristocracy, the upper class has, in Tucker's view, adopted the world outlook typically associated with such a class. This world outlook includes a hostility toward democracy, a fear of and resistance to progressive technological and social change, pessimism and a desire to protect economic and social privilege.[6] Tucker argued that it is this outlook that is the source of the environmentalist movement's disdain for growth and progress and that is the reason for the connection between environmentalism and social privilege.

In Tucker's view,

> the impulse to slow growth, to suspect invention, and to place natural or agrarian values above material progress has been the consistent pattern of aristocratic politics wherever and whenever it has asserted itself.[7]

Environmentalism, Tucker argued, "is the ideas of aristocratic conservatism translated onto a popular scale."[8]

Aristocrats see material progress as irrelevant or as a threat.[9] Tucker:

> Sitting at the top of the economic heap, aristocracies naturally do not want to see too much economic or social rearrangement. Having made it to the top, they become far more concerned with preventing others from climbing the ladder behind them than in making it up a few more rungs themselves.[10]

The opposition to progress is expressed in the form of a defense of nature.[11] As we will see below, it is likely that in a psychological and ideological way the term "nature" actually refers to the oligarchic elements of the upper class, or the upper class in general.

---

[5] Tucker, 1982, p.7.
[6] Ibid., pp. xvi, 15, 36, 42, 84.
[7] Ibid., p. 42.
[8] Ibid., p. 32.
[9] Ibid., p. 32.
[10] Ibid., p. 15.
[11] Ibid., pp. 11-12, 121, 125.

Tucker analyzed romanticist and reactionary aspects of environmentalism. He observed that the "mystique of wilderness" that has been a component of environmentalism is "little more than a revival of Rouseau's romanticisms about the 'state of nature.'" He went on to say that

> At bottom, as many commentators have pointed out, environmentalism has been striking some of the same chords as the German Romanticism of the nineteenth and early twentieth centuries that sought to shuck of the Christian (and Roman) traditions and revive the old Teutonic gods because they were 'more in touch with nature.'[12]

Tucker has introduced a variety of themes here. Among which are connections between environmentalism and the following: opposition to progress, economic self-interest, maintenance of power, and the subjective appeal of environmentalism. I think this puts us on the right track and we will pursue these ideas further. Tucker made some additional observations about the politics of environmentalism in the United States in the early-1980s.

Challenging the then common assumption that big business was hostile to environmentalism, Tucker observed that large corporations had been quite receptive to environmentalism. He pointed out that environmental policy and regulation had had a much greater impact on smaller businesses. The additional cost of doing business are more easily absorbed by larger companies so that environmentalism has the effect of improving the competitive situation of big business. The cost of environmental measures is spread over a much larger output for a big company and/or the cost can be passed along to the customers where prices are administered, i.e., arranged or fixed.[13] Tucker also suggested that the corporate executive may find himself attracted to the environmentalist world view in his private life even though he resents at times the additional costs it creates for business.[14]

The mass base of environmentalism, according to Tucker, is drawn from the upper-middle class (lawyers, academics, journalists, etc.), particularly from those living in the suburbs. While the old rich have provided the ideas and values for environmentalism, the upper-middle class has contributed its numbers and the skills it possesses by virtue of education and occupation. The economic and social message of environmentalism, with its emphasis on limits to growth, has proven unattractive to the poor, to African-Americans and many segments of organized labor.[15]

Tucker observed that environmentalism had been absorbed into the political mainstream by injecting an essentially conservative tendency into liberal politics and by providing a radical tinge to conservative politics. The adoption of environmentalism by large numbers of both liberals and conservatives has the effect of reducing whatever

---

[12] Ibid., p. 149.
[13] Ibid., pp. 66-76.
[14] Ibid., p. 36.
[15] Ibid., pp. 31-38.

differences might exist between them on matters relating to technological progress and economic growth.[16]

RICHARD NEUHAUS

Shortly after the national environmentalist movement began to take shape, Richard Neuhaus, a Lutheran clergyman and social activist, published a general indictment of environmentalism entitled *In Defense of People* (1971). Neuhaus was convinced that environmentalism represented a very definite political force.

> To whom, politically speaking, does the environmental issue belong? To the aristocrats certainly. To the monied, misanthropic aristocrats who live in the city as much as need compels them but find their 'real life' in getting away from it all. The presumably radical eco-tacticians of the 1970s are in large part the heirs of a conservationist history that, in a thousand variations, has peddled the proposition that 'only man is vile.'[17]

Neuhaus' conclusion was based on his assessment of the views of leading environmentalists and his observations of the forces that gathered around the environmentalist movement.

Neuhaus pointed out that the promoters of Malthusian population views and the supporters of the environmentalist movement's first Earth Day included the executives of leading corporations and banks and members of the upper class. He observed that companies such as Atlantic Richfield and Proctor and Gamble bought advertising space for the 1970 Earth Day not to defend themselves against environmentalism, but to promote its message. Similarly, he noted that a 1970 ad proclaiming the severity of environmental deterioration and attributing that deterioration to overpopulation included the signatures of such Establishment luminaries as World Bank president and former Defense Secretary Robert McNamara, Lamot duPont Copeland and George Champion of Chase Manhattan.[18]

The heart of Neuhaus' argument was in the demonstration that environmentalist values and policies reflected an elitist disregard for or an active hostility toward most of humanity, hallmarks of aristocracies and oligarchies. What many people might have thought was a radical challenge to established powers was in Neuhaus' view a movement so reactionary that he found its substance and meaning similar to that of Nazism.[19] Neuhaus' assessment of the political implications of environmentalism may be even more severe than Tucker's later critique, but both saw environmentalism as an expression of the aristocratic political inclinations of the upper class.

---

[16] Ibid., pp. 10, 34.
[17] Neuhaus, 1971, p. 30.
[18] Ibid., pp. 18-19, 81-84.
[19] Ibid., pp. 151-161.

SIMON, DEMERATH AND OTHERS

In his 1981 refutation of contemporary Malthusianism, entitled *The Ultimate Resource,* Julian Simon presented some evidence linking this movement to the upper class, but he seemed reluctant to draw any inferences from that evidence and did not attempt much explanation. As was noted earlier, Simon pointed out that between 1965 and 1976 the leading funders of international population control activities were, in descending order, the United States government, the Ford Foundation, Sweden, Norway, and the Rockefeller Foundation. During this time the Ford and Rockefeller Foundations not only contributed 246 million dollars to these activities but also encouraged government and government agencies to become more involved in population control.[20] Simon also mentioned that among those signing a newspaper ad claiming that "World food production cannot keep pace with the galloping growth of population" were the likes of oilman J. Paul Getty, Time, Inc. executive and owner Henry Luce III and Reader's Digest founder Dewitt Wallace.[21] Simon also identified many private organizations involved in domestic and international population control activities, but he did not emphasize or explain the apparent connections to elements of the American upper class.[22] He also noted that there had been for decades a close relationship between the eugenics movement and the population control movement,[23] but he failed to pursue the implications of this relationship and never entertained the possibility of an ideological or class interest factor in all of this. Others have at least noted this.

In his 1976 book entitled *Birth Control and Foreign Policy: The Alternative to Family Planning*, Nicholas J. Demerath was far less critical than Julian Simon of the goals of the population control movement but he was much clearer about the forces behind the movement. For example, Demerath observed that the

> family planning establishment is a visible and respectable spin off of the more general Eastern Establishment, that influential and polished combination of 'old boys,' talented professionals, and great wealth that operates in so many circuits of top U.S. power. The family planning establishment represents the Eastern Establishment's interests in population, particularly in foreign population growth. These interests run mainly to the control of natural resources, raw materials, investments, and markets, all of which tend to get translated by the Eastern Establishment as the need for law-and-order and national security.[24]

Apparently following the lead of the article by Barclay, Enright and Reynolds discussed earlier, Demerath went on to say that six organizations were responsible for the promotion of family planning, or birth control, overseas. The six are the Population Council, Ford Foundation, Rockefeller Foundation, Rockefeller Brothers Fund,

---

[20] Simon, 1981, pp. 292-293.
[21] Ibid., pp. 54-55.
[22] Ibid., pp. 298-301.
[23] Ibid., p. 323.
[24] Demerath, 1976, p. 34.

Population Crisis Committee and the International Planned Parenthood Federation. At the center of this network, according to Demerath, is the Eastern Establishment dominated Council on Foreign Relations (CFR). The CFR has been dominated by upper class banking and business interests since its creation. The Rockefellers have played a significant role in this organization during most of its history.[25] Organizationally, this population control establishment can be traced back to the American Birth Control League established by Margaret Sanger in 1921 and renamed the Planned Parenthood Federation of America in 1942. The American organization was inspired by the British Malthusian League founded in 1878 by Charles Bradlaugh and theosophist Annie Besant. That organization was absorbed into the Society of Constructive Birth Control in 1927.[26]

Demerath noted that the development of government involvement in international population control was parallel to the increasing activities of the private groups, such as the Rockefeller and Mellon-Scaife interests and the major foundations. Demerath suggested that the growing U. S. government commitment to population control expressed the family planning establishment's interests, and, hence, also the general interest of the Eastern Establishment.[27]

Similar observations were made by Peter Bachrach and Elihu Bergman. They suggested that one motive behind the upper class' promotion of population control was "a desire to secure a future in which their own privileged positions and life-styles will be preserved."[28] According to them, it is private individuals, making up the "old boy network," who develop the policy agenda and priorities for population policy. These private influentials also play a role in policy implementation as leaders of foundations and private associations and as part of the flow of people between private and public population control organizations.[29] Bachrach and Bergman observed that remarks made by representatives of the Population Establishment "conjure up an institutional image that is exclusive, restrictive, noncompetitive, elitist, self-sustaining, and, perhaps, even conspiratorial."[30] They advise their readers that they should not be disturbed by this because the goals of the Population Establishment are valid. That conclusion is not shared by James Weber, who argued in his 1977 book, *Grow or Die!*, that the population control movement is dangerously elitist and perhaps racist.[31]

President Richard Nixon reportedly arrived at a similar conclusion about environmentalism by the end of 1971. After giving public support to it for almost three years, Nixon came to the view that the environmental movement served the rich and that it was radically reactionary. Nixon then adopted a tactic of opposing environmentalism behind the scenes while avoiding public confrontation with environmentalists.[32] Why Nixon thought there was advantage in such a tactic is not clear. Given the nature of the forces supporting environmentalism, it is clear that they would have known immediately

---

[25] Quigley, 1966; Shoup and Minter, 1977.
[26] Demerath, 1976, pp. 30-35.
[27] Ibid., pp. 39, 45-51.
[28] Bachrach and Bergman, 1973, p. 98.
[29] Ibid., pp. 3-4, 55.
[30] Ibid., pp. 77-78.
[31] Weber, 1977, pp. 173-177.
[32] Flippen, 2000, pp. 136-146, 157, 180, 227.

of his opposition. Perhaps Nixon viewed the public opinion war as hopeless on the issue of environmentalism and decided that his only option was to pretend to be friendly to it. On an issue of this magnitude, that is a very opportunistic approach, apparently one of the President's primary flaws.

There are similar observations about the antinuclear activities of the environmental movement. In his 1982 book, *The War Against the Atom*, Samuel McCracken argued that the antinuclear movement was animated by a deeply held elitism. He suggested that while the environmentalist movement is a reaction to some real problems, it also expresses a concern for "improving the class privileges of the wealthy."[33] Unfortunately, McCracken had little else to say on this and concentrated on a handful of environmental leaders such as Barry Commoner and Ralph Nadar.

Also writing in defense of nuclear energy, Petr Beckman argued that the antinuclear movement was promoted by "members of a class who want to freeze society in the state where they occupy privileged positions."[34] Beckman accused the Ford Foundation's antinuclear Energy Policy Project of engaging in ideological economics and he charged the media with an antinuclear bias. However, Beckman ended up saying that the primary opponents of "economic growth, free enterprise and technology" are upper-middle-class intellectuals who feel that their status and life-style are threatened by growth.[35]

There are arguments that acknowledge upper class involvement in the environmental movement, but claim that the involvement is one or another type of co-optation. It has been suggested, for example, that foundation and corporate support for environmentalism gives the elite a means by which to control and channel movement activities. Others claim that while big business actually built the environmental movement, rather than coopting an existing one, its purpose in doing so was to prevent the emergence of a radical environmentalist movement which would get in the way of big business' growth oriented exploitation of nature.[36] As has been shown here, the origins of environmentalism are upper class in nature as are the movement's primary financial backers today. Those backers, of course, do not want an environmental movement which is independent of them. Their agenda is social, economic and political in nature and they will continue to "exploit nature" where that is in their interests. Environmentalist policy is adapted to those interests and environmentalism as a set of ideas function as an ideology.

ENVIRONMENTALISM AS IDEOLOGY

In some regards the idea that environmentalism is an ideology is one of the least controversial points of the present work. This is so because some of the most articulate promoters of environmentalism claim that it is an ideology. Others refer to environmentalism as a world view or a paradigm, both close cousins to ideology.

---

[33] McCracken, 1982, pp. 96, 100.
[34] Beckman, 1980, p. xvii.
[35] Ibid., pp. 236-240.
[36] Barkley and Weissman, 1970, pp. 48-58; Humphrey and Buttel, 1982, p. 127.

If one consults an unabridged dictionary, one will find many different meanings for the term "ideology." The social sciences and political writers have added still other definitions. Concern here will be only with those meanings of the term ideology which are relevant to our primary focus - the relationship between environmentalism and the needs, fears and interests of the wealthy and powerful groups that have promoted it.

In one of the most famous of social science books, *The Social Construction of Reality: A Treatise in the Sociology of Knowledge*, Peter Berger and Thomas Luckman defined ideology as a set of "ideas serving as weapons for social interests."[37] They also suggested that "an ideology is taken on by a group because of theoretical elements that are conducive to its interests." That is, the members of the group do not necessarily promote, accept or believe all elements of an ideology.

Over the long term, the most influential work on ideology may be the 1936 book by Karl Mannheim, *Ideology and Utopia*. Mannheim distinguished between two general types of ideology, which at times may be intertwined - the particular and the total. A particular ideology features ideas or representations that are "more or less conscious disguises of the real nature of a situation." To anticipate a little, an example might be where a group wishes to suppress the advances of others for self-interested reasons, but claims it is done to conserve resources. The need is to stop the advances. Resource conservation is the ideology; it acts to disguise self interest. Mannheim went on to emphasize that particular ideologies may range from "conscious lies to half-conscious and unwitting disguises; from calculated attempts to dupe others to self-deception."[38] In psychology, particular ideology might be analyzed as rationalization, perhaps also involving repression or sublimation.[39] Rationalization occurs where an individual or group devises "reassuring or self-serving, but incorrect, explanations for behavior." In our example above, conserving resources is a rationalization for opposing economic progress. Such thinking may also facilitate repression. That is, if one thinks and talks enough about conserving resources, one can repress the awareness of the self-interest involved. A form of sublimation may also occur, involving the "diversion of unacceptable impulses into those that are more socially acceptable." Protecting nature and conserving resources are more socially acceptable than preventing the progress of other groups or nations. The psychological mechanisms that would allow individuals to embrace an ideology are pretty well understood.

The concept of "total ideology" refers to the total structure of the mind or a whole outlook associated with a particular period of time or with a "concrete historico-social group." Mannheim suggested that the outlook or worldview of the group can only be understood "in the light of the life-situation" of those expressing the ideas. In pursuing such an interpretation, one is treating the worldview as an ideology.[40]

Among those friendly to environmentalism who readily identify it as an ideology is Lester W. Milbrath. Discussing environmentalism as a "paradigm" Milbrath quotes the following from Steven Cotgrove.

---

[37] Berger and Luckman, 1966, p. 6.
[38] Mannheim, 1936, pp. 55-56.
[39] Marsh, 1992, p. 142.
[40] Mannheim, 1936, pp. 55-56, 59.

Paradigms are not only beliefs about what the world is like and guides to action; they also serve the purpose of legitimating or justifying courses of action. That is to say, they function as ideologies. Hence, conflicts over what constitutes the paradigm by which action would be guided and judged to be reasonable is itself a part of the political process. The struggle to universalize a paradigm is part of a struggle for power.[41]

Elsewhere, Cotgrove has focused on what he calls the utopian elements of environmentalism, these serving as levers to promote social change.[42] Although Cotgrove wrongly associates utopian environmentalism with the middle class, he correctly identifies it as a challenge to economic progress.[43] The ideology of environmentalism can be partly understood as an expression of reactionary utopianism. That is, as an effort to contain or prevent progressive changes that threaten the position of a dominant group, a "concrete historico-social group."[44] Utopianism is the idea of a world with no opposition, threats, or impediments.

The concrete historico-social group for which environmentalism functions as an ideology is the Anglo-American Establishment. This has been true for over one hundred years. Environmentalism is an outgrowth of that group's world view. As an ideology environmentalism can only be understood through an understanding of its connection to that group's interests and its life-situation. At the individual level repression and sublimation may be involved. On specific issues, more or less conscious deception may also come into play. We will focus on it as an ideology.

Environmentalism is an ideology that expresses the goals of that Establishment. The central goal is the maintenance and reproduction of the power of that Establishment. Central to that is the need to prevent the rise of other centers of wealth and power. That is, progress has to be limited, particularly the progress of other national groups. Opposition to progress, economic self-interest and maintenance of power are all involved and are intertwined with each other. This is probably most obvious in international affairs, although it is also evident in domestic matters. William Tucker, discussed above, noted, almost in passing, that environmentalists have an "instinctive resistance" to economic development in the Third World. Tucker also noted that environmentalist leaders such as Paul Ehrlich and Barry Commoner were opposed to the U.S. sharing its technological progress with the rest of the world.[45] This makes sense.

ENVIRONMENTALISM, COLONIALISM AND GLOBALISM

The essential nature and purpose of colonialism, the forerunner of today's globalism, was clearly defined in the mid-1800s by the American economist Henry C. Carey.

---

[41] Milbrath, 1986, p. 101.
[42] Cotgrove, 1976, p. 25.
[43] Ibid., p. 33.
[44] Mannheim, 1936, pp. 192-193, 229; Milbrath, 1986, p. 101.
[45] Tucker, 1982, pp. 107-108, 121.

Carey's discussion of the central issues was sharper and more insightful than his left-wing contemporaries and their successors. We need to focus on this because the leaders of preservationism and environmentalism have been virtually identical with the leaders of American neo-colonialist policy over the last century. It makes sense that this would be so.

Carey clearly argued that the central purpose of colonialism was the prevention of economic development and progress in the dominated or colonized areas. Carey described examples of this in the following.

> In 1710, the House of Commons declared, 'that the erecting of manufactories in the colonies had a tendency to lessen the dependence upon Great Britain.' Soon afterwards complaints were made to Parliament, that the colonists were setting up manufactories for themselves, and the House of Commons ordered Board of Trade to report upon the subject, which was done at great length. In 1732, the exportation of hats from province to province was prohibited, and the number of apprentices to be taken by hatters was limited. In 1750, the erection of any mill or other engine for splitting or rolling iron was prohibited; but pig-iron was allowed to be imported in England duty free, that it might then be manufactured and sent back again. At a later period, Lord Chatham declared, that he would not allow the colonists to make even a hob-nail for themselves. Such is a specimen of the system, with regard to these colonies. That in relation to the world at large shall now be given.[46]

Carey went on to say that

> We see thus, that the whole legislation of Great Britain, on this subject, has been directed to the one great object of preventing the people of her colonies, and those of independent nations, from obtaining the machinery necessary to enable them to combine their exertions for the purpose of obtaining cloth or iron, and thus compelling them to bring to her their raw materials, that she might convert them into the forms that fitted them for consumption, and then return to the producers a portion of them, burdened with great cost for transportation, and heavy charges for the work of conversion. We see, too, that notwithstanding the revocation of a part of the system, it is still discretionary with the Board of Trade, whether or not they will permit the export of any machinery of any description.
>
> Had it not been that there was a natural tendency to have the producer of iron and cloth, and hats, to take his place by the side of the producer of food and wool, there could never have arisen any necessity for such laws as those passed in relation to Ireland and the colonies, and had that tendency not existed, the laws prohibiting the export of machinery would never have been required. It did exist, and it does everywhere exist, and it was for the purpose of preventing the gradual development of a natural state of things, and bringing about an unnatural one, whereby Great Britain might be made 'the work-shop of the world.' that those laws were passed. The object of protection has been, and is, to restore the natural one.[47]

---

[46] Carey, 1967, pp. 52-53.
[47] Ibid., p. 53.

England's general policy toward the rest of the world, both colonies and independent nations, was, and is, to prevent or limit economic progress. In the colonies England could dictate policy. With formally independent nations the strategy would come to be known as free-trade imperialism or neo-colonialism. That is, England would demand free trade so that it could use its early success and superiority to destroy or take over rising competitors in other nations.[48] One reaction to that, as noted by Carey, would be protectionism.

As John Gallagher and Ronald Robinson pointed out in the early-1950s, free trade was an alternative means to achieve the same ends as colonialism.[49] Both colonialism and free trade were aimed at converting foreign territories into "complimentary satellite economies, which would provide raw materials and food for Great Britain." The informal and more indirect domination produced by free trade could be, where necessary, backed with military force, as in British actions in Guatemala and Columbia in the 1870s and in Mexico and Honduras between 1910 and 1914.[50] The use of force or coercion to impose free trade policies has been repeated in recent decades. A modern version is in the demands made by the International Monetary Fund (IMF) on indebted countries and the methods used to enforce those demands.

The IMF was created in 1944 at a conference held at Bretton Woods, New Hampshire.[51] Ostensibly created to help countries deal with short term financial and trade problems, the IMF became a, probably the, major enforcer of free trade and free enterprise policies. After the mid-1960s, dozens of countries would be pressured to adopt IMF policies, known as Conditionalities, or conditions for loans.[52]

The standard set of policies demanded of the indebted and cash strapped nations include major reductions in the role played by government in both domestic and international economic processes, except where government would be needed to suppress consumption and labor demands. The IMF demands that national governments reduce domestic spending and withdraw from efforts to shape imports and exports. Control over what leaves and enters a country can be used to promote development. Countries are also asked to open up their economies to foreign investment.[53] In making and enforcing these demands the IMF does what Thomas Balogh, an adviser to the British government, said it does - it "fulfills the role of the colonial administration of enforcing the rules of the game."[54] That assessment was confirmed in 2000 by Joseph Stiglitz, a former chairman of the President's Council of Economic Advisors and, briefly, chief economist of the World Bank. Stiglitz observed that the imposition of Conditionalities is "a continuation of the colonial mentality."[55]

---

[48] Ibid., pp. 54, 101.
[49] Gallagher and Robinson, 1953, pp. 4-6.
[50] Ibid., pp. 8-11.
[51] McMichael, 2000; Shoup and Minter, 1977, pp. 166-169.
[52] Gibson, 1994, pp. 45-117; Payer, 1974.
[53] Payer, 1974, p. 38.
[54] Balogh, 1966, p. 29.
[55] Komisar, 2000, p.36.

Gallagher and Robinson pointed out that the attempt to use free trade to achieve both political and economic influence in the victim country has not always been successful. They cite the United States as an example.

> In the United States, for example, British business turned the cotton South into a colonial economy, and the British investor hoped to do the same with the Mid-West. But the political strength of the country stood in his way. It was impossible to stop American industrialization, and the industrialized sections successfully campaigned for tariffs, despite the opposition of those sections which depended on the British trade connexion. In the same way, American political strength thwarted British attempts to establish Texas, Mexico and Central America as informal dependencies.[56]

The early opposition of the United States to free trade imperialism, or neo-colonialism, makes it all the sadder that the U.S. was turned into a neo-colonial power after the end of the nineteenth century.

Henry Carey pointed out that Malthus' ideas about population had been used to explain the underdevelopment of the victims of the free trade imperialism and the colonial systems. Without using the word ideology, Carey is giving us an example of Malthusianism functioning as an ideology.

> We thus have here, first, a system that is unsound and unnatural, and second a [Malthusian] theory invented for the purpose of accounting for the poverty and wretchedness which are its necessary results. The miseries of Ireland are charged to over-population, although millions of acres of the richest soils of the kingdom are waiting drainage to take their place among the most productive in the world, and although the people of Ireland are compelled to waste more labour than would pay, many times over, for all the cloth and iron they consume. The wretchedness of Scotland is charged to over-population when a large portion of the land is so tied up by entails as to forbid improvement, and almost to forbid cultivation. The difficulty of obtaining food in England is ascribed to over-population, when throughout the kingdom a large portion of the land is occupied as pleasure grounds, by men whose fortunes are due to the system which has ruined Ireland and India. Over-population is the ready excuse for all the evils of a vicious system, and so will it continue to be until that system shall see its end, the time for which is now rapidly approaching.[57]

Against Malthus, Carey argued that development was beneficial for all.

> The labourers of the world have one common interest, and that is that labour should become everywhere productive and valuable. The more wheat produced in return to a given quantity of labour, the more of it will the shoemaker obtain for his work, and the more advantageously the shoemaker can apply his labour, the more readily will the farmer provide himself and his family with shoes. Such, likewise, is the case with nations. It is to the interest of all that labour in all should become productive, and if the

---

[56] Gallagher and Robinson, 1953, p. 10.
[57] Carey, 1967, pp. 64-65.

labour of the cotton-growing nation become unproductive, that of the sugar or wheat-growing nation feels the effect in an increased difficulty of obtaining clothing.[58]

Further on, Carey returned to Malthusianism and he directly attacked England's use of "free trade" as a cover for its neo-colonial policy. For those familiar with recent discussions of these and related issues it is worth mentioning again that these observations by Carey were published in 1851. He was not only more accurate than latter-day leftists and, of course, apologists for the system, but he also addressed these issues about half a century or more before any serious Marxist or left-wing analysis appeared. Referring to Malthusianism as the modern school, Carey pointed out that

> The modern school of political economy says, 'Be not fruitful; do not multiply. Population tends to increase faster than food.' It prescribes disobedience to the earliest of God's commands. Obedience thereto, in those who are poor, is denounced as improvidence; and to those who are so improvident as to marry, 'with no provision for the future, no sure and ample support even for the present.' it is thought 'important to pronounce distinctly that, on no principle of social right or justice, have they any claim to share the earnings or the savings of their more prudent, more energetic, more self-denying fellow citizens.' To have a wife for whom to labour, and with whom to enjoy the fruits of labor, is a luxury, abstinence from which is placed high among the virtues. To have children to develope all the kindly and provident feelings of the parents, is a crime worthy of punishment. Charity is denounced as tending to promote the growth of population. To rent land at less than the full price, is an error, because it tends to increase the number to be fed. To clear the land of thousands whose ancestors have lived and died on the spot is 'improvement.'
>
> Cottage allotments are but places for breeding paupers.
>
> Southey denounced the Byronian school of poetry as satanic,' and so may we fairly do with the school of political economy that has grown out of the colonial system, and the desire to make England 'the work-shop of the world.' It teaches every thing but Christianity, and that any feelings of kindness towards those who are so unfortunate as to be poor should still remain in England, is due to the fact that those who teach it have not in their doctrine sufficient faith to practice what they preach.
>
> The direct tendency of the existing monopoly of machinery which it is the object of free trade to maintain, is toward barbarism.[59]

Free trade was an alternative strategy for the then superior English economy. It was a different way of accomplishing the goals that motivated the creation of the colonial empire. That is, suppress development in other lands in order to prevent the rise of competitors and to keep countries in a situation of economic dependence and backwardness. That also meant that it would be very difficult for the colonized or dominated land to mount a military resistance to the exploitation. It is hard to create a modern military with little or no industrial base. Keeping countries open to U.S. and English upper class investment is useful for several purposes. Obviously, it is an

---

[58] Ibid., p. 130.
[59] Ibid., p. 201.

opportunity for profits. It is also useful in that Anglo-American interests can get into other countries to take over assets and prevent the rise of independent and competing interests. The economic presence can also be parlayed into political influence. Entry into other nations' economies seems to be the priority of globalism.

Globalization, the suppression of economic development, and free trade have all become explicitly linked to environmentalism. The environmental movement went global in an organizational sense with the creation of private groups such as the International Union for the Conservation of Nature and Natural Resources, the World Wide Fund for Nature, Friends of the Earth International and Greenpeace International.[60] Environmental issues were the focus of the 1972 United Nations Conference on the Human Environment, also know as the Stockholm Conference. This was followed twenty years later by the U.N. Conference on Environment and Development, also called the Earth Summit or the Rio Summit.[61]

While "free market" policies and environmentalism often appear as opposing viewpoints in U.S. domestic politics, they have been clearly joined in the global arena. The 1992 Rio Declaration promoted an open "international economic system" and claimed that trade liberalization, or free trade, and environmental protection go together.[62] The goal of this free-trade environmentalism is something called "sustainable development." While this and related terms were never given clear definition, two things are pretty clear. First, the goals of sustainable development include the idea of minimizing the use of energy and technology[63] and are, therefore, completely consistent with the goals of colonialism and free-trade imperialism. Second, many in the poorer countries see it in that way.[64] That is, they view "sustainability" as an ideological concept serving the global designs of the Anglo-American Establishment.

THE ANGLO-AMERICAN CONNECTION

The historic connection between the U.S. and English upper classes was enhanced and expanded after 1900. The U.S. upper class joined England in neo-colonial efforts, or free-trade imperialism, thus intensifying the longstanding linkages between the two groups that go back to the colonial era. The two upper classes were tied together in a variety of ways.

Through both education and marriage the ties between the two upper classes were deepened around 1900. Much of the prep school system that educates the U.S. upper class was created around this time. Both the schools created in earlier times and the ones established around 1900 were modeled after the elite English schools. These schools provided what amounted to an Anglophile education.[65]

---

[60] Elliot, 1998, pp. 133, 136.
[61] Ibid., pp. 7-8.
[62] Ibid., pp. 184, 208-211.
[63] Ibid., pp. 13-14, 108, 180-181.
[64] Ibid., pp. 108, 174, 177.
[65] Cookson and Persell, 1985, pp. 4-30.

There were a host of marriages linking the wealth of the United States to European and, particularly, English aristocracy. By 1915, nearly 500 upper-class American women had married aristocrats, yielding 42 American princesses, 33 marchionesses, 136 countesses, 19 viscountesses, 64 baronesses, 46 ladies and 17 dutchesses. Hundreds of other similar marriages followed, indicating a deep and widespread American upper class desire to acquire titles and aristocratic status.[66]

In addition to the links provided by education and marriage there were ties through upper-class social clubs. The elite clubs created in the U.S. were modeled after White's of London. Many of the members of American clubs were English men.[67]

In two areas of business of central importance in the modern world, oil and banking, there have been long standing relationships between English and U.S. interests. By the 1920s, the major oil interests of the two countries became closely intertwined through joint ventures and cooperation. This brought such important U.S. families as the Rockefellers and the Mellons into close working relationships with the British upper class. Appropriately enough, one of the early agreements involving U.S. and English oil interests was worked out at a castle in Scotland.[68]

American and British banking have also had enduring relationships. For example, in the mid-1800s Drexel, Morgan and Company and also Kidder, Peabody and Company acted as intermediaries between American railroads and English banks.[69] In the second half of the 1900s, U.S. and English financial interests have worked closely together in creating and running such important international institutions as the International Monetary Fund, the World Bank, and Bank for International Settlements.

The American and English upper classes are also linked through the private policy making organizations. For example, the Council on Foreign Relations in New York was started in the early 1920s through cooperative efforts of upper-class figures from the U.S. and England. The council has ever since maintained a close relationship with its sister organization in England, the Royal Institute of International Affairs.[70] Americans and Englishmen also come together every year since 1954 at the Bilderberg Society meetings. There they are interacting with elite Europeans such as environmentalist Prince Bernhard of the Netherlands, who was also a founder of the Bilderberg Society and for many years its chairman. When Bernhard retired in the mid-1970s, the chairmanship was passed to former British Prime Minister Lord Hume. Members of the Rockefeller family and other upper-class families have been regular participants in these meetings.

Finally, the intelligence communities of England and the United States are thoroughly intertwined. This has been clearly true since World War Two when British intelligence helped to create the Central Intelligence Agency.[71] Britain is even a participating partner in the United States National Security Agency.[72]

---

[66] Lacey, 1983; Lundberg, 1937, p. 9.
[67] Landry, 1938, pp. xi, 1, 5, 9-12, 19, 45, 47, 201, 205.
[68] Blair, 1976; Engdahl, 1992; Sampson, 1975; Sherrill, 1983.
[69] Kotz, 1978, pp. 26-27.
[70] Quigley, 1981, pp. 168, 190-191.
[71] Mahl, 1998.
[72] Bamford, 2001, p. 40.

It is a tragedy of the modern world that the United States became in the early-1900s most of what Carey and other anti-colonialist Americans were opposed to, that is, a neo-colonial power. Once the United States embarked on a neo-colonial policy it became committed to the goals of colonialism and "free-tade imperialism." That is, the globally oriented, American neo-colonialist became committed to suppressing the industrialization and development of other nations, particularly those in Africa, Latin America and Asia. Not all American businessmen or political leaders have been committed to this and there have been conflicts over it,[73] but it has been the dominant tendency for a century.

Part of the education of the upper class is learning that protection and furtherance of class interests means preventing the rise of competing elites or the rise of the underclasses.[74] The problem with development and industrialization, especially if it is to be accomplished quickly, is that new elites appear both in the process of achieving progress and as a result of the progress.

Rapid progress, especially but not only if it takes off from a low level of development, is rarely if ever achieved without a strong role for government.[75] When societies are mobilized by the state for purposes of development or quick economic growth, there is a growing role in decision making for experts, technicians, planners, bureaucrats, managers, scientists, engineers, politicians, and growth oriented business people.[76] In fact, the whole enterprise might be sold as a democratic undertaking and in this way most of the population is enlisted in its support. That means that private wealth and power, heredity, privilege and status and class become less important and less dominant. It also means that the upper class' wealth and influence may be significantly undermined and eroded over the long haul.

Growth and progress, whether it is within a nation or global, gives rise to new centers of wealth and influence which may become competitors to older ruling groups. If they cannot be absorbed into the existing establishment in subservient roles, they will reduce the influence and power of the existing oligarchy. Development and rapid economic progress pose a threat to the power of those seeking to constitute themselves as an oligarchy or modern day aristocracy. Environmentalism expresses their fear of and opposition to that development.

We might add that this whole business of progress brings to the fore a set of values that makes the hereditary powers feel deeply threatened. Applied science, public planning, raising the standard of living, improving mass education, and increasing democracy taken together are a challenge to the very existence of a ruling elite anchored in heredity and privilege.

Both the methods of achieving rapid progress, or perhaps any progress, and the results of such progress pose a threat to any oligarchy or hereditary ruling clique. In the modern world the most important oligarchy of the last century is the Anglo-American Establishment. The environmentalist movement and environmentalism are saturated with

---

[73] Gibson, 1994, pp. 35-76.
[74] Cookson and Persell, 1985, p. 24.
[75] Herman and McChesney, 1997, p. 30.
[76] Apter, 1965, pp. 439-442, 446, 448, 459; Bluestone and Harrison, 2000, pp. 20, 37-49; Gibson, 1994, pp. 19-51.

their fears, values and interests. Environmentalism is their ideology. Free trade imperialism and the upper class' environmentalism share a basic objective - limit development and bring economic processes under their control or influence.

Chapter Eight

THE ARISTOCRATIC OPPOSITION TO PROGRESS: A CONCLUSION

Steven C. Rockefeller, chairman of the Rockefeller Brothers Fund and Professor Emeritus of Religion at Middlebury College in Vermont, contributed an essay, "Faith and Community in an Ecological Age," to a 1992 book entitled *Spirit and Nature, Why the Environment Is a Religious Issue*. Rockefeller, who also co-edited the book, is the son of the former governor of New York and vice-president of the United States Nelson Rockefeller. Steven Rockefeller is a highly educated man and on the surface a most civilized man. He reportedly gained the reputation within the large Rockefeller clan of being the conscience of the fourth generation, descending from John D. Rockefeller, Sr., the founder of the fortune.[1] He is precisely the kind of person who can demonstrate the depth of the upper class fear of and animus toward economic and technological progress. He is a thoughtful and apparently gentle man. He is also oblivious to the need for and value of progress. He is a gentleman capitalist in all of the worst possible meanings of that term.

In the tradition of Lynn White and Arnold Toynbee, Rockefeller believes that the solution to the "environmental crisis" will have to be, in part at least, a religious solution. Such an effort supposedly will also help us deal with our spiritual problems. Rockefeller says that the "integration of the moral and religious life with a new ecological worldview, leading to major social transformations, is a fundamental need of our time."[2]

According to Rockefeller, the sources of and the solutions for the environmental crisis can be found in aspects of Judeo-Christian thought, Greek philosophy, and modern science. A cause of the crisis is the idea in Christianity that humans were created in God's image and were consequently given dominion over the earth. Rockefeller does not explain what is meant by humans being in the image of god. Instead, he quickly emphasizes that Christianity did not assign intrinsic value to nature, only to humans.[3]

---

[1] Collier and Horowitz, 1976, p. 613.
[2] Rockefeller, 1992, pp. 141, 145.
[3] Ibid., p. 148.

Referring to the Judeo-Christian concept of God, man and nature as a "set of problematical ideas," Rockefeller continues by arguing that Plato contributed to the problem with his idea that there is a radical separation between the spiritual world and nature. The allegedly anti-nature tendencies of Platonism and Christianity were then intensified by the modern scientific revolution. Particularly problematic, in Rockefeller's view, was Rene Descartes' concept of the human ego, a concept that included a celebration of rationality. This Cartesian outlook fed the industrial revolution by transforming the non-human world into an object of rational analysis, manipulation and control. The Cartesian world view, according to Rockefeller, wound up contributing to massive social change. Rockefeller:

> The development of the Cartesian ego also contributed to the Western drive toward the independence of the self, encouraging new demands for intellectual, social, and economic freedom. When aspirations for democratic social change were joined with the forces of industrialization and technology, the idea of progress was born, leading to a new secular faith that emerged as a powerful social force in the late eighteenth and nineteenth centuries. Mastery over nature and democratic social transformation promised not only material well-being, but a new way to salvation, the realization of an ideal society of freedom, justice, and equal opportunity on earth.[4]

Of all the great figures in western history, Rockefeller arbitrarily selected Descartes and Sir Isaac Newton as the sources of the revolution of industrialism and democracy. Whether they deserve this credit, or the blame assigned to them by Rockefeller, or are Rockefeller's strawmen, is not of immediate concern. What is Rockefeller's attitude toward all of this.

Without pausing to acknowledge any value in these revolutionary changes, Rockefeller quickly moves to the argument that the modern scientific outlook and the "anthropocentric attitudes at work in Christianity" have combined to alienate humans from nature and to secularize our relationship to nature. Old "supernaturalistic interpretations of events" have been abandoned.[5] Rockefeller, by implication, appears to believe that humanity was much better off in a premodern, pre-industrial, pre-democratic life of superstition and irrationality. That is, people were better off when they were in awe of and submitted to the forces of nature, or is it the forces of oligarchy and aristocracy. Rockefeller's view of these events is not of course the only one. D.S.L. Cardwell, for example, argues that Christianity's role in the explosion of technological creativity, a good thing, was the emancipation of the human spirit and the rejection of the fatalism that was central to "so many ancient and Eastern religions."[6] Rockefeller prefers those religions.

What vision of life does Rockefeller offer up against the evil modern world? Without a trace of embarrassment, he offers up, among others, Carl Jung, Martin Heidegger and John Muir. Against "rationalism and scientific materialism" he quotes Jung. Without

---

[4] Ibid., p. 150.
[5] Ibid., p. 151.
[6] Cardwell, 1972, p. 7

mentioning Jung's affinity for Nazism, he looks to Jung for guidance on man's loss of harmony with nature.

When Jung wasn't predicting the "coming aeon of Aquarius"[7] or speculating on the visitations of UFOs,[8] he was pondering the ethical necessity of doing evil.[9] Along the way, Jung also presented his own misanthropic version of environmentalism. Jung:

> Nothing could persuade me that 'in the image of God' applied only to man. In fact it seemed to me that the high mountains, the rivers, lakes, trees, flowers, and animals far better exemplified the essence of God than men with their ridiculous clothes, their meanness, vanity, mendacity, and abhorrent egotism...[10]

This is one of the people Rockefeller looks to for a new outlook.

Like early German ecologists, Rockefeller is attracted to the idea that everything has equal importance. Sounding much like Moritz Arndt in 1815, Rockefeller says the following in relationship to the Chinese Taoist tradition:

> Each and everything is an interdependent interacting part of the continuous cosmic process, which is called the 'great transformation' (ta-hua). The fundamental reality in this process is a vital force or power (ch'i), which embraces both the physical and spiritual aspects of the world. Rocks and trees as well as humans are manifestations of this vital force. It is omnipresent and preserves the interconnectedness of all things in the ongoing process of growth and transformation which is the universe. Humans are not superior to this natural process but integral parts of its functioning.[11]

There is no indication that Rockefeller is aware of the German forerunner to this. He does refer positively to the philosopher Martin Heidegger.[12] According to Peter Staudenmaier,[13] the anti-technology Heidegger was an active member of the Nazi party who lived into the 1970s without ever indicating that he had any regrets concerning that involvement. He was something of an ecologist.[14]

A 1982 article celebrating John Muir as a "deep ecologist" included the following quote celebrating Heidegger:

> Heidegger claims that the real threat of technology for man is not atomic weaponry or other destructive devices. These can destroy us physically, but to live as human beings under the sway of the technological view of reality might well destroy the spiritual essence of man. Heidegger (sees) the new discussion of Being will involve 'releasement' of the human being from the will to power. Such releasement...would allow man to dwell within the world, NOT as its master, but as its servant endowed with the gift of letting the

---

[7] Jung, 1965, p. 339.
[8] Ibid., p. 334.
[9] Ibid., pp. 60, 329-330.
[10] Ibid., p. 45.
[11] Rockefeller, 1992, p. 157.
[12] Ibid., p. 160.
[13] Staudenmaier, 1995, pp. 12-13.
[14] Bramwell, 1989, p. 250.

beings of the world display themselves in all their glory. Instead of seeing the world as a manipulatable object thrown and held on against us as subject, we would cultivate the world by letting being BE what they are and how they are, and not as they are according to power-oriented viewpoint of the subject.

The recent rise of 'ecological consciousness' might be a harbinger of such a change in our apprehension of the Being of beings. This movement arose in large measure as a result of the growing awareness man was about to destroy himself because of his destruction of the environment. Heidegger would certainly agree with many of the axioms of this new consciousness, including its desire to halt the senseless pillaging of nature for profit.[15]

This discussion of the supporter of Nazism manages to end up with a leftish jab at profits.

With intellectual inspiration coming from the likes of Jung and Heidegger, it probably should not be surprising that the Rockefeller essay ends up with an outburst of irrational, eco-babble and one world jargon. For example, Rockefeller observes that

a holistic and relational view of the human self suggests that in a real sense the whole earth is a person's extended body and the consciousness of the individual is a focal point of the earth's emerging self-consciousness.[16]

Rockefeller looks to organizations such as the International Union for Conserving Natural Resources to help lead the new "Great Awakening," a reference to the eighteenth century religious fervor. This awakening encompasses

diverse religious visions, moral democracy, various holistic philosophies, the new physics, the science of ecology, reverence for life, deep ecology, the practice of I and thou, feminism, and the ethics of sustainable development.[17]

Rockefeller later pointed to the important role faith will play in the transformation and went on to say that "Faith has the power to take self beyond itself to a new self." Rockefeller called on the world's religions to "take to heart the ecological idea of global interdependence." The last paragraphs of the essay are taken up with calls for an ecologically inspired global community.

Throughout this discussion, Rockefeller shows no awareness that life for much of the world's people is a matter of survival. He indicates absolutely no appreciation for science, industry or modernization. He casually associates himself with ideas or people that range from goofy to sinister and evil. His treatment of Jung and Heidegger is disturbing. This scion of one of the country's and the world's wealthiest and most influential families wants to create a "whole earth community" in order to bring plants into the moral community. If these kinds of ideas affect national goals and policy, the country is surely doomed.

---

[15] Devall, 1982, p. 77.
[16] Rockefeller, 1992, p. 165.
[17] Ibid., p. 167.

What Rockefeller is engaged in here is an act of rationalization in which sin is elevated to virtue. Bernard Lonergan has observed that dominant groups may delude "mankind by the rationalization of their sins."[18] His family has for many decades been a leading force within the upper eschelons of America's globally oriented upper class. They have long desired a global economy directed by them and their allies. They have been involved in neo-colonial activities for a century.[19] When he says he wants a global community based on ecological values (i.e., limited growth, less technology), he is actually restating long exisitng goals but with a new rational. The sin, global dominance, has been transformed into a virtue, protection of the global ecology.

Steven Rockefeller's uncle has linked these together a little more clearly. In a foreward to a 1991 Trilateral Commission book entitled *Beyond Interdependence,* David Rockefeller suggested that people need to move beyond the economic idea of international interdependence to a recognition of the "meshing of the world's economy and the earth's ecology."[20]

Rockefeller's forward was followed by a brief introduction by Maurice Strong, Secretary General of the United Nations Conference on Environment and Development. One of the three authors of the book had been a longtime advisor to Strong. Strong said the following.

> The authors demonstrate that the world has now moved beyond economic interdependence to ecological interdependence - and to an intermeshing of the two. They argue persuasively that this interlocking of the world's economy and the earth's ecology is the new reality of the century, with profound implications for the shape of our institutions of governance, national and international.[21]

These remarks echo those made in 1963 by Sir Frank Fraser Darling who said that "In a world where the only hope for man is internationalism, nationalism is the political ecological factor which prevents any constructive action to curb population increases."[22]

Behind these new world order comments of Steven Rockefeller, David Rockefeller, Sir Frank Darling and Maurice Strong are assumptions and purposes of longstanding. The Anlgo-American Establishment wants a global economic system under their control, meaning that new or independent centers of influence and power have to be prevented, coopted, absorbed or destroyed. The global system should be largely a private affair, featuring generally weak and passive national governments, i.e., what people such as this mean by free markets or free enterprise.[23] They are not opposed to managed or manipulated markets or to intervention into markets as long as it is private manipulation and intervention or government action at the behest of private interests. One of the roles for government in this scheme is to promote environmentalism.

---

[18] Lonergan, 1970, p. 239.
[19] Gibson, 2000, pp. 182-188; Quigley, 1966, 1981.
[20] MacNeill, Winsemius and Yakushiji, 1991, p. v.
[21] Ibid., p. ix.
[22] Lowe and Worboys, 1978, p. 14.
[23] Frank, 2000; Greider, 1997, pp. 137-138.

Environmentalism poses no threat to the Anglo-American upper class. Their roles as founders, leaders, supporters and financial backers make it impossible for environmental organizations to act against that upper class. The environmental movement has never challenged upper class property interests, wealth or influence and power. It has never even criticized their consumption or life styles. The occasional problem, like paying for an oil spill, is mere nuisance compared to the ideological and policy value of a belief system that says that material progress is essentially over.

This oligarchy, which features significant remnants of the English aristocracy, spawns both one world eco-babble, such as the above examples from Steven Rockefeller, and the openly vicious commentaries of a Henry Fairfield Osborn or Frederick Osborn. Environmentalism, however it is expressed, is a means to an end, it is not an end in itself. The end is the perpetuation and expansion of the influence, power and wealth of the Anglo-American Establishment and its allies and servants. The vocabulary of environmentalism is full of terms and ideas that have political and social meanings.

THE ESSENCE OF ECOLOGY AND POLITICS

Certain core ideas that had more than one meaning appeared early in the development of ecological thought and are still to be found in contemporary environmentalism. As suggested before, they can be understood as expressions of the desires, fears and hatreds of the groups that promoted them.

As we saw in Chapter Two, there was in German ecology an idea that nature is a complex and fragile web of relationships. Any disruption of even a part of this balanced ecosystem threatens the whole system. Let me suggest the obvious. The concept of ecosystem actually refers simultaneously to two things. It is an assertion about or an opinion about nature. As an image of nature it probably vastly overstates the static nature of nature and hugely understates the violence and destructiveness of natural forces. The other thing that it refers to is social relationships. That is, the fragile system about which elite ecologists were worried was actually the economic, political and social relationships that underlay or allowed for the continued status of upper class groups. It is their privilege and influence that is endangered. Industrialism and urbanization no doubt did threaten forests and landscapes, but the most important systems threatened were those involving status and power.

When Malthus wrote about the limits of a natural order related to land and population, he was also talking about limits created by the economic and social order of England. In Malthus' mind, the attempt to overcome the limits of nature would lead to attacks on the social order. In fact, as pointed out, Malthus at one point actually substituted the "law of property" for the law of nature.[24] When Malthus shifted his discussion to the law of property, it was government and government action that Malthus worried about. The fear that Malthus gave voice to was that government would override existing property interests in an attempt to stimulate economic production.

The British aristocracy's disdain for industrial technology and applied science expressed and expresses the outlook of a class rooted in a time when the preservation of a caste like class order was paramount. Most or all of the changes stimulated by industrialization were threatening to a system based on hereditary privilege, control of land and labor intensive agriculture. The conservationist and preservationist culture of the English upper class included preoccupation with stability and a hostility toward industrialism and materialism. The protection of the class order and the protection of the countryside were thoroughly interwoven.

Such interweaving also occurred in the United States, beginning in the early years of conservationism. Conservationists, and even more so preservationists, were opposed to the growing role of the machine, industrialism and urbanism. As in England, there was an attraction to nature and the countryside. In the U.S. and England the anti-modern and anti-materialist sentiments became intertwined with racial and ethnic prejudice, both expressed in aspects of the eugenics movement.

When Fairfield Osborn, a close associate of Steven Rockefeller's uncle Laurance, complained that humans act as if they do not have to live by nature's principles, he was also complaining that people do not accept an existing social and economic order, but constantly seek to alter it and improve it. When Osborn promoted adaptation to nature, as did right-wing German ecologists,[25] he was also proposing that people adapt to the existing socio-economic order. That idea was central to Malthus' thinking and to Social Darwinist thought. That is, the idea that natural selection takes place in relation to adaptability was a part of Malthus' view and was carried over into Darwinism and Social Darwinism. The problem with this, of course, is that humans to a considerable degree create their environment and don't just adapt to it. Contemporary environmentalism is shot through with ideas of adapting to the limits of resources and ecosystems.

The environmentalist idea of limits is an attempt to convince people that the human species, like animals, exists within a fixed environment. This argument is implicit in the widely used term 'natural resources.' Strictly speaking, the term is a logical contradiction. The concept of nature is itself a product of the human mind and was generated only after humans developed to the point where they recognized themselves as unique and as separate from their environment. In that sense, nature does not exist aside from the human mind even if what we call nature does have its own material existence, that is, it is not a figment of imagination. That said, what most of us understand by the term 'natural' is the sum total of all life forms and inert materials which do not owe their current form or existence to human activity. That is generally what is meant by natural. A resource is something different.

Resources are defined by human needs and human powers. The only resources which could be properly termed 'natural' are those which humans used when their powers were essentially the same as animals, that is, in the most primitive hunting and gathering society. Then, the water, vegetables, fruits and animals consumed by humans could be described as natural resources. All resources used beyond this primitive economic level

---

[24] Malthus, 1960, p. 370.
[25] Staudenmaier, 1995, pp. 25-26.

have been in varying degrees also products of human knowledge, ingenuity and technology. The development of these abilities allowed humans to escape a relationship to nature based entirely on need and to develop a relationship based on human creativity. Virtually everything referred to as a natural resource has no existence as a resource independent of human knowledge and activity. Hence, the term 'natural resource' is logically incoherent.

A whole vocabulary has been developed which promotes explicitly what is implied by the idea of natural resources. The phrases spaceship earth, lifeboat earth, finite world, finite resources and limits to growth all express what is implied by the idea of natural resources. They all suggest that humans exist or should exist in a passive, parasitical relationship to the natural world. These phrases are employed in the context of arguments about resource scarcity, overpopulation and environmental deterioration in a way that reinforces the specific arguments and drives home the notion that human creativity is nonexistent, irrelevant or destructive.

When Osborn warned that people cannot escape the laws of nature, he was trying to discourage them from pursuing change through advancements in science and technology. That is, Osborn promoted pessimism and fatalism. Such pessimism became an increasingly important part of American culture in the 1970s.[26] For most people, the consequences of this have to be negative. People who do not believe that generalized progress is possible will not seek it. A population that lives in awe of nature's forces, as Toynbee recommended, would be incapable of seeking either scientific or social progress. Environmentalist leader Max Nicholson hoped that decades of environmentalist propaganda would lead people to submit to "ecological laws."

Today's environmentalism represents no significant departure from these earlier views, views that are aristocratic in origin and nature and are deeply reactionary. The "higher values" that conservationists seek to protect[27] are the values of an aristocratic oligarchy, and "aristo-finance elite." What is to be conserved is a social order dominated by upper-class Anglo-American groups. Environmental arguments are made to serve those ends. Such arguments will be made with or without evidence. For example, even though there is no scientific evidence demonstrating that global warming is caused by humanly generated carbon dioxide, environmentalists assert this as an undisputed fact. On the web site for Earthday 2000 it is stated without qualification that the consumption of fossil fuels increases carbon dioxide in the atmosphere and this causes the temperature to rise.[28] Compare that to a statement from MIT Professor of meteorology Richard Lindzen, who was one of eleven scientists asked to prepare a special report on climate change for the National Academy of Sciences in 2001. Lindzen emphasized that "we are not in a position to confidently attribute past climate change to carbon dioxide or to forecast what the climate will be in the future."[29] This is typical. Environmentalists have an agenda to promote, often an extreme one. **Extremism Apparently Is A Virtue**

---

[26] Dunlap, 1989, pp. 21-22.
[27] Tucker, 1982, pp. 9-10.
[28] http://www.earthday.net/goals/, 22 April 2000.
[29] Lindzen, 2001.

The extremism of earlier ecological and preservationist thought has not disappeared. It is pervasive in today's environmentalism. It expresses the fears, desires and hatreds of that elite.

The hatred of the modern, industrial, technological world is clearly put in the following by Barry Commoner, perhaps the only "leftist" ever promoted by *Time* magazine.

> Air pollution is not merely a nuisance and a threat to health. It is a reminder that our most celebrated technological achievments--the automobile, the jet plane, the power plant, industry in general, and indeed the modern city itself--are, in the environment, failures.[30]

Commoner recommended that we substitute human labor for technology and for synthetic energy in order to achieve "harmony with the ecosphere."[31] In Commoner's mind, human creativity itself is an evil.

A similarly broad condemnation of the modern world is offered up by Robert Heilbroner.

> Now without going beyond the specific dangers of population growth, war and environmental deterioration, I must identify a fundamental element in the external situation--not so much a fourth independent threat as an unmentioned challenge that lies behind and within all the particular dangers we have singled out for examination. That is the presence of science and technology as the driving force of out age.[32]

This challenge is to be met by the "gradual abandonment of the lethal techniques, the uncongenial lifeways, and the dangerous mentality of industrial civilization itself," even if this abandonment means the violation of democratic principles.[33] According to Heilbroner, "life must be maintained within fixed rather than outward-moving material boundaries."[34] Heilbroner, like Willis Harman, Duane Elgin[35] and others, has used environmentalist arguments to promote an acceptance of post-industrialism. As noted before, this line of thinking was developed in a project at the Stanford Research Institute in the late-1960s and early-1970s.[36]

Paul Ehrlich's extreme statements could fill a chapter. Here is just one where he recommends the elimination of over 80 percent of the U.S. and world population.

> Its difficult to determine the ideal population. There probably is no such static figure, but many scientists think the population of the United States should eventually be reduced to well under 50,000,000 and that of the world to an absolute maximum of 500,000,000.[37]

---

[30] Commoner, 1972, p. 77.
[31] Ibid., pp. 288-289, 298.
[32] Heilbroner, 1980, p. 56.
[33] Ibid., pp. 106, 160.
[34] Ibid., p. 171.
[35] Elgin, 1982; Harman, 1976.
[36] Gibson, 1993; SRI International, 1974.
[37] Ehrlich, 1973, p. 17.

The renowned English anthropologist and think tank consultant, Margaret Mead, commented on Ehrlich and Commoner.

> Now, whatever it [the population] is going to reach, it is too many, so experts should stop arguing about details. These are the arguments between Commoner and Ehrlich, which is, again, a piece of nonsense, because if we didn't have as much population, we wouldn't have as much trouble. True. And if we did have the population without the technology, we wouldn't have as much trouble. True. And so what! We've got the population, we've got the technology; the technology has broken the chain of the relationship to nature and endangers the planet; the population continually puts pressure on the use of technology. They are both right.[38]

Perhaps nobody has been more hostile to modern technology and more enamoured with the idea that most people should spend their lives doing rudimentary physical labor than E. F. Schumacher. In his widely read book, *Small Is Beautiful*, Schumacher recommends that we reverse two centuries of technological progress and revert back to a low consumption, labor intensive economy. Schumacher:

> As I have shown, directly productive time in our society has already been reduced to about 3 1/2 percent of total social time, and the whole drift of modern technological development is to reduce it further, asymptotically to zero. Imagine we set ourselves a goal in the opposite direction -- to increase it sixfold, to about twenty per cent, so that twenty per cent of total social time would be used for actually producing things, employing hands and brains and naturally excellent tools. An incredible thought! Even children would be allowed to make themselves useful, even old people.[39]

If this isn't nostalgia for a premodern age, it is something close to it.

If anything, William Ophuls is even clearer about the idea of rolling back the clock to an earlier era. Ophuls:

> To take just one example, it seems evident that in the long run agriculture will become more labour-intensive, both because labor will be cheaper than energy in a frugal society and because horticultural agriculture as practised in many parts of Asia is less ecologically damaging than our current extensive, industrial agriculture. This is likely to mean that a larger proportion of the population will have to be 'peasants' in a low-energy steady state society (or, alternatively, that most of the population will have to be at least part-time peasants along Maoist lines), and this is a situation that may seem unpalatable and regressive to most moderns, for whom toil has always been an enemy.[40]

Ophuls, like many contemporary environmentalists, does not even feel a need to conceal his disdain for most people.

---

[38] Oltmans, 1974, pp. 22-23.
[39] Schumacher, 1973.
[40] Ophuls, 1977, pp. 164-170.

In their Club of Rome report published in 1974 as *Mankind At the Turning Point*, Mihajlo Mesarovic and Eduard Pestel began with a quote from a 1955 article entitled "The World Has Cancer and the Cancer Is Man."[41] Mesarovic and Pestel argued that we will need global institutions to solve the population-resource problems and they called for "harmony with nature" and for lifestyles adopted to an "age of scarcity."[42] Helibroner, quoted above, also referred to people as a cancer.[43] In a later Club of Rome report, 1991, the authors Alexander King and Bertrand Schneider concluded that the real enemy is "humanity itself."[44] The award for the most colorful example of aristocratic misanthropy probably goes to Harrison Brown who referred to the world's people as a "pulsating mass of maggots."[45] Various officials and leaders of population control organizations have proposed an assortment of sterilization programs to keep the cancers and maggots in check.[46] It is not at all surprising that many African and Latin American intellectuals and leaders view population control as a sister policy to neo-colonialism.[47]

In the view of some, the most significant intellectual figure of contemporary environmentalism has been Rene' Dubos.[48] Born in France, Dubos became a U.S. citizen in 1938. He was at Rockefeller University for many years and he was a member of the Century Association.[49] He was asked by Maurice Strong to prepare the "conceptual framework" for the 1972 Stockholm Conference on the Environment.[50]

In a 1975 New York Times editorial, Dubos said that "In any kind of society, the healthiest, happiest and most creative persons are likely to be found among those who consume least."[51] That would be street people or somebody like that. This is a totally absurd and hypercritical comment. Dubos went on in a similar vein about the use of energy.

> An abundant supply of energy is, of course, essential for the production of more and more industrial goods, but this is not all that there is to happiness and civilization. If one judges on the basis of civic virtue, sophistication of thought, quality of writing, charm of landscapes, architectural styles and perhaps even of average comforts, I see little evidence that our civilization has been made more appealing by the recent phenomenal increases in the use of energy.[52]

Compare those comments on energy with the following conclusion from the eminent anthropologist, Leslie White (no relation to Lynn White):

---

[41] Mesarovic and Pestel, 1974, p. 1.
[42] Ibid., pp. 127, 143-145.
[43] Heilbroner, 1980, p. 63.
[44] King, and Schneider, 1991, p. 115.
[45] Simon, 1981, p. 160.
[46] Weber, 1977, pp. 180-181.
[47] Bachrach and Berman, 1973, pp. 19-20.
[48] Efron, 1984, pp. 37-38.
[49] Marquis Who's Who, 1978-79.
[50] Efron, 1984, pp. 38-39.
[51] Dubos, 1975, p. 33.
[52] Ibid., p. 33.

We may summarize our discussion of energy and tools in the following law of cultural development: culture advances as the amount of energy harnessed per capita per year increases, or as the efficiency or economy of the means of controlling energy is increased, or both.[53]

Anyone seriously accepting the views of Dubos should get rid of their car and air conditioning and seek physical work using little or no technology or energy.

RADICAL ENVIRONMENTALISM?

With the above in mind, we should not be surprised to find that radical environmentalists have a lot of difficulty sounding radical, that is, separating themselves from such mainstream thinkers as Toynbee, Rockefeller and Heilbroner. In one attempt, a book of readings, to produce a Green or radical environmentalist agenda different from mainstream environmentalism, the editor ends up including many of the people who make up mainstream or Establishment environmentalism and the "radicals" who appear in the book offer little that is different.

The 1991 book, *The Green Reader*, was edited and introduced by Andrew Dobson of England's University of Keele. Dobson claimed that the book represented the ideas of the Green movement, a "successor to traditional environmentalism." According to Dobson this new more radical movement, the deep ecology or Green movement, was still in the early stages of development. This book, however, clearly demonstrates continuity between Establishment environmentalism and the supposedly more radical Green movement. The foreward to the book was written by a former official of the Sierra Club and the table of contents reads like a who's who of Establishment environmentalism.

Among the contributors are Rachel Carson, E. F. Schumacher, Donella Meadows, Garret Hardin, Ted Trainer, William Ophuls, Herman Daly, Aldous Huxley and Aldo Leopold - all spokemen for or associated with Establishment environmentalism. In other words, Dobson went in search of radicals and found them in the environmentalist mainstream. The contents of the book are radical - radically reactionary, radically aristocratic and radically misanthropic.

Here are a few examples of this successor to traditional environmentalism. In the following, Ted Trainer offers up a pessimistic and zero sum image of the world's future, giving his readers a choice between Social Darwinism and redistribution of permanently scarce resources. The message he is sending to middle-class people in Europe and North America is that the only way people in the rest of the world can make advances is by taking it away from that middle class.

Some savage implications follow from this analysis. Unless extremely implausible assumptions are made *there is no chance of all people ever rising to the levels of material affluence enjoyed by Americans in the late 1970s*, let alone to the levels Americans will

---

[53] White, 1959, p. 56.

reach if growth in material living standards continues. The corollary is that people in developed countries today are affluent because they are hogging scarce and dwindling resources; our way of life is only possible for the few who live in developed countries as long as we go on securing and consuming most of the materials produced each year. If we shared world resources equally the average American would have to get by on less than one-sixth of the present average energy now used....If these arguments are valid it follows that our affluent way of life is highly immoral and that we in rich countries must accept the idea of de-development; we should take immediate action towards reducing our material living standards in order to permit the Third World to have a fairer share of the available resources and to permit more of the Third World's productive capacity to be geared to the needs of its people.[54]

What kind of politics is this? One of the contributors to Dobson's book, Jonathon Porritt, provides an answer. Porritt was Director of Friends of the Earth, Britain. In the foreward to Dobson's book, Friends of the Earth is correctly labeled a "mainstream" environmental organization. Porritt:

> The claim made by Green politics that it's 'neither right, nor left, nor in the centre' has understandably caused a lot of confusion! For people who are accustomed to thinking of politics exclusively in terms of the left-right polarity, Green politics has to fit in somewhere. And if it doesn't, then it must be made to.
>
> But it's really not that difficult. We profoundly disagree with the politics of the right and its underlying ideology of capitalism; we profoundly disagree with the politics of the left and its adherence, in varying degrees, to the ideology of communism. That leaves us little choice but to disagree, perhaps less profoundly, with the politics of the centre and its ideological pot-pourri of socialized capitalism. The politics of the Industrial Age, left, right and centre, is like a three-lane motorway, with different vehicles in different lanes, but *all* heading in the same direction. Greens feel it is the very direction that is wrong, rather than the choice of any one lane in preference to the others. It is our perception that the motorway of industrialism inevitably leads to the abyss - hence our decision to get off it, and seek an entirely different direction.[55]

What Porritt and Dobson are promoting is a non-industrial, non-modern third way. What gives these ideas their aristocratic flavor is the obviously low regard in which are held all of the technical and scientific achievements of the last couple of centuries. These men are no doubt making full use of most or all of those achievements in their own lives.

Dobson himself took aim at the productive and creative potential of humanity in his introduction.

> Within a few weeks of each other, in 1986, the Chernobyl nuclear power plant in the Soviet Union and the American space shuttle, Challenger, both exploded. Despite mutterings on both sides which sought to place the blame for these accidents on the inefficiencies of bureaucratic centralism and disorganized capitalism respectively, many were left with the sneaking suspicion that no political system can contain the folly of our

---

[54] Dobson, 1991, pp. 66-68.
[55] Ibid., pp. 34-35.

Promethean aspirations. Prometheus stole fire from the gods and gave it to human beings. He was punished by Zeus by being chained to a rock and having his liver chewed by a vulture every day for thirty years. Prometheus was rescued by Heracles - we might not be so lucky....

Green politics settles human beings by humbling them first. The science of ecology teaches us that we are part of a system which stretches back into an unfathomable past and reaches forward into an incalculable future, and that the whole planetary community is bound by ties of interdependence which makes a mockery of mastery. There is no room for Prometheus here. The talk around the tables in vegetarian restaurants is of limits: not limits to industrial and population growth, but of the limits to human knowledge that produce the dark side of ingenuity. We take refuge in our ignorance, relieved at last of the awful responsibility of choosing a new future from a limitless number of designs. There is solace to be had once we realize that the wisdom of God passeth all understanding. Green politics responds to an age of uncertainty by teaching us to know our place.[56]

The Promethean spirit should be destroyed totally. Dobson and associates will teach us to know our place. This is the Green idea of radical politics. They are the new gods, Cronos and friends.

One finds reactionary, elitist and aristocratic politics in the eco-perspective with dependable regularity. For example, the term "biodiversity" appeared in the 1980s with an anti-establishment air about it. However, the man some credit with making the term current, E. O. Wilson, is a rather conventional Malthuisan and Social Darwinist whose fellow diversifiers include Paul Ehrlich and Lester Brown.[57] The concept of biodiversity is a hodgepodge of mysticism and Darwinism. It shares with post-modern thought the idea that the world is so complex and most people so inept that only a handful of experts, like biodiversity experts, can comprehend it.[58] They must serve as our guides. The idea of biodiversity was consciously developed as a weapon to be used against the aggressor - people.[59]

The examples cited above may be more strident than a Vogt, Carson or Osborn; probably they are not. Unable to clearly separate their goals and values from "mainstream" environmentalism, many deep ecologists have tried to adopt methods that are more extreme.[60] Others, like Dobson, end up associating deep ecology with Establishment greens like Lynn White or Rozak, or they try to out radical the mainstream by embracing the Nazi supporter Martin Heidegger.[61] Some deep ecologists may have greater desires to be at one with nature, but they will find it difficult to outdo the older movement's opposition to progress and its disdain for most people. A few environmentalists may even be troubled by that history.[62]

Given the nature of environmentalism, how did it become associated in many people's minds with "liberalism." It did so by helping to change the meaning of the term

---

[56] Ibid., pp. 7-8.
[57] Kevles, 1985, pp. 272-275; Takacs, 1996, pp. 128, 149, 327-331.
[58] Devine, 1996, p. 30.
[59] Takacs, 1996, pp. 1-3, 106-107.
[60] DeLucca, 1999, pp. 70-71, 73-78; Dryzek and Lester, 1989, pp. 315, 317.
[61] Devall, 1980, pp. 303, 307, 309; Manes, 1990, p. 143.
[62] Darnovsky, 1992, pp. 24-26.

"liberalism" and because opposition to environmentalism became an element of anti-government politics, something contemporary American conservatives are much more comfortable with.

LIBERAL ENVIRONMENTALISM

If there is any political consistency in the history of ecology, conservationism and environmentalism it is an association with upper class interests and an elitist bias against technological and economic progress. For the most part, the ideas have been the ideas of those with hereditary privilege and of those associated with such people. Environmentalism is their ideology.

In the middle third of the twentieth century, say from the early-1930s to the late-1960s, the term "liberal" often, but not always, referred to or was compatible with the politics associated with Franklin Roosevelt and John Kennedy. When it referred to FDR, JFK or similar people, the idea of liberalism included, among other things, the idea of using governmental powers to stimulate economic progress, creating more wealth and getting that wealth distributed to more people. Tax policy, budgetary decisions and the creation of money and credit were all supposed to facilitate the investment in and the development of new technology. Under FDR and JFK the government was an instrument of progress. The commitment to industrialism, science, technology, planning and to prosperity was close to absolute.[63]

In the same period that environmentalism became a major national issue, the liberals and the Democratic Party became less committed to industrialism and to that FDR-JFK approach. The two things appear to have happened together. They are associated with each other rather than one being the cause of the other. The language and priorities of environmentalism, however, virtually preclude a focus on technological and economic progress. The values and goals of environmentalism have little to do with the values and goals of the FDR-JFK tradition. It is difficult to focus on development and on the material needs of people when you are referring to them as a cancer. Environmentalism can do more than just inject a conservative note into liberal politics, it can help to eliminate the commitment to progress.

The focus on industry, science and technology and on the development of human creativity have been a prominent part of American cultural and political history. That has not been the province of any one political party. Its supporters, promoters and leaders have been Federalists, Whigs, Republicans and Democrats. The current association of environmentalism with "liberalism," or post-JFK liberalism, developed during the Carter-Reagan face off[64] and as a result of the development of a certain type of virulently anti-government conservatism.

Although Democratic President Jimmy Carter did not get particularly high grades form the environmental establishment, little better than presidential candidate George H.

---

[63] Bluestone and Harrison, 2000, pp. 27-49; Gibson, 1994.
[64] Tucker, 1982, pp. 36-39, 63.

W. Bush, Reagan was near the bottom of potential national leaders.[65] Reagan's anti-environmentalism was embedded in a broader anti-government politics. Reagan and then conservative media figures, most notably Rush Hudson Limbaugh III, carried a message to the general public that had been previously distributed to a smaller, more affluent audience by the *Wall Street Journal, Fortune* and other voices for Wall Street and high finance. Around 1980 Reagan and various business interests did much to make environmentalism an issue of big government.[66] In fairness to Reagan, it is also true that some of his appointees (e.g., Anne Burford) did briefly raise the issue of environmental elitism.[67]

The Republican party, particularly one its most famous presidents, Teddy Roosevelt, had been very supportive of conservationism. But in the 1980s there seems to have been at least three reasons for the conservatives and Republicans to adopt the anti-environmentalism cause. First, it could add a major element to the overall anti-government campaign carried on by the post-1960s Republican Party. Second, it is a real concession to interests in the Republican party who disagree with or are injured by environmental regulations. Among others, that would include the followers of conservative critics of environmentalism such as Julian Simon, Dixie Lee Ray and Edith Efron and, of course, self interested business people and landowners. Simon, Ray and Efron have provided some of the most thoughtful criticism of the anti-technology, anti-growth aspects of environmentalism. They have not been willing, however, to address the role of the Anglo-American elite in all of this. Third, as long as environmentalism is debated superficially and as long as it is treated primarily as an example of big government, it is a useful and safe issue for the Republican party and for the aristo-finance elite. This means that there are certain rules that must be followed. Conservative and Republican Party critics of environmentalism are never to mention past or present upper class support for environmentalism. No one is to acknowledge the elitist and reactionary nature of environmentalist ideology. Prominent figures should not focus on the lack of evidence for many environmental arguments. No one is to allude to it as an ideology. Silence on this issue is also in the interests of Democrats whose "liberal" credentials are now often based on stands taken on global warming or some other ecological crisis. Neither conservatives nor liberals want a full discussion of the characteristics and history of environmentalism.

All of this pays off in the world of pseudo-politics. Democrats can now oppose Republicans claiming that they will do a better job protecting nature and Republicans can campaign against the intrusiveness and irrationality of some of the government's environmental policy. Environmental organizations can come up with an endless list of problems to debate. Often with little scientific evidence and never with any apologies for previous errors or exaggerations, the environmental movement can promote an atmosphere of crisis around cancer scares, acid rain, alar, ozone holes and global warming and vague references to overpopulation and resources. Some of this crisis

---

[65] New York Times, 1980, p. 9.
[66] New York Times, 1980a, p. D14.
[67] Shabecoff, 1983, p. B12.

mongering, even when there is nothing to support it, ends up affecting government policies.[68]

Given the frequent flimsiness of so-called environmental science and given the cost of environmental policies to the country, trillions of dollars since the 1970s, it makes sense that many people will be upset. What most of the conservative critics do is give these offended individuals and groups someone to hate - government.

Hatred of government is pervasive in the anti-environmentalism movement. Hostility toward government is the atmosphere for all thinking about environmentalism. Environmentalism is virtually reduced to just one more reason to hate government. Ruling interests in this country have either been very shrewd or very lucky. A situation has developed which is a heads-they-win, tails-we-lose situation. If we buy into environmentalism, we essentially convince ourselves that progress is no longer possible. Along the way we absorb much in the way of aristocratic values and misanthropic attitudes. If we buy into the anti-government rhetoric of the conservative critics of environmentalism, we basically turn the future of the country and world over to the same oligarchic forces.

There are anti-environmentalist people among the following groups: "ranchers, miners, loggers, farmers, fishermen, trappers, hunters, off-road vehicle users, property rights advocates, industry associations, corporate front groups and right-wing activists."[69] Some of these have become part of the Wise Use movement, created at a 1988 Multiple-Use Strategy Conference. This conference was sponsored by the Center for the Defense of Free Enterprise and the founders of Wise Use included Exxon, DuPont and the Competitive Enterprise Institute.[70] Although competition has not always been a priority at Exxon and DuPont, they are certainly comfortable with the anti-government cause. Rabidly anti-government organizations such as the Heritage Foundation are also prominent in the anti-environmentalism campaign. The Wise Use movement is intertwined with another anti-government group, the property rights oriented Alliance for America, which emerged in the early-1990s.[71]

These developments have created a political climate in which the American citizen is often confronted with a choice between the rhetoric of the Wall Street Journal and that of the Friends of the Earth. In domestic politics, the upper class has cut Malthus in half, separating his hatred of active government from his hatred of progress. We can have a government with no commitment to progress or we can turn the future over to powerful private interests with no commitment to progress, or worse. That is not much of a choice.

---

[68] Coffman, 1994, pp. 31-32, 35-39, 47-51; Efron, 1984; Fumento, 1993, pp. 19-34; Hogan, 1997; Maduro and Schauerhammer, 1992; Rosenbaum, 1989, pp. 220-224.

[69] Rowell, 1996, p. 15.

[70] Ibid., pp. 16-17.

[71] Ibid., p. 25.

CONCLUSION

When William Tucker's *Progress and Privilege* was published in 1982 it was reviewed for the New York Times by Samuel Florman. Florman's own book defending modern technology, *Blaming Technology*, was published in 1981. Among other things, Florman criticized Tucker for failing to see that there were good reasons for the rise of environmentalism and that there were reasons that many scientists and engineers allied themselves with environmentalism. They did so, according to Florman,

> because of the things that Mr. Tucker has neglected to mention in his book, such as the rapaciousness of unchecked developers and the unattended spread of truly worrisome problems (such as soil erosion and the contamination of aquifers) and because environmentalism itself, properly viewed, is not an obstructionist philosophy but rather an expression of purpose, yearning and rising expectations, another chapter in the saga of human progress.[72]

There is in fact no way to view environmentalism as part of the saga of human progress unless it is disconnected from much of its history and from its present. One may imagine unicorns, but that does not make them real. One may imagine a history of environmentalism that is part of the saga of progress, but that is not the real history.

The problem with environmentalism is that it has little to do with the prevention of soil erosion. It is a political doctrine and its proponents talk about soil erosion in order to promote the political and social agenda, not to solve the soil problem. If Tucker erred, it was in not giving this enough emphasis. The leaders of environmentalism create or adopt issues because they fit with the economic and social program that is sponsored by the Anglo-American Establishment. They are, therefore, unaffected by facts and evidence. If it is proven that they misrepresent things (e.g., overpopulation in Africa and South America, imminent resource depletion, acid rain catastrophe, alar in apples), that proof has no effect on the broader message of environmentalism because that message is a political one. To the Anglo-American Establishment and its allies, rapid progress, and the enhanced role for other groups in society that progress requires and produces, is a threat to their power, influence and status.

This is the reason that so many of the core ideas of environmentalism are purely political ideas, not ones arising from observable phenomena or scientific reasoning. They disparage both the results of and the sources of generalized progress because they fear and oppose that progress. The possibility of a higher standard of living brought about by a commitment to the planned development and use of advanced technologies is to be denied because it threatens their power and privilege. High levels of consumption, industrialism, modern technology, and human creativity itself are attacked by environmentalists because they are in fact the targets, not actual damage to nature. Within the world of upper class environmentalism, the terms "ecosystem," "nature" and "environment" actually represent the upper class itself. It is they who are being defended

---

[72] Florman, 1982.

and conserved. The fatalism, passivity and pessimism promoted by modern Malthusian arguments discourage us from seeking a better world. That is a primary goal of contemporary environmentalism and it is the reason that the language and discourse of environmentalism is full of polemics, extremism, exaggeration, disregard of facts and of opposing views, devaluation of human life, contempt for technological achievement and for Western culture, and an underlying rigidity in message. A part of the population consequently becomes cynical about all environmental concerns, including the rational ones. There is two hundred years of this.

The core political ideas, the devaluation of material progress and the disparaging of reason, have their roots in aristocratic culture and were articulated by Malthus. The idea of a limited world is not based on science or physical facts, it is an expression of power relations, which are in a sense zero sum. The physical world is not in any practical sense finite, it changes with growth in human knowledge and capability. The world of social and economic power is finite. If groups outside of the Anglo-American upper class increase their power, it is at the expense of that upper class. It is the power relations that progress threatens to change.

The real goal of environmental*ism* and ecolog*ism* is the preservation and protection of the Anglo-American Establishment and its allies, junior partners, and minions. Environmental*ism* is a socio-political doctrine. Specific arguments about resources, population or pollution can change; such arguments can be abandoned. What does not and will not change are the sources of and purposes of those arguments. It is time for the majority to reassert the Promethean tendency celebrated by Aeschylus 2500 years ago.

BIBLIOGRAPHY

Aeschylus. 1961. *Prometheus Bound, The Suppliants, Seven Against Thebes, The Persians.* Trans. and Intro. by Philip Vellacott. New York: Penguin Books.

Allen, Michael Patrick. 1987. *The Founding Fortunes: A New Anatomy of the Super-Rich Families in America.* New York: Truman Talley Books/E. P. Dutton.

American Council of Learned Societies. Various years. *Dictionary of American Biography.* New York: Charles Scribner's Sons.

Anderson, Walt (Ed.). 1970. *Politics and Environment: A Reader in Ecological Crisis.* Pacific Palisades, CA: Goodyear Publishing Co.

Apter, David E. 1965. *The Politics of Modernization.* Chicago, IL: University of Chicago Press.

Bachrach, Peter and Elihu Bergman. 1973. *Power and Choice: The Formulation of American Population Policy.* Lexington, MA: Lexington Books/D.C. Heath and Co.

Baltzell, E. Digby. 1964. *The Protestant Establishment: Aristocracy and Caste in America.* New York: Vintage Books/Random House.

Bamford, James. 2001. *Body of Secrets.* New York: Doubleday.

Banks, J. A. 1972. *The Sociology of Social Movements.* London: Macmillan.

Barclay, William, Joseph Enright and Reid T. Reynolds. 1970. "Population Control in the Third World." *NACLA Newsletter*, Vol. IV (December): 1-18.

Barkan, Steven E. 1979. "Strategic, Tactical and Organizational Dilemmas of the Protest Movement Against Nuclear Power." *Social Problems* 27: 19-37.

Barkley, Katherine and Steve Weissman. 1970. "The Eco- Establishment." *Ramparts* 8 (May): 48-54.

Barnett, Harold J. and Chandler Morse. 1963. *Scarcity and Growth: The Economics of Natural Resource Availability.* Baltimore, MD: Johns Hopkins Press/Resources for the Future.

Barney, Gerald O. (Ed.). 1977. *The Unfinished Agenda.* New York: Thomas Y. Crowell.

Bates, Marston. 1960. "The Population Explosion: There's a New Chicago Every Month." *New York Times*, Book Review (November 13): 3.

Becher, Anne. 2000. *American Environmental Leaders: From Colonial Times to the Present.* Santa Barbara, CA: ABC-CLIO, Inc.

Beckmann, Petr. 1980. *The Health Hazards of Not Going Nuclear*. New York: Ace Books/Grosset & Dunlap.

Bedford, Sybille. 1973. *Aldous Huxley: A Biography*. New York: A. Knopf/Harper & Row.

Berger, Peter L. and Thomas Luckman. 1966. *The Social Construction of Reality: A Treatise in the Sociology of Knowledge*. Garden City, NY: Doubleday & Co.

Berger, Peter L., Brigitte Berger and Hansfried Kellner. 1973. *The Homeless Mind: Modernization and Consciousness*. New York: Vintage Books/Random House.

Bickerstafffe, Julia and David Pearce. 1980. "Can There Be a Consensus on Nuclear Power?" *Social Studies of Science* 10: 309- 344.

Bird, Kai. 1992. *The Chairman: John J. McCloy and the Making of the American Establishment*. New York: Simon & Schuster.

Birmingham, Stephen. 1987. *America's Secret Aristocracy*. Boston, MA: Little, Brown and Company.

Blair, John M. 1976. *The Control of Oil*. New York: Vintage Books/Random House.

Blau, Eleanor. 1973. "Humanist Manifesto II Offers a 'Survival' Philosophy." *New York Times* (August 26): 1, 51.

Bluestone, Barry and Bennett Harrison. 2000. *Growing Prosperity: The Battle for Growth with Equity in the Twenty-first Century*. New York: Houghton Mifflin Co.

Blumer, Herbert. 1974. "Social Movements." Pp. 4-20 in R. Serge Denisoff and Robert K. Merton (Eds.) *The Sociology of Dissent*. New York: Harcourt Brace Jovanovich.

Boyd-Orr, John and David Lubbock. 1964. *The White Man's Dilemma*. New York: Barnes and Noble, Inc.

Bracker, Milton. 1955. "Scholars Gather To Discuss World." *New York Times* (August 2): 21.

Bramwell, Anna. 1989. *Ecology in the 20th Century: A History*. New Haven, CT:

Buxton, William J. 1999. "Reaching Human Minds: Rockefeller Philanthropy and Communications, 1935-1939." Pp. 177-192 in Theresa Richardson and Donald Fisher (Eds.) *The Development of the Social Sciences in the United States and Canada: The Role of Philanthropy*. Stamford, CT: Ablex Publishing Corp.

Cain, P. J. and A. G. Hopkins. 1986. "Gentlemanly Capitalism and British Expansion Overseas: I. The Old Colonial System, 1688-1850." *Economic History Review*, Vol. xxxix (November): 501-25.

--. 1987. "Gentlemanly Capitalism and British Expansion Overseas: II. New Imperialism, 1850-1945." *Economic History Review*, Vol. xl (February): 1-26.

Caldwell, John and Pat Caldwell. 1986. *Limiting Population Growth and the Ford Foundation Contribution*. Dover, NH: Frances Pinter.

Camilleri, Joseph A. 1984. *The Stae and Nuclear Power*. Seattle, WA: University of Washington Press.

Campbell, John L. 1988. *Collapse of an Industry: Nuclear Power and the Contradictions of U.S. Policy*. Ithaca, NY: Cornell University Press.

Cardwell, D. S. L. 1972. *Turning Points in Western Technology*. New York: Science History Publications/Neale Watson Academic Publications.

Carey, Henry. 1967 (1851). *The Harmony of Interests: Agricultural, Manufacturing & Commercial*. New York: Augustus M. Kelly.

Carey, John. 1992. *The Intellectuals and the Masses*. New York: St. Martin's Press.

Carmin, Joann. 1999. "Voluntary Associations, Professional Organizations and the Environmental Movement in the United States." pp. 101-121 in Christopher Rootes (Ed.) *Environmental Movements: Local, National and Global*. London: Frank Cass.

Carrel, Alexis. 1935. *Man The Unknown*. New York: Harper & Brothers.

Carson, Rachel. 1962. *Silent Spring*. New York: Fawcett Crest Books.

Caulfield, Henry P. 1989. "The Conservation and Environmental Movements: An Historical Analysis." Pp. 13-56 in James P. Lester (Ed.) *Environmental Politics and Policy: Theories and Evidence*. Durham, NC: Duke University Press.

Chase, Allan. 1982. *Magic Shots*. New York: William Morrow and Co.

Childe, V. Gordon. 1942. *What Happened In History*. New York: Penguin Books.

--. 1951. *Man Makes Himself*. New York: Meridian Book/New Americam Library.

Coffman, Michael S. 1994. *Saviors of the Earth?* Chicago, IL: Northfield Publishers.

Cole, H. S. D., Christopher Freeman, Marie Jahoda and K. L. R. Pavitt (Eds.). 1973. *Models of Doom: A Critique Of The Limits To Growth*. New York: Universe Books.

Collier, Peter and David Horowitz. 1976. *The Rockefellers: An American Dynasty*. New York: Signet/New American Library.

Commoner, Barry. 1971. *The Closing Circle: Nature, Man & Technology*. New York: Bantam Books.

Cookson, Peter W. and Caroline Hodges Persell. 1985. *Preparing for Power: America's Elite Boarding Schools*. New York: Basic Books, Inc.

Cortesi, Arnaldo. 1961. "Stabilizing of World Population Is Advocated by Rockefeller 3d." *New York Times* (November 7): 1, 17.

Cotgrove, Steven. 1976. "Environmentalism and Utopia." *Sociological Review* 24: 23-42.

Council on Foreign Relations. 1963. *Annual Report, Council on Foreign Relations*. New York: Harold Pratt House.

Cronon. William. 2001. "When the GOP Was Green." *New York Times* (January 8):

Darnovsky, Marcy. 1992. "Stories Less Told: Histories of US Environmentalism." *Socialist Review*, Vol. 22: 11-54.

Davies, Clarence J. III. 1970. *The Politics of Pollution*. New York: Pegasus.

Davies, Lawrence E. 1969. "Naturalists Get A Political Arm." *New York Times* (September 17): 21.

DeLuca, Kevin Michael. 1999. *Image Politics: The New Rhetoric of Environmental Activism*. New York: The Guilford Press.

Demerath, Nicholas J. 1976. *Birth Control and Foreign Policy: The Alternatives to Family Planning*. New York: Harper and Row.

Devall, Bill. 1980. "The Deep Ecology Movement." *Natural Resources Journal*, Vol. 20: 299-322.

--. 1982. "John Muir As Deep Ecologist." *Environmental Review*, Vol. 6: 63-86.

Devine, Philip E. 1996. *Human Diversity and the Culture Wars*. Westport, CT: Praeger.

Devlin, John C. 1962. "Philip and Bernhard Appeal Here for Aid to Wildlife." *New York Times* (June 8): 1, 21. --. 1963. "Bronx Zoo's Farm to Be Refuge For Species Facing Extinction." *New York Times* (October 4): 1.

Dewar, Elaine. 1995. *Cloak of Green*. Toronto: James Lorimer & Co.

Dickson, Paul. 1971. *Think Tanks*. New York: Atheneum.

Dobson, Andrew (ed.). 1991. *The Green Reader: Essays Toward A Sustainable Society*. San Francisco, CA: Mercury House.

Domhoff, G. William. 1978. *The Powers That Be*. New York: Vintage Books/Random House. --. 1983. *Who Rules America Now? A View for the 80s*. Englewood Cliffs, NJ: Prentice-Hall, Inc. --. 1998. *Who Rules America? Power and Politics In The Year 2000*. Mountain View, CA: Mayfield Publishing Company.

Dominick, Raymond H., III. 1992. *The Environmental Movement in Germany*. Bloomington, IN: Indiana University Press.

Dryzek, John S. and James P. Lester. 1989. "Alternative Views of the Environmental Problematic." Pp. 314-330 in James P. Lester (Ed.), *Environmental Politics and Policy: Theories and Evidence*. Durham, NC: Duke University Press.

Dubos, Rene. 1975. "Less Energy, Better Life." *New York Times* (January 7): 33.

Dunlap, Riley E. 1989. "Public Opinion and Environmental Policy." Pp. 87-134 in James P. Lester (Ed.), *Environmental Politics and Policy: Theories and Evidence*. Durham, NC: Duke University Press.

Dye, Thomas R. 1983. *Who's Running America? The Reagan Years*. Englewood Cliffs, NJ: Prentice-Hall, Inc.

Ebbin, Steven and Raphael Kasper. 1974. *Citizen Groups and the Nuclear Power Controversy*. Cambridge, MA: MIT Press.

Eder, Richard. 1960. "Family Planning Is Goal of Drive." *New York Times* (March 20): 32.

--. 1960a. "Population Curb Gets Private Aid." *New York Times* (March 21): 8.

Efron, Edith. 1984. *The Apocalyptics: Cancer and the Big Lie*. New York: Simon and Shuster.

Ehrlich, Paul. 1968. *The Population Bomb*. New York: Ballantine Books.

--. 1973. "Playboy Interview, 1970." Pp. 13-28 in Edward Pohlman (Ed.), *Population: A Clash of Prophets*. New York: Mentor Book/New American Library.

Elliott, Lorraine. 1998. *The Global Politics of the Environment*. Washington Square, NY: New York University Press.

Engdahl, F. William. 1992. *A Century of War: Anglo-American Oil Politics and the New World Order*. Concord, MA: Paul & Company Publishers Consortium.

Erskine, Hazel. 1972. "The Polls: Pollution and Its Costs." *Public Opinion Quarterly* 36: 120-135.

Falk, Jim. 1982. *Global Fission: The Battle Over Nuclear Energy*. New York: Oxford University Press.

Ferguson, Marilyn. 1980. *The Aquarian Conspiracy*. Los Angeles, CA: J.P. Tarcher.

Fischer, Erika J. and Heinz D. Fischer. 1994. *John J. McCloy: An American Architect of Postwar Germany*. New York: Peter Lang.

Fisher, James, Noel Simon and Jack Vincent. 1969. *Wildlife in Danger*. New York: Studio Book/Viking Press.

Fiske, Edward B. 1970. "The Link Between Faith and Ecology." *New York Times*, Week In Review (January 4): 5. --. 1970. "Christianity Linked to Pollution." *New York Times* (May 1): 12.

Flippen, J. Brooks. 2000. *Nixon and the Environment*. Albuquerque, NM: University of New Mexico Press.

Florman, Samuel C. 1981. *Blaming Technology: The Irrational Search For Scapegoats*. New York: St. Martin's Press.

--. 1982. "The Environmental Elite: Progress and Privilege." *New York Times* (August 8): VII, 8, 16.

Foundation Center. Various years. *Annual Report*. New York: The Foundation Center.

--. Various years. *The Foundation Grants Index*. New York: The Foundation Center.

Fowle, Farnsworth. 1963. "Ford Fund Is Adding 2.8 Million For Research on Birth Control." *New York Times* (April 17): 1, 12.

Fox, Stephen. 1981. *The American Conservation Movement*. Madison, WI: University of Wisconsin Press.

Frank, Thomas. 2000. *One Market Under God: Extreme Capitalism, Market Populism, and the End of Economic Democracy*. New York: Doubleday.

Fumento, Michael. 1993. *Science Under Siege*. New York: Quill/William Morrow.

Gallagher, John and Ronald Robinson. 1953. "The Imperialism of Free Trade." *The Economic History Review*, Vol. VI: 1-15.

Garrity, John A. and Mark C. Carnes (Eds.). 1999. *American National Biography*. New York: Oxford University Press.

Gibson, Donald. 1990. "The Role of the Establishment in the Antinuclear Movement." *Sociological Spectrum* 10: 321-340. --. 1992. "The Environmental Movement: Grass-Roots or Establishment?" *Sociological Viewpoints*, Vol. 8 (Fall): 92-124. --. 1993. "Post-Industrialism: Prosperity Or Decline?" *Sociological Focus*, Vol. 26: 147-163.

--. 1994. *Battling Wall Street: The Kennedy Presidency*. New York: Sheridan Square Press, Inc.

Golub, Robert and Joe Townsend. 1977. "Malthus, Multinationals and the Club of Rome." *Social Studies of Science*, Vol. 7: 210-222.

Gormley, William T., Jr. 1983. *The Politics of Public Utility Regulation*. Pittsburgh, PA: University of Pittsburgh Press.

Gunn, Jennifer. 1999. "A Few Good Men: The Rockefeller Approach to Population, 1911-1936." Pp. 97-114 in Theresa Richardson and Donald Fisher (Eds.) *The Development of the Social Sciences in the United States and Canada: The Role of Philanthropy*. Stamford, CT: Ablex Publishing Corp.

Hardin, Garrett. 1974. "The Case Against Helping the Poor." *Psychology Today* (September): 38-43, 123-126.

Harman, Willis. 1976. *An Incomplete Guide to the Future*. New York: W. W. Norton & Co.

Hays, Samuel P. 1980. *Conservation and the Gospel of Efficiency: The Progressive Conservation Movement, 1890-1920*. New York: Atheneum.

Hayward, Steven. 2000. "Environmentalism Isn't Just for Liberals." *Wall Street Journal* (April 21): Op Ed.

Herberle, Rudolf. 1951. *Social Movements: An Introduction to Political Sociology*. New York: Appleton-Century-Crofts.

Herman, Edward S. and Robert W. McChesney. 1997. *The Global Media: The New Missionaries of Corporate Capitalism*. London: Cassell.

Hill, Gladwin. 1969. "A Sterility Drug In Food Is Hinted." *New York Times* (November 25): 19.

Hofstadter, Richard. 1955. *The Age of Reform*. New York: Vintage Books/Random House.

Hogan, James P. 1997. "Ozone Politics: They Call This Science?" Pp. 161-168 in *Taking Sides: Clashing Views on Controversial Issues in Science, Technology, and Society*. Guilford, CT: Dushkin Publishing/Brown & Benchmark..

Hugh Moore Fund. 1963. "Population Explosion Nullifies Foreign Aid." *New York Times* (June 9): 10E.

--. 1964. "Threat to 'The Great Society'." *New York Times* (December 13): E3.

Humphrey, Craig R. and Frederick R. Buttel. 1982. *Environment, Energy, and Society*. Belmont, CA: Wadsworth.

Hyman, Sidney. 1975. *The Aspen Idea*. Norman, OK: University of Oklahoma Press.

Ingham, Geoffrey. 1984. *Capitalism Divided? The City and Industry in British Social Development*. London: MacMillan Education Ltd.

Inglehart, Ronald. 1981. "Post-Materialism in an Environment of Insecurity." *American Political Science Review* 75: 880-900.

Ingram, Heken M. and Dean E, Mann. 1989. "Interest Groups and Environmental Policy." Pp. 135-157 in James P. Lester (Ed.), *Environmental Politics and Policy: Theories and Evidence*. Durham, NC: Duke University Press.

Johnson, Lyndon. 1965. "Natural Beauty of our Country." *House Documents, 89th Congress, 1st Session*. Washington DC: Government Printing Office.

--. 1965a. "National Wilderness Preservation System." *House Documents, 89th Congress, 1st Session*. Washington, DC: Government Printing Office.

--. 1966. "State of the Union Message." *House Documents, 89th Congress, 2nd Session*. Washington, DC: Government Printing Office.

--. 1967 (1964). "The Goals." Pp. 15-19 in Marvin E. Gettleman and David Mermelstein (Eds.) *The Great Society Reader*. New York: Vintage Books/Random House.

Johnson, Robert Underwood. 1923. *Remembered Yesterdays*. Boston, MA: Little, Brown and Co.

Jones, Holway R. 1965. *John Muir and the Sierra Club: The Battle for Yosemite*. San Francisco, CA: Sierra Club.

Jung, C. G. 1965. *Memories, Dreams, Reflections*. Edited by Aniela Jaffe. New York: Vintage Books/Random House.

Kennedy, David M. 1970. *Birth Control In America: The Career of Margaret Sanger*. New Haven, CT: Yale University Press.

Kennedy, John F. 1961. Edited and intro. by Allan Nevins. *The Strategy of Peace*. New York: Popular Press.

--. 1962. "Our Conservation Program." *House Documents, 87th Congress, 2nd Session, Doc. No. 348*. Washington, DC: Government Printing Office.

Kevles, Daniel J. 1985. *In the Name of Eugenics: Genetics and the Uses of Human Heredity*. Los Angeles, CA: University of California Press.

Kihss, Peter. 1962. "Ford Foundation to Stress U.S. Needs in Next Decade." *New York Times* (July 1): 1, 32.

Killian, Lewis M. 1973. "Social Movements: A Review of the Field." Pp. 9-53 in Robert R. Evans (Ed.) *Social Movements: A Reader and Source Book*. Chicago: Rand McNally.

King, Alexander and Bertrand Schneider. 1991. *The First Global Revolution: A Report by the Council of the Club of Rome*. New York: Pantheon Books.

Kline, Benjamin. 1997. *First Along the River: A Brief History of the U.S. Environmental Movement*. San Francisco, CA: Acada Books.

Komisar, Lucy. 2000. "Taking On The Debt Collectors, The Progressive Interview - Joseph Stiglitz." *The Progressive* (June): 34-38.

Kotz, David M. 1978. *Bank Control of Large Corporations in the United States*. Los Angeles, CA: University of California Press.

Krier, James E. and Edmund Ursin. 1977. *Pollution and Policy*. Berkeley, CA: University of California Press.

Krock, Arthur. 1961. "Troubles At Home." *New York Times*, Sec. IV (July 24): 9.

Lacey, Robert. 1983. *Aristocrats*. Boston: Little, Brown & Co.

Landry, Stuart O. 1938. *History of the Boston Club*. New Orleans, LA: Pelican Publishing Co.

Laqueur, Walter. 1974. *Weimar: A Cultural History*. New York: G.P. Putnam's Sons/Capricorn Books.

Lauer, Robert H. 1976. "Introduction: Social Movements and Social Changes: The Interrelationships." Pp. xi-xxvii in Robert H. Lauer (Ed.) *Social Movements and Social Change*. Carbondale, IL: Southern Illinois University Press.

Lewis, Anthony. 1970. "British Naturalist Says U.S. Is World's Biggest Polluter." *New York Times* (November 18): 3.

Lewy, Guenther. 1980. "Millenarianism as a Revolutionary Force." Pp. 168-209 in Harold D. Lasswell, Daniel Lerner and Hans Speier (Eds.) *Propaganda and Communication in World History, Volume II, Emergence of Public Opinion in World History*. Honolulu: University of Hawaii Press.

Life. 1970. "Ecology Becomes Everybody's Issue." *Life* (January 30): 22-30.

Lindzen, Richard S. 2001. "Scientists' Report Doesn't Support The Kyoto Treaty." *Wall Street Journal* (June 11): A22.

Lipset, Seymour Martin. 1968. *Revolution and Counterrevolution: Change and Persistence in Social Structures*. New York: Basic Books.

Loftus, Joseph A. 1948. "Population Outgrows Food, Scientists Warn the World." *New York Times* (September 15): 1, 34.

Lonergan, Bernard J. F. 1970. *Insight: A Study of Human Understanding*. New York: Philosophical Library.

--. 1974. *A Second Collection*. Edited by William F. J. Ryan and Bernard J. Tyrrell. Philadelphia, PA: Westminster Press.

Long, Tania. 1955. "Population Rise Held U.S. Peril." *New York Times* (March 16): 16.

Lowe, Philip and Michael Worboys. 1978. "Ecology and the End of Ideology." *Antipode*, Vol. 10: 12-21.

Lundberg, Ferdinand. 1937. *America's 60 Families*. New York: Vanguard Press.

--. 1968. *The Rich and the Super-Rich*. New York: Bantam Books.

Maduro, Rogelio A. and Ralf Schauerhammer. 1992. *The Holes in the Ozone Scare.* Washington, DC: 21st Century Science Associates.

MacArthur, John R. 2000. *The Selling of "Free Trade": NAFTA, Washington, and the Subversion of American Democracy.* New York: Hill and Wang/Farrar, Straus and Giroux.

MacNeill, Jim, Pieter Winsemius and Taizo Yakushiji (Eds.). 1991. *Beyond Interdependence: The Meshing of the World's Economy and the Earth's Ecology.* New York: Oxford University Press.

Mahl, Thomas E. 1998. *Desperate Deception: British Covert Operations in the United States, 1939-44.* Washington, DC: Brassey's.

Malthus, Thomas Robert. 1960. *On Population.* New York: Modern Library.

Mannheim, Karl. 1936. *Ideology and Utopia.* New York: Harvest Book/Harcourt, Brace and World.

Margolis, Jon. 1970. "Our Country 'Tis of Thee, Land of Ecology..." *Esquire* (March): 124, 172-179.

Marquis Who's Who, 1910-11. *Who's Who in America.* Chicago, IL: Marquis Who's Who.

--. 1940-41. *Who's Who In America.* Chicago, IL: Marquis Who's Who.

--. 1962-63. *Who's Who In America.* Chicago, IL: Marquis Who's Who.

--. 1973. *Who Was Who In Anemic*, Vol. V. Chicago, IL: Marquis Who's Who.

--. 1978-79. *Who's Who In America.* Chicago, IL: Marquis Who's Who.

--. 1988-89. *Who's Who In America.* Chicago, IL: Marquis Who's Who.

--. 2000. *Who's Who in America.* Chicago, IL: Marquis Who's Who.

Marsh, Diane T. 1992. *Families and Mental Illness: New Directions in Professional Practice.* NY: Praeger.

Marx, Karl. 1969. *Theories of Surplus Value, Part II.* London: Lawrence & Wishart.

--. 1972. *Theories of Surplus Value, Part III.* London: Lawrence & Wishart.

McCarthy, John D. and Mayer N. Zald. 1987. "Appendix: The Trend of Social Movements in America: Professionalization and Resource Mobilization." Pp. 337-391 in Mayer N. Zald and John D. McCarthy (Eds.) *Social Movements In An Organizational Society.* New Brunswick, NJ: Transaction Books.

McCracken, Samuel. 1982. *The War Against the Atom.* New York: Basic Books.

McDonald, Forrest. 1982. *Alexander Hamilton: A Biography.* New York: W. W. Norton & Co.

McMichael, Philip. 2000. *Development and Social Change: A Global Perspective.* Thousand Oaks, CA: Pine Forge Press.

Meek, Ronald L. (Ed.) 1971. *Marx and Engels on the Population Bomb.* Berkeley, CA: Ramparts Press Inc.

Mesarovic, Mihajlo and Eduard Pestel. 1974. *Mankind At The Turning Point: The Second Report To The Club Of Rome.* New York: New American Library/Times Mirror.

Middleton, Drew. 1965. "United Nations Hail Pontiff, Kennedy Quoted." *New York Times* (October 5): 1,2.

Milbrath, Lester W. 1986. "Environmental Beliefs and Values." Pp. 97-138 in Margaret G. Hermann (Ed.) *Political Psychology.* San Francisco: Jossey-Bass, Publishers.

Mitchell, Robert Cameron. 1981. "From Elite Quarrel to Mass Movement." *Transaction/Society* 18: 76-84.

Mosse, George. 1964. *The Crisis of German Ideology, Intellectual Origins of the Third Reich*. New York: Universal Library/Grosset and Dunlap.

--. 1966. *Nazi Culture*. New York: Schocken Books.

Nagai, Althea, Robert Lerner, and Stanley Rothman. 1994. *Giving for Social Change: Foundations, Public Policy, and the American Political Agenda*. Westport, CT: Praeger.

National Academy of Sciences. 1877-2000. *Biographical Memoirs*. Washington, DC: National Academy of Sciences.

Nelkin, Dorothy and Michael Pollak. 1981. *The Atom Besieged: Extra Parliamentary Dissent in France and Germany*. Cambridge, MA: MIT Press.

Neuhaus, Richard. 1971. *In Defense of People*. New York: Macmillan.

Newsweek. 1970. "Special Report: The Ravaged Environment." *Newsweek* (August 3): 3, 31-47.

Newton, Scott and Dilwyn Porter. 1988. *Modernization Frustrated: The Politics of Industrial Decline in Britain since 1900*. Boston: Unwin Hyman.

New Yorker. 1957. "The Talk of the Town." *The New Yorker* (March 9): 23-24.

New York Times. 1948. "Conservation Unit Set Up to Warn U.S." *New York Times* (April 6): 25.

--. 1950. "Mrs. Sanger Urges U.S. Sterility Plan." *New York Times* (October 26): 26.

--. 1951. "Population Curb Held Key To Peace." *New York Times* (October 25): 42.

--. 1953. "Parenthood Units Told To Seek Aims." *New York Times* (May 8): 22.

--. 1953a. "A Study of Mankind's Future." *New York Times* (August 17): 14. --. 1954. "Most Pressing Problem." *New York Times* (September 8): 13.

--. 1959. "Population Rise Held Youth Peril." *New York Times* (December 7): 4.

--. 1960. "Fund Chairman Named" *New York Times* (April 9): 45.

--. 1960a. "Action Is Demanded On Population Rise." *New York Times* (May 20): 11.

--. 1960b. "Population Curbs Urged By Draper." *New York Times* (November 15): 23.

--. 1961. "U.S. Shuns Moves On Birth Control." *New York Times* (July 24): 41.

--. 1961a. "People Are His Cause." *New York Times* (November 7): 17.

--. 1961b. "Casals In Atom Plea." *New York Times* (November 15): 18.

--. 1963. "Ford Foundation Gives India 5 Million For Family Planning and Health." *New York Times* (July 5): 2.

--. 1963a. "Rockefeller Fund Revises Program." *New York Times* (September 25): 45.

--. 1964. "Population and Poverty." *New York Times* (January 30): 28.

--. 1964a. "Horace C. Montgomery to Marry Mrs. Erickson." *New York Times* (February 28).

--. 1964b. "Threat to 'The Great Society.'" *New York Times* (December 13): E3. --. 1967. "Rockefeller 3d Wins Sanger Award." *New York Times* (October 9): 42.

--. 1968. "Man vs. Nature." *New York Times* (January 1): 14.

--. 1968a. "Rusk Tells of Pride In Helping Prevent A Nuclear Conflict." *New York Times* (January 11): 2.

--. 1968b. "To Save a Nation." *New York Times* (March 12): 42.

--. 1968c. "Ford Foundation Grants Millions to Spur Training in Ecology." *New York Times* (June 30): 29.

--. 1968d. "William Vogt, Former Director Of Planned Parenthood, Is Dead." *New York Times* (July 12): 31.

--. 1968e. "Rusk Is Reported To Direct Population Study." *New York Times* (November 22): 23.

--. 1969. "Fairfield Osborn, the Zoo's No. 1 Showman, Dies." *New York Times* (September 17): 47.

--. 1969a. "Huxley Sees 1980's As A Perilous Time." *New York Times* (October 12): 11.

--. 1971. "Environmental Institute Is Founded." *New York Times* (January 10): 52.

--. 1971. "Slowdown on Family Planning." *New York Times* (February 1): 30.

--. 1971. "Planner of Global Talks, Maurice Frederick Strong." *New York Times* (September 23): 22.

--. 1972. "Population Rebuff..." *New York Times* (May 11): 44.

--. 1978. "Democrats Found To Back Environmental Issues." *New York Times* (May 1): B10.

--. 1980. "Ratings by Conservationists Put Kennedy at the Top." *New York Times* (April 19): 9.

--. 1980a. "The Candidates' Stands on the Economy, Defense and Other Issues." *New York Times* (November 3): D14.

New York World-Telegram. 1959. *The World Almanac, 1959*. New York: World-Telegram.

Nicholson, Max. 1970. *The Environmental Revolution: A Guide for the New Masters of the World*. New York: McGraw-Hill.

Oltmans, Willem L. (Ed.) 1974. *On Growth*. New York: Capricorn Books/G. P. Putnam's Sons.

Ophuls, William. 1977. "The Politics of the Sustainable Society." Pp. 164-170 in D. Pirages (Ed.), *The Sustainable Society: Implications for Limited Growth*. New York: Praeger.

Osborn, Fairfield. 1948. *Our Plundered Planet*. Boston: Little, Brown and Company.

--. 1953. *The Limits of the Earth*. Boston: Little, Brown and Company.

--. (Ed.) 1962. *Our Crowded Planet*. Garden City, NY: Doubleday.

Osborn, Frederick. 1960. "Frederick Osborn." Pp. 83-138 in Thomas Malthus, Julian Huxley and Frederick Osborn, *Three Essays On Population*. New York: Mentor Books/New American Library.

--. 1968. *The Future of Human Heredity: An Introduction To Eugenics in Modern Society*. New York: Weybright and Tulley.

Outdoor Recreation Resources Review Commission. 1962. *Outdoor Recreation for America*. Washington, DC: Outdoor Recreation Resources Review Commission.

Pace, Eric. 1970. "Philip Sees Crisis In Pollution War." *New York Times* (February 10): 8.

Pector, Jeff. 1978. "The Nuclear Power Industry and the Anti-Nuclear Movement." *Socialist Review* 8: 9-35.

Pepper, David. 1984. *The Roots of Modern Environmentalism*. New York: Routledge.

Perrot, Roy. 1968. *The Aristocrats*. New York: Macmillan Co.

Perry, Joseph B., Jr. and David Meredith Pugh. 1978. *Collective Behavior: Response To Social Stress*. New York: West Publishing.

Petersen, Anna. 1959. "Population Curb by U.N. Proposed." *New York Times* (November 20): 33.

Petulla, Joseph M. 1987. *Environmental Protection in the United States*. San Francisco, CA: San Francisco Study Center.

--. 1988. *American Environmental History*. Columbus, OH: Merrill Publishing.

Pinchot, Gifford. 1998 (1947). *Breaking New Ground*. Washington, DC: Island Press.

Piotrow, Phylis Tilson. 1973. *World Population Crisis: The United States Response*. New York: Praeger.

Poore, Charles. 1960. "Books of the Times." *New York Times* (November 10): 45.

Powis, Jonathan. 1984. *Aristocracy*. New York: Basil Blackwell, Inc.

Price, Jerome B. 1982. *The Antinuclear Movement*. Boston, MA: Twayne.

Pringle, Peter and James Spigelman. 1981. *The Nuclear Barons*. New York: Avon Books.

Quigley, Carroll. 1979. *The Evolution of Civilizations*. Indianapolis, IN: Liberty Press. --. 1981. *The Anglo-American Establishment*. New York: Books in Focus.

Ray, Dixie Lee. 1993. *Environmental Overkill: Whatever Happened to Common Sense?* New York: Harper Perennial/Harper Collins.

Raymont, Henry. 1970. "Technology Topic Of Cultural Panel." *New York Times* (July 30): 37.

Reston, James. 1959. "Kennedy Opposes Advocacy By U.S. Of Birth Control." *New York Times* (November 28): 1, 12.

--. 1961. "Washington." *New York Times* (July 21): 22.

--. 1963. "Washington: The Population Problem and Foreign Aid." *New York Times* (February 27): 6.

--. 1965. "Washington: The President Recognizes the Population Problem." *New York Times* (January 8): 28.

--. 1966. "Washington: The Politics of Birth Control." *New York Times* (June 10): 44.

--. 1971. "Primary and Secondary Questions." *New York Times* (February 14): IV, 11.

--. 1991. *Deadline: A Memoir*. New York: Random House.

Richardson, Theresa and Donald Fisher. 1999. "Introduction." Pp. 3- 21 in Theresa Richardson and Donald Fisher (Eds.) *The Development of the Social Sciences in the United States and Canada: The Role of Philanthropy*. Stamford, CT: Ablex Publishing Corp.

Ridgeway, James. 1970. *The Politics of Ecology*. New York: E. P. Dutton & Co.

Rienow, Robert and Leona Rienow. 1968. "Conservation For Survival." *The Nation* (August 26): 138-142.

Robinson, Marshall. 1993. "The Ford Foundation: Sowing the Seeds of a Revolution." *Environment* (April): 11-15, 38-41.

Rockefeller, Laurance. 1972. "My Most Unforgettable Character." *Reader's Digest* (October): 137-141.

Rockefeller, Steven. 1992. "Faith and Community in an Ecological Age." Pp. 139-171 in Steven C. Rockefeller and John C. Elder (Eds.), *Spirit and Nature: Why the Environment Is a Religious Issue*. Boston, MA: Beacon Press.

Rosenbaum, Walter A. 1989. "The Bureaucracy and Environmental Policy." Pp. 212-237 in James P. Lester (Ed.), *Environmental Politics and Policy: Theories and Evidence.* Durham, NC: Duke University Press.

Rosenberg, Charles (Ed.). 1984. *The History of Hereditarian Thought - A Decade of Progress in Eugenics, 1932.* New York: Garland Publishing.

Ross, Douglas. 1968. *Robert F. Kennedy: Apostle of Change.* New York: Pocket Books.

Rowell, Andrew. 1996. *Green Backlash: Global Subversion of the Environmental Movement.* New York: Routledge.

Rozak, Theodore. 1969. *The Making of a Counter Culture.* New York: Anchor Books. --. 1975. *Unfinished Animal: The Aquarian Frontier and the Evolution of Consciousness.* New York: Harper Colophon/Harper & Row.

Sadler, A. E. (Ed.). 1996. *The Environment: Opposing Viewpoints.* San Diego, CA: Green Haven Press.

Sale, Kirkpatrick. 1993. *The Green Revolution.* New York: Hill and Wang/Farrar Straus.

Sampson, Anthony. 1975. *The Seven Sisters and the World They Shaped.* New York: Bantam Books.

Schoenfeld, A. Clay, Robert F. Meier and Robert J. Griffin. 1979. "Constructing a Social Problem: The Press and the Environment." *Social Problems*, Vol. 27 (October): 38-61.

Shabecoff, Philip. 1977. "Tensions Increase Between Labor and Environmentalists Over Jobs." *New York Times* (May 28): 22.

--. 1980. "Earth Day '80 Dawns Tomorrow Amid Reflection and Plans for a New Decade." *New York Times* (April 21): A16.

--. 1981. "Poll Finds Strong Support for Environmental Code." *New York Times* (October 4): 30.

--. 1983. "Environmentalists Come of Age." *New York Times* (October 13): B12.

Shelley, Mary. 1975 (1818). *Frankenstein or, The Modern Prometheus.* New York: Dell Publishing Co.

Sherrill, Robert. 1983. *The Oil Follies of 1970-1980.* Garden City, NY: Anchor Press/Doubleday.

Shuster, Alvin. 1968. Briton Foresees A Hell On Earth." *New York Times* (November 24): 25.

Simon, Julian L. 1981. *The Ultimate Resource.* Princeton, NJ: Princeton University Press.

SRI International. 1974. *Changing Images of Man.* Menlo Park, CA: Center for the Study of Social Policy, SRI International.

Staudenmaier, Peter. 1995. "Fascist Ecology: The 'Green Wing' of the Nazi Party and Its Historical Antecedents." In Janet Biehl and Peter Staudenmaier, *Ecofascism: Lessons From the German Experience.* San Francisco, CA: AK Press.

Strouse, Jean. 1999. *Morgan: American Financier.* New York: Random House.

Taft Corporation. 1978. *Taft Foundation Reporter.* Washington, DC: Taft Corporation.

Takacs, David. 1996. *The Idea of Biodiversity: Philosophies of Paradise.* Baltimore, MD: Johns Hopkins University Press.

Talbot, Allan R. 1972. *Power Along the Hudson.* New York: E. P. Dutton & Co.

Tebbel, John and Mary Ellen Zuckerman. 1991. *The Magazine in America, 1741-1990.* New York: Oxford University Press.

Teltsch, Kathleen. 1949. "Population Gains Held To Be Danger." *New York Times* (August 18): 15.

--. 1990. "Rockefeller Foundation Starts Ecology Effort." *New York Times* (July 24): C10.

Theobald, Robert and Stephanie Mills (Eds.). 1973. *The Failure of Success*. New York: Bobbs-Merrill Co.

Thompson, Peter. 1980. "Bilderberg and the West." Pp. 157-189 in Holly Sklar (Ed.) *Trilateralism*. Boston, MA: South End Press.

Time. 1964. "The American Civilization." *Time* (May 29): 18.

--. 1965. "The Land." *Time* (February 19): 54-55.

--. 1965a. "Natural Resources." *Time* (June 4): 16-17.

--. 1965b. "The Land." *Time* (September 17): 62-71.

--. 1970. "Environment: Fighting to Save the Earth from Man." *Time* (February 2): 56-63.

Tolchin, Martin. 1968. "Buckley Urges More Federal Aid for Wildlife." *New York Times* (September 28): 20.

Touraine, Alain. 1981. *The Voice and the Eye*. Translation by Alan Duff. New York: Cambridge University Press.

Toynbee, Arnold J. 1973. "The Genesis of Pollution." *New York Times* (September 16): IV, 15.

Tucker, William. 1982. *Progress and Privilege*. Garden City, NY: Anchor Press/Doubleday.

Twelve Southerners. 1951. *I'll Take My Stand: The South and the Agrarian Tradition*. New York: Peter Smith.

United States Bureau of the Census. 1984. *Statistical Abstract of the United States, 1985*. Washington, DC: Department of Commerce.

Van Doren, Carl. 1991 (1938). *Benjamin Franklin*. New York: Penguin Books.

Vellacott, Philip. 1961. "Introduction." Pp. 7-18 in Aeschylus, *Prometheus Bound, The Suppliants, Seven Against Thebes, The Persians*. New York: Penguin Books.

Vogt, William. 1948. *Road To Survival*. New York: William Sloane Associates, Inc.

Walter, Edward. 1981. *The Immorality of Limiting Growth*. Albany, NY: State University of New York Press.

Warwick, Paul. 1985. "Did Britain Change? An Inquiry into the Causes of National Decline." *Journal of Contemporary History*, Vol. 20: 99-133.

Wasserman, Harvey. 1979. "The Nonviolent Movement versus Nuclear Power." Pp. 147-162 in Severyn T. Bruyn and Paula M. Rayman (Eds.) *Nonviolent Action and Social Change*. New York: Irvington.

Weber, James A. 1977. *Grow or Die!* New Rochelle, NY: Arlington House.

Wertham, Fredric. 1967. *A Sign for Cain*. New York: Macmillan Co.

--. 1980. *The German Euthanasia Program*. Cincinnati, OH: Hayes Publishing Co.

White, Leslie A. 1959. *The Evolution of Culture: The Development of Civilization to the Fall of Rome*. New York: McGraw-Hill.

White, Lynn, Jr. 1967. "The Historical Roots of our Ecologic Crisis." *Science*, Vol. 155 (March): 1203-1207.

Wiener, Martin J. 1981. *English Culture and the Decline of the Industrial Spirit, 1850-1980*. New York: Cambridge University Press.

Wilkinson, Paul. 1971. *Social Movements*. New York: Praeger.

Winks, Robin W. 1997. *Laurance Rockefeller: Catalyst for Conservation*. Washington, DC: Island Press.

Wolfe, Linnie Marsh. 1978. *Son of the Wilderness: The Life of John Muir*. Madison, WI: University of Wisconsin Press.

Zlotnick, Jack. 1961. "Population Pressure and Political Indecision." *Foreign Affairs*, Vol. 39 (July): 683-694.

INDEX

Y

Z

A Five-Star Review for This Book

Awesome Book Which Exposes Those in Big Business that Funded, Created, and Crafted Environmentalism, and Why

By Mark Fegley, Amazon.com, August 23, 2006

This is a fantastic book; it easily receives 5 stars for the superb content and analysis. Dr. Gibson is simply a guy with terrific work who does not receive the attention he should. I highly recommend reading Gibson's "Battling Wall Street: The Kennedy Presidency" first that way you can become familiar with Gibson's work.

This book goes into great detail about the money that created the environmental movement and why. Environmentalists may not like this book; if you are an environmentalist, read with an open mind. Dr. Gibson shows how big oil and other so-called opponents of environmentalism actually created and fund the movement in the past and today. Gibson demonstrates the stranglehold by which these individuals and companies still control and manipulate the movement...

Gibson demonstrates that the individuals and companies who fund the movement have specific economic and ideological goals. One of the core messages behind the environmental movement is to stop the progress of technology. Technology is the largest economic force of redistribution of power and wealth in society. Many economists and social scientists acknowledge this reality. This is one of the many factors Gibson demonstrates as to explain why big business pushes the environmental movement.

The book emphasizes the Rockefeller and Ford connections to the environmental movement, as well as the many extreme environmentalists who believe that the world's population should be reduced by 80%, and call for a return back to oppressive and intense labor. The book offers a terrific explanation as to why the environmental movement is against religions such as Christianity.

Gibson investigates the origins of Earth Day and how it was originally perceived as a corporate buyout and propaganda model. If you are environmentalist and consider yourself to dislike oil companies, the Ford corporation, and other companies seemingly destructive to the environment; then prepared to have your mind blown as you find out these are the very companies that control, created, fund, and shape the entire environmental movement. If you end up reading this book and like it or want to know more about the power groups involved in the book, I recommend you to read both "Battling Wall Street" and "Communication, Power and Media" by Donald Gibson.

Overall this is a truly fantastic book, the information presented is hard to come by, well researched, and very honest.

Progressive Press Books

In bookstores, online, or on sale from ProgressivePress.com

Six by Webster Griffin Tarpley

9/11 Synthetic Terror: Made in USA — by a network of moles, patsies, killers, corrupt politicians and media. The authoritative account of 9/11. "Strongest of the 770+ books I have reviewed" – R. Steele. 5th ed., 569 pp, $19.95. In Spanish: ***11-S Falso Terrorismo***. 408 pp, $19.95.

George Bush: The Unauthorized Biography Vivid X-ray of the oligarchy dominating U.S. politics, with a full narrative of GWHB's long list of crimes. How Skull-and-Bonesmen Bush and Brown Bros Harriman made fortunes building up Hitler's war machine. Bush Sr is linked to Iran-Contra, Watergate, and genocide in Iraq after luring Saddam Hussein to attack Kuwait. 700 pp, $19.95.

Just Too Weird: *Bishop Romney and the Mormon Putsch Against America: Polygamy, Theocracy and Subversion.* Mormonism exposed as part of the British-neocon financier plot to take back the colonies. 284 pp, $16.95.

Barack H. Obama: the Unauthorized Biography The abject corruption of a Wall Street lackey, and a richly detailed profile of the finance oligarchy. 595 pp, $19.95.

Obama – The Postmodern Coup: Making of a Manchurian Candidate. The Obama puppet's advisors are radical reactionaries. This study distills decades of astute political insight and analysis. 320 pp, $15.95.

Surviving the Cataclysm, ***Your Guide through the Greatest Financial Crisis in Human History***, by W.G. Tarpley. The unwinding of the hedge funds and derivatives bubble, and with them, life as we knew it in the USA. Richly detailed history of the financier oligarchy, how they plunder our nation. Plus, How to cope with the crisis. 668 pp, $25.

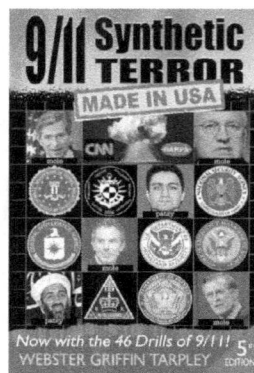

Five by F. Wm. Engdahl

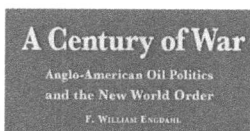

A Century of War: Anglo-American Oil Politics and the New World Order. The classic exposé; the empire controls the oil to control the world. 352 pp, $25.

Full Spectrum Dominance: Totalitarian Democracy in the New World Order. They are out for total control: land, sea, air, space, cyberspace, media, money, movements. 258 pp, $23.95.

Gods of Money: Wall Street and the Death of the American Century. The banksters stop at nothing: setting world wars, plunging our world in chaos and corruption. 390 pp, $24.95.

Seeds of Destruction: The Hidden Agenda of Genetic Manipulation. A corporate gang is out for complete control of the world by patenting our food. Inside the corporate boardrooms and science labs, a world of greed, intrigue, corruption and coercion. 340 pp, $25.95.

Target China: How Washington and Wall Street Plan to Cage the Asian Dragon. The secret war on many fronts to thwart the Chinese challenge. 256 pp, $24.95.

Three by Michel Chossudovsky

Towards a World War III Scenario: The Dangers of Nuclear War. The Pentagon is preparing a first-strike nuclear attack on Iran. 103 pp, $15.95.

The Global Economic Crisis: The Great Depression of the XXI Century, by Prof. Chossudovsky, with a dozen other experts. 416 pp, $25.95.

The Globalization of Poverty and the New World Order. Brilliant analysis how corporatism feeds on poverty, destroying the environment, apartheid, racism, sexism, and ethnic strife. 401 pp, $27.95.

Two by Henry Makow

Illuminati: Cult that Hijacked the World tackles taboos like Zionism, British Empire, Holocaust. How international bankers stole a monopoly on government credit, and took over the world. They run it all: wars, schools, media. 249 pp, $19.95. ***Illuminati 2: Deception & Seduction***, more hidden history. 285 pp, $19.95

History

Two by George Seldes, the great muckraking journalist, whistleblower on the plutocrats who keep the media in lockstep, and finance fascism. ***1,000 Americans Who Rule the USA*** (1947, 324 pp, $18.95) Media concentration is nothing new! ***Facts and Fascism*** (1943, 292 pp, $15.95) How our native corporatist élite aimed for a fascist victory in WW2.

Two by Prof. Donald Gibson. ***Battling Wall Street: The Kennedy Presidency***. JFK: a martyr who strove mightily for social and economic justice. 208 pp, $14.95. ***The Kennedy Assassination Cover-Up***. JFK was murdered by the moneyed elite, not the CIA or Mafia. 375 pp, $19.95.

Two by Stewart H. Ross. ***Global Predator: US Wars for Empire***. A damning account of the atrocities committed by US armed forces over two centuries. ***Propaganda for War: How the US was Conditioned to Fight the Great War*** Propaganda by Britain and her agents like Teddy Roosevelt sucked the USA into the war to smash the old world order. 350 pp and $18.95 each.

Afghanistan: A Window on the Tragedy. An eloquent photo essay on life amidst the ruins of war. 110 pp, $9.95.

Enemies by Design: Inventing the War on Terrorism. A century of imperialism in the Middle East. Biography of Osama bin Ladeen; Zionization of America; PNAC, Afghanistan, Palestine, Iraq. 416 pp, $17.95.

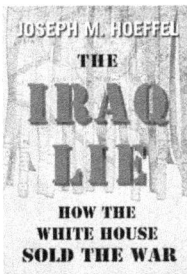

The Iraq Lie: How the White House Sold the War, by former congressman Joseph M. Hoeffel. Bush Lied about WMD — and went ahead with war. $14.95

The Nazi Hydra in America: Suppressed History of a Century by Glen Yeadon. US plutocrats launched Hitler, then recouped Nazi assets to erect today's police state. Fascists won WWII because they ran both sides. "The story is shocking and sobering, and deserves to be widely read." – Howard Zinn. 700 pp, $19.95.

Inside the Gestapo: Hitler's Shadow over the World. Intimate, fascinating Nazi defector's tale of ruthlessness, intrigue, and geopolitics. 287 pp, $17.95.

Sunk: The Story of the Japanese Submarine Fleet, 1941-1945. The bravery of doomed men in a lost cause, against impossible odds. 300 pp, $15.95.

Terrorism and the Illuminati, A 3000-Year History. "Islamic" terrorists are tentacles of western imperialism. 332 pp, $16.95.

Troublesome Country. Throughout its history the US has failed to live up to our guiding democratic creed. 146 pp, $12.95.

Psychology: Brainwashing

The Rape of the Mind: The Psychology of Thought Control, Menticide and Brainwashing. Conditioning in open and closed societies; tools to defend against torture or social pressure. Classic by Dr Joost Meerloo, survivor of Nazism and McCarthyism. 320 pp, $16.95.

The Telescreen: An Empirical Study of the Destruction of Consciousness, by Prof. Jeffrey Grupp. How mass media brainwash us with consumerism and war propaganda. Fake history, news, issues, and reality steal our souls. 199 pp, $14.95. Also by Grupp: ***Telementation: Cosmic Feeling and the Law of Attraction***. Deep feeling is our secret nature and key to self-realization. 124 pp, $12.95.

Conspiracy, NWO

Corporatism: the Secret Government of the New World Order by Prof. Jeffrey Grupp. Corporations control all world resources. Their New World Order is the "prison planet" that Hitler aimed for. 408 pp, $16.95.

Descent into Slavery. How the banksters took over America and the world. The Founding Fathers, Rothschilds, the Crown and the City, world wars, globalization. 310 pp, $16. Also by Des Griffin: ***Fourth Reich of the Rich***, 316 pp, $16.

Dope Inc.: Britain's Opium War against the United States. "The Book that Drove Kissinger Crazy." Underground Classic, new edition. 320 pp, $12.95.

Ecology, Ideology and Power by Prof. Donald Gibson. Ulterior motives of the reactionary elite pushing population and resource control. 162 pp., $14.95

Final Warning: A History of the New World Order by D. A. Rivera. Classic, in-depth research into the Great Conspiracy: the Fed, the Trilateral Commission, the CFR, and the Illuminati. 360 pp, $14.95.

How the World Really Works by A.B. Jones. Crash course in conspiracy. Digests of 11 classics like *Tragedy and Hope, Creature from Jekyll Island*. 336 pp, $15.

Killing us Softly: *the Global Depopulation Policy* by Kevin Galalae, 146 pp., color. The Why and How of the covert, indirect war on the people. $15.95.

The Money Power: Empire of the City and Pawns in the Game. Two classic geopolitics books in one. The illuminist Three World Wars conspiracy: to divide us on ethnic and political lines to conquer humanity. 320 pp, $16.95

The Triumph of Consciousness by Chris Clark. The real Global Warming and Greening agenda: more hegemony by the NWO. 347 pp, $14.95.

Conspiracy: False Flag Operations

9/11 on Trial: The W T C Collapse. 20 proofs the World Trade Center was destroyed by controlled demolition. 192 pp, $12.95.

Gladio, NATO's Dagger at the Heart of Europe: The Pentagon-Mafia-Nazi Terror Axis. The blood-red thread of terror by NATO death squads in Europe, from WW2 up to 2012. 484 pp, $16.95.

Conspiracies, Conspiracy Theories and the Secrets of 9/11, German best-seller explores conspiracy in history, before tackling competing theories on 9/11. 274 pp, $14.95.

Grand Deceptions: Zionist Intrigues. The Neocon World Order, from Herzl, to the world wars, Bolshevism, 9/11, Al-qaeda, and media tyranny. 177 pp., $13.95.

In Search of the Truth: An Exposure of the Conspiracy, by Azar Mirza-Beg. A portrait of our times, society and religion, and the threat we face. 208 pp, $17

JFK-911: 50 Years of Deep State., by Laurent Guyénot. The Greater Israel strategy behind the JFK and 9/11 murders. 238 pp, $15.95.

Subverting Syria: How CIA Contra Gangs and NGO's Manufacture, Mislabel and Market Mass Murder. Syrian "uprising" is a cynical US plot using faked news, provocateurs, opportunists, mercenaries, and Wahhabi fanatics. 116 pp, $10.00

Terror on the Tube: Behind the Veil of 7/7, an Investigation, by Nick Kollerstrom. The glaring evidence that all four Muslim scapegoats were completely innocent. 7/7 clinched the assault on our rights. 3rd ed, 322 pp, $17.77.

The War on Freedom. The seminal exposé of 9/11. "Far and away the best and most balanced analysis of September 11th." – Gore Vidal. 400 pp, $16.95.

Truth Jihad: My Epic Struggle Against the 9/11 Big Lie. Kevin Barrett's profound and humorous autobiographical testament. 224 pp, $9.95.

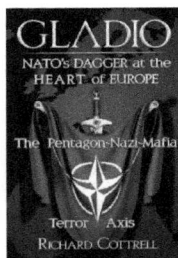

Coming Soon

A Prisoner's Diary, by Hussain Mohammed Al-Amily
Myth of the Arab Spring, by Chris Macavel
Subjugating the Middle East and *Ukraine: The Attack on Russia and the Eurasian Union* by Takis Fotopoulos.

E-Books

9/11 Synthetic Terror; Barack Obama Unauthorized Biography; Gladio, NATO's Dagger at the Heart of Europe, Grand Deceptions; In Search of the Truth; Iraq Lie; JFK-911; Just Too Weird; Killing Us Softly; Nazi Hydra; Subverting Syria; Surviving the Cataclysm; Target: China.

www.ingramcontent.com/pod-product-compliance
Lightning Source LLC
Chambersburg PA
CBHW080049280326
41934CB00014B/3264